PRODUCTION
STAGE
MANAGEMENT
for broadway

PRODUCTION STAGE MANAGEMENT
for broadway

From **idea** to opening night **& beyond**

PETER LAWRENCE

FOREWORD BY MIKE NICHOLS

Quite Specific Media Ltd.
Los Angeles

For Steve, Kaddee, Emma, Meg

Book Design: Jeffrey Cohen
Editor: Judith Durant
Cover Design: Richard Carlow/C2C Studio, Inc.
A Pat MacKay Project

Library of Congress Cataloging-in-Publication Data
Lawrence, Peter,
Production stage management for Broadway : from idea to opening night and beyond /
Peter Lawrence.
     pages   cm
  Includes bibliographical references and index.
  ISBN 978-0-89676-293-0
1. Stage management. 2. Theater—Production and direction. I. Title.
  PN2085.L39 2015
  792.02'3—dc23
                                        2014042774

Quite Specific Media Group Ltd.
An imprint of Silman-James Press, Inc.
www.silmanjamespress.com
info@quitespecificmedia.com | info@silmanjamespress.com

Contents

Snatching Order from Chaos

A Foreword by Mike Nichols

I know what stage managers do because I've seen it all my life. They call the curtain and the light cues. They keep order. They organize rehearsals and write the show reports. They are in charge of the backstage, not only in technical issues but in solving the day-to-day problems on a long-running show.

But the real thing stage managers do is to reassure. A group that is putting on a play, no matter how successful, by definition needs reassurance. Even the most experienced Broadway professionals, the most glittering stars, feel unsure of themselves sometimes—actually, most of the time. A good stage manager knows how to look calm at all times, no matter what's happening in his or her gut. They can make all of us feel not only safe in our work but also slightly confident and hopeful that we're on the right track.

Stage managers are conversant with every aspect of a production. I've seen them go over the budget with the general manager, the score with the conductor, the light plot with the lighting designer and the design plans with the scenic designer. They, after all, will time the cues, the beginning of the scenes, the end of scenes, the blackouts, the effects, the music cues—everything that happens during the course of the play that hasn't been happening already, i.e., the scene onstage now.

What it boils down to is that the stage manager is the pulse of the production. The actors are responsible for the pace of the scenes. The stage manager is responsible for the pulse of the show. I've seen them encourage and praise the actors and calm down the producers. I've seen them guide the stagehands, rehearse the understudies and come out and make an announcement stopping the show in an emergency. The most important things are the private things they do with any member of the company, including the director who may get discouraged or angry about passing sirens and loud air conditioners. I depend on my stage manager to let me know what is really going on in productions having a long run, what in the politics of a theatre company I should be dealing with and what I should leave alone. This can be invaluable.

In different companies different people can be the beating heart of a production. It can of course be the leading lady or the leading man, it can be an author who drops by frequently, it can be a young girl or boy wrestling with eight shows a week and that bane of child actors' existence, a tutor with any of these, you can be sure that the responsibility for connecting with and soothing them falls to the stage manager.

When a stage manager knows what he is doing the cast tends to feel happy and secure. Schedules are observed. There is laughter during tech, sometimes ideas. I am able to do my work. Cast members don't have to keep checking the flies for a loose sandbag. Stagehands move quietly and efficiently. The producer and general manager aren't always worried about overtime and making the first preview on time. The theatre becomes a relatively calm and tentatively happy place. I like coming to work.

I also know what happens when you don't have a good stage manager. A feeling of slight chaos overtakes a production. Things crash at tech. Designers and stagehands blame each other. Previews are called off. The cast feels deserted. There is no one to remind everyone that it's all going to turn out okay.

I've been lucky to work with terrific stage managers, many who became friends as well as colleagues. Most have thought about the play or musical as much as the actors in the production. Stage managers all have a good sense of humor. It's pretty much required with the combination of excitement and fear that runs previews, tryouts, opening nights, new actors joining the production or the President coming to see the show.

Peter Lawrence's book is an excellent guide about how one snatches order from chaos. His point of view remains positive. He doesn't approach a show with fear but rather with love. And he has the experience to back up what he says. Pete and I have done eight shows and a television series together. He knows what he's talking about.

New York
August 2014

Introduction

The theatre cannot be taught—but it can be learned. Mentoring, trial and error, and real world empirical experience are the ways. Theatre is a personal, highly subjective cottage industry practiced by people with a respect for the traditions of the theatre as well as an utter disregard for old, hidebound practices. In reality, the theatre is no fit place for an adult. It defies logic, business models, and stereotypes. And it demands passion, curiosity, and a lifelong commitment.

I've always believed that we are tapped by the theatre. For some inexplicable reason, we feel at home in the theatre. We are drawn in by an undeniable power. Some might say if you can possibly avoid going into the theatre, do so. If, however, you are one of us who has no choice but to respond to the call, the theatre will tell you how you may serve. Whatever your vocation—welder, actor, hairdresser, accountant, visual artist, musician, or money hustler—the theatre can put you to work.

This book is about American-style stage management for the commercial theatre. In the United States, the stage manager is responsible for everything that happens upstage of the proscenium arch—directorial, managerial, personal, and technical. Calling cues and writing reports is a small part of what a US stage manager must do. The complete welfare of the backstage and daily interaction with all the elements of a production are the jobs of the American stage manager. Others base their style on the US or UK method and add in their own local twists.

An important word about the title "Stage Manager." Stage managers are members of Actors' Equity Association (AEA) and covered by their contracts. Interestingly, Actors' Equity does not yet recognize or use the title "Production Stage Manager," although that is the term most of us now use for the very subject of this book.

Technically, "production stage manager" is an honorific connoting the original stage manager in charge of the show during its production period. Many now use the term for any head stage manager, whether original or replacement. In this book we will use "production stage manager" (PSM) and "stage manager" (SM) interchangeably to mean the original stage manager who takes the show from idea to opening night and beyond.

This book is a map showing how to get from the beginning of a production to the end. It is a standard working template and includes a wealth of charts and calendars at the back to illustrate my methods. But this is my own personal way of working. There is no attempt to be balanced here. Take what you can use and reject the rest. Use these pages as a reference point to develop your own style. I encourage you to let this book challenge your methods and make you decide for yourself how you want to handle the distribution of information, your relationships with fellow professionals, and your working style. Like acting or directing, production stage management is a craft that you refine to maximize your own skills and working methods.

Production Stage Management for the Broadway: From Idea to Opening Night and Beyond is intended for a wide range of theatre professionals. Both a beginning stage manager with high school or college experience and an assistant stage manager working in the commercial theatre may use this book. It is a book for those with a basic working understanding of stage management, and it speaks to those who want to deepen their understanding of the craft. It is a book for stage managers who want a standard of professional behavior.

A Story

When I began as a stage manager, I had to make it all up. I had no mentors. I had to invent my own working methods, many of which were pointless or confusing. Over the years, I have learned from my mistakes and have continued to adapt my calling scripts, report forms, calendars, and correspondence. I have never stopped adapting.

Peter Lawrence
New York
August 2014

1
The Idea of Stage Management

Director Mike Nichols says that everyone serves the production. The play is the center of the event and each member of the production team contributes to expressing the idea of the play. But no one—not the producer, the author, the director, or the star—is above the play.

When I first began to work in the commercial theatre, stage managers were often dancers who had been injured or they were professional understudies who just drifted into stage management. We joked that if you could tell time and sweep a stage, you could be a stage manager! Off-Broadway you didn't even need to be able to tell time. All that has changed.

As of this writing, the average Broadway musical costs $15 million and the average play costs $3 million—and costs keep climbing. During technical rehearsals, the orchestra seats are filled with more computers than most lawyers' offices. The commercial theatre is a 19th-century art form presented with 21st-century technology. And the production stage manager has to understand how to coordinate all elements—technical, legal, and artistic—of the production without ever losing sight of the goal: to serve the live event, the play, or the musical.

The production stage manager is at the very center of the play, from beginning to end. The PSM is the only person who knows and understands all the elements of the production, from casting to design choices to directorial ideas to budgeting. Whether coordinating with marketing, running the show, or balancing personality conflicts, the stage manager is the one unifying element.

The US–style of production stage management is based on the idea that once a show has opened, everything upstage of the proscenium arch is controlled by the stage manager. All technical, artistic, safety, timing, and personality issues are in the hands of the stage manager. All eyes turn to the stage manager during the run of the show.

And let's make it fun! Creative energy is easily dampened, and one of the production stage manager's primary jobs is to keep the rehearsal room, the tech rehearsals, the dress rehearsals, and the daily running of the show light and easy.

A Story

I once worked the revival of a musical that was on tour for a year before coming into New York. I was being paid a lot of money, and I had a child in college. I felt I couldn't leave the job, but I was miserable—mostly because of the star. One day after opening I visited some friends who were in tech rehearsal for a new musical. They were laughing and having a wonderful time. The work was creative, playful, and trusting. I'd actually forgotten that I went into the theatre to have a good time and to serve the play, not to make money or to cater to difficult stars. I gave notice that same day. Several days later, a general manager friend called, saying he had a new play with no title. It was five hours long and was going to a regional theatre, with no possibility of coming to New York. The cast was a bunch of movie stars and it paid virtually nothing. I asked why I would take such a show. The general manager replied, "Because Mike Nichols is directing it." I leapt at the job, which became *Hurlyburly*. And I've continued to work with Mike Nichols ever since—26 years and counting. We're not meant to be miserable in the theatre, nor are we in it only for the money.

2
The Cast of Characters

The Idea

A play is usually written by one person, and a musical by two or three. Once the rather solitary job of writing and composing is finished to their creative satisfaction, an army of professionals is employed to launch the project commercially.

Usually, the author first has to interest a producer or producers in taking on the project. The producers then set about hiring the army to realize the vision agreed upon by the authors and the producers. The authors supply the material; the producers supply not only the money but the organizational oversight.

Who does what in the commercial theatre is hard to figure out, especially since the responsibilities that come with each job title keep shifting.

Playwright

This is self-explanatory. However, if the playwright is a member of the Dramatists Guild of America and signs a Dramatists Guild contract, then the playwright becomes the employer—that is, the playwright employs the producer. The playwright owns the property. Changes may only be made in the play or musical with the consent of the playwright. The producer does not employ the playwright; it is the other way around.

Lead Producers

Most productions today have not one but a number of producers. The lead producers are often also the general partners, and are therefore responsible for financing the production.

They find the project, secure the rights to the project, attract other investor-producers, and hire the creative team. Lead producers are theatrical professionals and they set the tone for a production, since they decide what sort of creative team will be hired.

Investor-Producers

In the 21st century, there are many investor-producers on most projects—you see them all trouping up to the stage at the Tony Awards. They will not only give money to the lead producers but will also give their opinions regarding all aspects of the production to the lead producers. While the lead producers will speak directly with the creative/technical team, the investor-producers will not. Generally, investor-producers come from outside the theatre and are there to make money and to bring in other investors.

General Manager

At one time, the general manager (GM) worked for the producer—often in the same office—and was responsible for the distribution of the funds raised by the producer and for the weekly payroll. However, in the modern commercial theatre, general managers usually maintain their own offices and are hired for each individual production. They are paid a production fee plus weekly maintenance and office expenses, and they often get a percentage of the profits. Nowadays, it is the GMs who do much of the nuts and bolts of producing. They hire much of the creative and technical team, as well as budget the production, the weekly operating expenses, and the day-to-day operations of the show. General managers are usually, but not necessarily, members of the Association of Theatrical Press Agents and Managers, (ATPAM). PSMs and SMs negotiate their contracts with the general manager.

Company Manager

The company manager works for the general manager and usually works from the GM's office. The company manager prepares the weekly payroll for all employees of the production as well as royalty payments to the creative team and producers. While GMs do most of their work from their own office, the company manager spends a great deal of time in the theatre building, and has a one-on-one relationship with everyone at the theatre. The company manager is responsible for the business operation of the production inside the theatre building and is also a member of ATPAM.

Director

Directors have the full responsibility of the production on their shoulders. As the production stage manager, you are serving the vision of the director, both technically and artistically. In rehearsal, never leave the director's side. Your job during rehearsal is to serve the director—not in the getting-coffee sense of serving, but in the advising, reminding, encouraging, and listening sense. Don't succomb to getting caught up in the necessary office work, the daily reports, script changes, and phone calls instead of being at the director's side. Producers, designers, managers, actors, and press are all vying for the director's time. You must help allocate this time wisely and protect the director from unnecessary distractions. Directors are members of the Stage Directors and Choreographers Society (SDC).

Associate Director

Until the British began producing extensively in the US commercial theatre, there were no associate directors in the United States. Duties that are now linked to associate directors were performed exclusively by stage managers. Now, a production stage manager is frequently also the associate director. In the British theatre system, stage managing is a purely technical function, and the artistic dimension of stage management is entrusted to resident directors or associate directors—same job, different titles.

Associate directors have no technical or organizational duties; their only function is to note and redirect the actors in the absence of the director. My view is that since many, if not most, American stage managers are trained as directors, a separate associate director is a waste of money and effort. Associate directors are not covered by any union or guild.

Assistant Director

The assistant director really does "serve" the director. Bringing coffee, doing personal chores, making phone calls. Organizing the director's outside life is the assistant's job. Assistant directors have no artistic or technical function on a production, although they often observe rehearsals and frequently move on to become associate directors, directors, or stage managers. Assistant directors are covered by no union or guild.

Choreographer

The choreographer is responsible for all dances and musical staging in a musical production. I've also done a number of plays, for example *The Graduate*, that had a choreographer for a specific small musical sequence. Often, the choreographer also works out the transitions from scene to scene, especially if actors are involved in the transition and/or the transitions are timed to music. I always assign one of my assistants to work closely with the choreographer because I'm focusing on the director. That way the choreographer has one dedicated SM to whom they can turn. The needs of the choreographer must be served with the same detail as those of the director. Choreographers, like directors, are members of the Stage Directors and Choreographers Society (SDC).

Associate Choreographer and Assistant Choreographer

These positions are to the choreographer exactly what the associate director and assistant director are to the director. However, a production stage manager is almost never the associate choreographer. But sometimes the dance captain functions as the associate choreographer. Associate and assistant choreographers are covered by no union or guild.

Dance Captain

The job of the dance captain is to note and maintain the choreography of the show in the absence of the choreographer or associate choreographer. This is often an overlooked and under-appreciated job on musicals.

The dance captain is almost always a member of the dancing ensemble. Ideally, the dance captain should be one of the swings (who understudies several roles). Because they are already covering them, the swings already know multiple choreographic routines and can readily learn all the remaining choreography in a show. Also, a swing watches the choreography being taught (rather than being a part of the dance) and so can observe and note patterns more easily. The swing also actually has time to write down and draft the choreographic patterns—ensemble members do not.

The dance captain and the production stage manager are natural partners. They are both responsible for the staging of the show and for the idea of the show. The PSM takes on the scenes and overall storytelling while the dance captain handles the direction of the dances. If, during a long run, the dances begin to look mechanical, it's time to get the dance captain to pay closer attention.

In doing almost any musical I rely heavily on the dance captain, eliciting their advice not only about the dances but about the scenes. The dance captain is the PSM's partner and should be nurtured and protected. Because dance captains are in the cast, they are members of Actors' Equity Association (AEA).

Musical Director

The musical director is responsible for all the music played in the pit or sung on stage. They organize the music for distribution, teach the music to the cast, rehearse the orchestra, and conduct most of the performances. In the case of a new musical, the musical director works closely with the composer, with the arranger, and with the orchestrator. Like the production stage manager, the musical director interacts with everyone: cast, orchestra, director, choreographer, and creative team. The musical director is an artist, diplomat, and athlete—it's very strenuous work conducting a musical. Like the dance captain, the musical director should be the stage manager's best friend. When running a musical, most of the stage manager's cues come from the musical director, so you need to know exactly how they conduct. Musical directors are members of the American Federation of Musicians (AFM).

Musical Arranger

The arranger takes the music the composer has written and adapts it to fit the specific needs of the production. On a new musical, the arranger works closely with the composer, choreographer, and musical director during rehearsals. There may also be a separate dance arranger working with the choreographer to extend and rewrite certain musical passages for dance numbers. The best arrangers add personality, humor, and drive to the music. They are responsible for the style of the piece. In the rehearsal hall, the arranger is an integral member of the creative team and is constantly rewriting the score—with the approval of the composer. Arrangers are usually members of AFM.

Orchestrator

The orchestrator is not usually a part of the rehearsal hall creative team. They will come to the rehearsal hall when the composer, arranger, and musical director think a particular song or dance number is finished. The orchestrator will watch that number being performed, usually record it, and then go to a separate studio to write the parts for all the musical instruments. The orchestrator adds flesh to the bare bones of a song. Orchestration is a creative function specific to the orchestra and separate from the rehearsal hall process. The orchestrator is responsible to the composer.

The number of instruments and players available to be orchestrated depends on negotiation with the producers, general manager, and composer. Orchestrators are usually members of AFM.

Scenic Designer

The scenic designer is responsible not only for the design of the environment on stage, but also for the design of the props. The lead time for approving and drafting a scenic design will be taken up later in chapter 4. The director, choreographer, and scenic designer must have all details of the stage space, the movement of scenery, and actor-related details worked out well in advance of the beginning of rehearsals. The initial design approved by both the designer and director will often have to be modified quickly, once the cost bids come back from the scenic shops. Given the complexity of most contemporary stage design, the sets are in the shop being built before the show goes into rehearsal. And so, while small changes may be made during rehearsals, large changes become time and/or cost prohibitive. Scenic designers are members of IATSE Local USA (aka United Scenic Artists) 829.

Associate Scenic Designer

The associate scenic designer is responsible (often with multiple assistants) for drafting the working drawings for the scenery. The scenic designer sets the overall look and feel of the show, and the associate designer supplies all the details—how many inches there are between pieces of scenery, the exact width of each wing, and the exact height and weight of each piece of moving scenery. It's part of the PSM's responsibility to work closely with the associate designer, working out the exact scenic details and keeping the director up to speed on changes that might affect the staging. The associate scenic designer and stage manager must make sure that all the scenery will fit on the stage, that the actors have enough room, and that the director knows exactly how much space is available in which to work. A great associate designer is as important to a production stage manager as a great designer is to a director. Like scenic designers, associate scenic designers are members of IATSE Local USA 829.

Lighting Designer

The lighting designer is responsible not only for the lighting design of the show itself, but also for any lighting built in to the set. Often the lighting designer attends a number of rehearsal studio run-throughs—it helps in getting a good idea of the tone of each scene as well as the staging and/or choreography. You'll find that many lighting designers, especially the British, will actually give the stage manager the cue placements before dry tech (technical rehearsal without actors) begins. Each lighting designer has a very particular way of working, both in dry tech and during tech with actors. A little research on the methodology and amount of time each lighting designer needs to light a show will save many headaches in your production schedule. Lighting designers are members of IATSE Local USA 829.

Associate Lighting Designer

The associate lighting designer is usually responsible for drafting lighting design and working with the associate scenic designer to negotiate the space being allotted both overhead and offstage for lighting and for scenery. During tech, the associates keep the paperwork that tracks each cue, light, color, and intensity. On a musical, there is usually an associate who is responsible solely for cueing and tracking follow spots. Associate lighting designers are usually members of IATSE Local USA 829.

Costume Designer

The costume designer not only designs the clothes for the show but also is present at virtually every fitting for each actor's multiple costumes. It is a very time-consuming job, one that requires great tact in balancing actors' egos and self-images with the needs of the show. Once the director has approved the overall design, it will be put out to bid at various costume shops. During rehearsal, each costume will be altered accordingly. Does the garment need pockets or protective padding? Do we need special fabric because it's now worn in a dance number?

British designers frequently design both scenery and costumes. Before the 1960s in American commercial theatre, is was not unusual to see the set designer double as the lighting or costume designer. Today if you are planning for a show with one designer crossing over multiple disciplines, you need great associates so the designer can perform multiple functions. Costume designers are members of IATSE Local USA 829.

Associate Costume Designer

There are often several costume associates, each handling a specific area. Male and female actors may have a different associate. Frequently there is an associate who only handles shoes. The number of associates depends on the number and complexity of the costumes—and of course, the budget. Associate costume designers are usually members of IATSE Local USA 829.

Hair Designer

A big musical can easily require several hundred wigs once all the swings and understudies are figured in. Each wig needs to be designed, approved, and then often built from scratch. Like costumes, this building process requires multiple fittings. Usually, the costume designer is integral to the hair design process and often approves the choice of hair designer. Also like costume design, hair design requires great tact. Hair designers are usually members of a Theatrical Wardrobe Union local of IATSE.

Makeup Designer

The complexity of the role for this design team member depends on the show itself. It could be as simple as bringing in a designer during tech to advise the actors on how to do their makeup and then leaving the actors to apply their own makeup for each show. Or makeup could be as complicated as *Shrek The Musical,* which requires a full-time makeup department of four and includes film-quality prosthetics. The range of possibilities in makeup design and execution is huge. It's very important for the stage manager to understand the scope of the makeup design in order to allow sufficient time for consultations and design as well as fittings for prosthetics, if required. Like hair designers, makeup designers are members of a Theatrical Wardrobe Union local of IATSE.

Sound Designer

In 1975, *The Wiz* was a noteworthy Broadway musical for its use of radio mics actually worn on the actors' bodies. By 1984, *On Your Toes* was notable for not using mics on the actors. A complete revolution in the use of sound had taken place in less than 10 years.

Sound designers are responsible for the amplification of the actors and orchestra, as well as the playback of any sound effects. They are also responsible for all communication elements, using both headset and wireless devices, as well as any live video feeds used during the show.

This design field is evolving so quickly that last year's state-of-the-art equipment is this year's junk. The sound designer is not only an artist, but also a technician of the highest order. Sound designers are members of IATSE Local USA 829.

Video and Projection Designer

This is a separate area from the video monitoring that is part of the sound department. Many plays and musicals use video and projection as a way of enhancing either the lighting design or the scenic design. In some cases this could be so subtle as to be almost unnoticed. In other cases there might be nothing subtle about the projections at all—projection mapping and LED screens enhance and become the scenery.

Like the sound designer, the video and projection designer is both artist and technician, responsible for not only the image projected to the stage, but also for the delivery system to get it there. And like sound equipment, this year's latest projection solution is next year's junk. The quality of the image on the stage is only as good as the equipment. Video and projection designers are members of IATSE Local USA 829.

Musical Coordinator

The musical coordinator is responsible for hiring the orchestra for a musical. They are members of the American Federation of Musicians local chapter that has jurisdiction over the theatre building that houses your show. Think of the musical coordinator as a casting director for the orchestra. The coordinator will also hire or approve all the subs, deal with any orchestra union issues, and oversee the local coordinators on national tours. Usually, the musical coordinator is a former working musician and pays very close attention to the needs of the score; for example, *Gypsy* needs a great first trumpet but the guitar book is quite easy. Musical coordinators are members of American Federation of Musicians (AFM).

Casting Director

It's impossible to overstate the crucial role of the casting director. Yes, the director (and choreographer and musical director in a musical) makes the final casting decisions. But the range of actors, singers, and dancers brought in for the creative team to review and audition completely depends on the casting director.

Casting is not just about finding actors who are right for the role, but it also means finding new and surprising choices. A good casting director trolls showcases and off-off-Broadway theatres to find those new artists who will surprise both the creative team and the audience. For every hour the casting director spends in session with the creative team, many more hours are spent seeing new faces and narrowing the list of possibilities to present to the creative team.

As production stage manager you should attend all casting sessions and keep your own sets of notes—more about that in chapter 4. If the show is a long run, you will find yourself making casting choices in the absence of the director, so you must know the criteria for each role. Casting directors are usually members of the Casting Society of America (CSA).

Fight Director

If there is any staging in a show that goes beyond normal blocking or choreography, it is wise to hire a fight director. Potentially dangerous staging could include sword fighting, falls or jumps, simulated punching or wrestling, pratfalls, or any other unusually physical staging. Good and qualified fight directors and are best found by asking colleagues who have used them in the past. Fight directors are not unionized.

Child Guardian (formerly Wrangler)

For legal and safety reasons, there must be a guardian any time a child under 18 years of age is employed on a production. The guardian should be separate from the stage management staff, and have the care of the children as their only duty. The guardian will be with the children at all times, not only supervising them in the dressing room, but also taking them to and from the stage.

The number of guardians on a show depends upon the number of children and whether or not the children perform as a group or have individual times onstage. Child guardians are now a part of IATSE.

Animal Wrangler

Any time live animals are used in a production, an animal wrangler is required to be responsible for their safety, care, feeding, and performance. Usually, the agency providing the animals will also provide the wrangler. This is a job for a professional and should not be handled by anyone other than a trained animal handler. Animal wranglers are not covered by any union or guild.

Technical Director/Production Supervisor/ Production Manager

These terms are often used interchangeably. This position is responsible for hiring the "pink contract" crew (see below), working out the production calendar with the stage manager and general manager, budgeting and supervising the load-in, and overseeing the building of the set in the shop. In years past, former pink contract carpenters generally held this position, but more recently men and women with more experience building and budgeting scenery have been given the position. On smaller shows, the pink contract crew may act as their own production manager. The technical director or production manager is usually a member of IATSE, but not necessarily so.

Pink Contract Crew

The pink contract crew is made up of those carpenters, electricians, props, wardrobe, and hair personnel who work for the production directly and who are paid by the production directly. They may or may not belong to the IATSE local responsible for the theatre where the show is playing, but they must belong to an IATSE local somewhere. They are hired by the production manager and work hand-in-hand with the production stage manager, general manager, and production manager to set schedules and solve the problems of the production. They are usually highly trained, with extensive knowledge of computers, rigging, stage machinery, and availability of materials.

The maximum number of pink contracts on a show are:
- Seven on a musical opening without an out-of-town tryout
- Eight on a musical opening in New York with an out-of-town tryout
- Four on a play

As stage manager, these pink contract crew are your lifeline to the local theatre crew and should be treated with the utmost respect.

Local Crew

In virtually every theatre there are stagehands, called house heads, who work directly for the theatre. They are responsible for the care and maintenance of the theatre itself, for turning in the payroll hours for each local stagehand in their department, and for advising the pink contract crew on the idiosyncrasies of their theatre. Often the pink contract crew will meet with the house heads far in advance to ensure that there is enough weight, pipe, cable, and electrical power available in the theatre. House heads are appointed by the owner of the theatre but are members of the IATSE Local. This is a highly political position and the stage manager must never get on the bad side of a house head.

Local stagehands are hired on an "as needed" basis by the house head for each department for every show. The local crew works at the behest of the house head and are loyal to that person first, and to the show second. Local stagehands usually have a specialty—carpenter, flyman, props, electrics—but may work in different departments on different shows.

Wardrobe Crew

The wardrobe crew is responsible for the maintenance of the costumes. They are members of IATSE's Theatrical Wardrobe Union. The wardrobe supervisor, in consultation with the costume designer and general manager, will determine the number of dressers needed for any production.

Dressers

Dressers are members of the wardrobe crew. They have one of the most personal jobs in the theatre. They prepare the actors' costumes for each performance and then help them in and out of these costumes—usually in close quarters and at high speeds. Dressers must be personable but not intrusive, and very detail-oriented. On a musical, there may be more than a dozen dressers. Dressers are members of IATSE's Theatrical Wardrobe Union.

Star dressers are assigned to only one person and are usually responsible for that star's perks, in addition to the usual functions of a dresser. A star dresser may escort guests to the star's dressing room, prepare tea or coffee, and run small errands. Usually stars choose their own star dressers.

Production Stage Manager
and Stage Managers

Although these terms are often used interchangeably in contemporary theatrical practice, the production stage manager is, technically, the original stage manager who was in charge of the show during its pre-production period up to and through opening. Actors' Equity Association does not yet use this title. Frequently you will also hear a replacement stage manager who is the team lead referred to as a PSM.

On touring productions under the aegis of AEA or on all Broadway shows, there is a mandated minimum number of stage managers:

- For a play, one stage manager and one assistant stage manager
- For a musical, one stage manager, one assistant stage manager, and one second assistant stage manager

Production stage management is a big job, but a rewarding one, filled (under the right circumstances) with passion, energy, friendship, comradery, comedy, accomplishment, and applause. The following chapters are my suggestions and methods for taking the show from idea, to opening, and beyond.

3
Getting the Job

If you can figure this one out, you can make millions. Getting the job is hard, and unlike most professions, it doesn't get any easier the longer you've worked or the more credits you have on your résumé. Even if a director or a general manager you've worked with before wants you on the show, there are others who must also sign off on you before you get hired. So no matter how experienced you may be, every interview is starting from scratch, every inquiry is a new introduction.

And since the cast of characters changes frequently, most of the people doing the hiring will never have heard of you—no matter how many productions you've done. There is no seniority in the theatre; you're always starting over again.

Who Hires You?

Like everything else in this book—it depends. Powerful directors often insist on their choice of stage managers. I have managed multiple shows for Mike Nichols, Gene Saks, Marcia Milgrom Dodge, and Graciela Danielle. Often, a production stage manager is put forward by the director, to be agreed upon by the producer and management.

Equally as often, the general manager will put forward the name of the stage manager they think best suited to this particular show. Then the director may accept or reject this suggestion. General managers used to have in-house stage managers that they would use for every show, but this is much less common now.

Powerful producers, with their own producing offices, may also have stage managers they insist do their productions. Regional theatres like the Manhattan Theatre Club and the Roundabout have a stable of stage managers they try use on their shows. Directors going into those theatres know in advance that they will be handed one of several stage managers.

But whoever it is that suggests the PSM/SM whether it's the director, producer, general manager, or choreographer—the team all have to sign off on the final choice. Production stage managers almost always hire their own assistants in consultation with the general manager.

Getting Your First Job

There are many paths, most involving a good deal of luck. But here are a few of the most reliable.

PRODUCTION ASSISTING

Being a PA, a production assistant, is a great entry-level job for a would-be stage manager. The job usually begins on the first day of rehearsal and ends on opening night. It requires working the same hours as a stage manager and performing many of the same tasks. However, the pay is terrible and there are no benefits like health insurance or vacation pay. It is cheap stage management labor. The advantages are that you'll quickly learn how a commercial production is put together, you'll meet an enormous number of people who may hire you on their next show, and, most importantly, you may become a substitute stage manager if the show has a substantial run.

SUBBING

As soon as a commercial production opens, the production stage manager will begin to train substitute stage managers, or subs. A sub will usually learn to run one or both sides of the stage deck and will come in to work on short notice when a stage manager is ill or must be out of the building during a performance. When a stage manager takes a vacation, a sub is brought in, usually for a week at a time. A stage manager may be a sub on a number of different shows at the same time, but of course not on the same night. This is a great way to get to know the cast, crew, and management of the running show and to be a logical choice for a replacement when one of the permanent stage managers leaves a show. A wise production stage manager will make the production assistant into the sub on a show. The PA already knows the intricacies of the show, so the training time is minimal. And since subbing pays the same as regular stage managing, the production stage manager is in essence paying back the PA for the slave wages earned during production. The PSM will get much better and happier PAs if the sub jobs go to them.

A Story about Long-Term Relationships

I have been working with one of my assistants, Jim Woolley, for over 30 years and hope to keep doing so. By now he's really more a business partner. More recently, when I was doing a seminar at North Carolina School of the Arts (now called University of North Carolina School of the Arts), I met a student, Rachel Wolff, who wanted to work with me when she graduated. She kept in touch, asked for an interview on a new musical I was doing, and I hired her as a PA. Then she subbed on that show. On the next show, I hired her as a second assistant and then as a stage manager for the national tour of the same show. On a third show, I hired her as the first assistant. She kept proving herself and I kept moving her up the chain of responsibility. Most recently she replaced me as the lead SM on the Broadway revival of *Annie* when I left the show.

There are very few directors, general managers, production managers or producers whom I have I worked with only once. Building long-term relationships in the commercial theatre is essential, in both directions. Do your best to work multiple times with those who hire you; it looks good on your resume and you know each others' style. And if you find assistants who work well with you—and compensate for your weak areas—keep working with them. Turn to your long-term colleagues to ask for advice, and ask them to alert you to upcoming jobs.

ACTORS' EQUITY ASSOCIATION

AEA has job postings on their website every week. Even if you're not a member of AEA yet, you probably know someone who is. The job listings are quite valuable, not just for the individual listings, but also for following trends about which theatres and which areas of the country are doing the most hiring.

STAGE MANAGERS' ASSOCIATION

The SMA was founded in 1985 as a way for stage managers to meet each other, to share ideas and ask for help, and to lobby for a greater voice within Actors' Equity Association. Over the years, it has also become a job referral service and a great way for younger stage managers to meet and learn from more experienced ones. You don't have to be in AEA to join. It's low-key and fun—and it helps stage managers find work.

ONLINE SITES

Certain websites, like Playbill (playbill.com), have job listings as well as casting notices. And, of course, you should check the social media sites like Linkedin, Facebook, Twitter or whichever is the current favorite. I have tracked down many of the people I was interested in hiring using one of these sites.

Negotiating Your Contract

This could be its own book and may not be appropriate for a general discussion, but here's the gist. Scale salaries are relatively good, especially under the AEA/Broadway League production contract. These are the weekly stage management salaries as of September 29, 2014:
- Stage manager for a musical: $3,058
- Stage manager for a play: $2,628

- 1st assistant stage manager for a musical: $2,416
- 1st assistant stage manager for a play: $2,148
- 2nd assistant stage manager for a musical: $2,019

However, in addition to salary, the following items are up for negotiation:

- *Billing.* Where does your name appear on the Playbill? On the poster? In the album? In newspaper ads? On the website? Does it appear at all? Early in my career, I wanted people in the business to know my name and so I gave up a higher salary for better billing. I wanted those who do the hiring to get used to seeing my name.
- *Class of Transportation.* When traveling by plane, producers will naturally fly you coach, unless business or first class airfare is negotiated. It is common for production stage managers to negotiate business or first class airfare for flights to Europe or Asia or for flights of over three hours duration within the United States.
- *Housing.* If you are traveling with a pet, a significant other, a bicycle or motorcycle, or anything unusual, this must be negotiated into your contract. You may or may not have to pay for the privilege of traveling with these extras. Also, you may be able to negotiate a housing upgrade.
- *Notice for Termination.* The standard AEA contract calls for you to give a two-week notice if you are planning to leave the show. Most general managers will ask for at least four weeks' notice because they need time to replace you. You may want to ask for something in return for this longer notice.
- *Choice of Assistants and PAs.* Producers and general managers often have friends who are stage managers. It's not unusual for them to want to do those friends a favor by hiring them as your assistant. My advice is to negotiate approval of all your assistants. You should agree to interview and consider anyone the producers or general managers may recommend—but the final hiring decision should be yours.
- *Directorial Rights for Subsequent Companies.* If there is no associate director on a show, and if the original director is not going to direct subsequent productions, then the logical person to direct is the original production stage manager. This must be negotiated.
- *Ancillary Contracts.* The stage manager often has a role to play in recording the cast album and TV commercials, as well as in TV appearances and the Tony Awards. These are items you want to consider in your negotiations.

How much you choose to insist on controlling each of these items depends upon how much power you perceive you have in the negotiation. But remember: You cannot negotiate with power unless you're willing to lose the job. Don't bluff.

Beginning the Job

Like everything else in the commercial theatre, there is no standard start time for a production stage manager. When I first began in the business, I would get a call for a job, and then six weeks later I would be on contract and getting paid. Now I get a call for a job and paid work on that commercial production might not begin until two to three years later. The time between the initial call and the actual production is taken up with readings, workshops, and endless meetings—often while the producers are out raising money to finance the show.

A stage manager is required by Actors' Equity Association to receive two weeks' salary prior to the first day of actor rehearsal. This extra salary is meant to compensate for the meetings, auditions, and design conferences that may stretch on for over a year. Workshops and readings pay very little, usually $100 per week. So unless you can negotiate a pre-production fee, you will work a long time on a new production before you ever make any money from it. And, of course there is always the possibility that investors take a pass and the show never goes on. This is why so many stage managers are doing workshops and readings while running their Broadway show.

However, the pre-production period is the most valuable time for production stage managers, since this is when all the basic decisions are made. Whether you are being paid properly or not, the stage manager's input is critical during pre-production. You must insist on being involved and simply do your best to negotiate fair pre-production money.

4

Pre-Production

The Idea

Pre-production, one of the most valuable and least-understood segments of the production process, includes everything that happens before a show goes into rehearsal.

This is the crucial time when the author, director, choreographer, designers, producers, general manager, and production stage manager hammer out exactly what kind of production they want to create.

The pre-production period can be as short as six months or last as long as several years. Cameron Mackintosh, arguably the finest producer of the current era, has a 52-week rule. From the moment he hires the creative team and commits the money, it should take no more that 52 weeks to open the first preview. Any less rushes the project. Any more takes the urgency away from the project.

The producer 's choice of material, director, designers, and physical theatre will set the scope of the production. Will this be an off-Broadway show, a Broadway show in a small house, a multi-set show in a large house, or something in between? This really means setting the budget for the show and asking the creative team to adhere to its limitations.

Meetings with the Director/Producer/ General Manager

These sessions work out the most basic parameters of the show. Before anything else happens, discussions and decisions will be made about all of the issues discussed here.

A Story

Here is a story about *Cats*, Andrew Lloyd Webber and Tim Rice's blockbuster based on T.S. Elliot's *Old Possum's Book of Practical Cats*. When the director, Trevor Nunn, was first handed the script, he thought it was a children's show destined for schools and regional theatres. Lloyd Webber said, "Think bigger." Result: it became the biggest production ever mounted at that time. And until recently the longest-running Broadway show of all time, grossing over $2 billion worldwide.

CAST SIZE

This is a major decision for both management and the creative team since it affects both budget and creativity. For dramas, cast size is easy—how many characters are there and how many understudies are needed? But for musicals, the size of the ensemble is a negotiated item. For *Spamalot*, choreographer Casey Nicholaw originally wanted eight men and eight women for the ensemble—but the general manager had budgeted for four men and four women. They ended up with six men and six women. They reached the compromise when the choreographer described what he could and could not do with various ensemble sizes, while the general manager described the cost effect on the weekly operating expenses. Always remember—the higher the weekly operating expenses, the less likely the show is to have a long run.

An early casting decision is whether or not to have stars in the production. Stars bring high visibility to a show and deliver a major lift to ticket sales, but they also generate many costs: high salaries, transportation, star dressers, assistants, housing, and daily perks.

PRODUCTION CALENDAR

Any production calendar must start with a format, and I'm sorry to say that as of this writing, there isn't a good one.

Many of us use Calendar Creator, a PC program by Broderbund that does not work on Mac. It is the clearest of all the calendar programs and is preferred by many general managers because they're used to it. Its advantages are its familiarity and relative quickness. Its disadvantages are that it must be used on a PC. The only way to share the calendar with your team is as a PDF attachment. If you're working on a PC, this is currently the best choice.

I've recently started doing my calendars on iCal because I work on a Mac. You can fit almost as much information onto iCal as you can onto Calendar Creator, but it is more difficult to print out clearly. The chief advantage is that it can be stored in iCloud so it's always up-to-date for anyone who has a Mac, iPhone, or iPad. Google Calendar is also a good choice and works with either Mac or PC. And because it is web-based, it too is always up-to-date, but has similar printing problems to iCal. There are also calendar templates on Microsoft Word and Excel, but I've always found them to be clumsy. My advice is to work with all three and see which you like best.

The bare bones of the production calendar are worked out in these early production meetings. The producer and general manager will decide the following:

- What is the targeted opening night whether in New York or some other point of origin?
- How long is the casting period?
- How many weeks of rehearsal are necessary and affordable?
- How many weeks of tech are necessary and affordable?
- How many preview performances should be played before opening night?
- Will there be an out-of-town tryout? If so, will the show come directly into the point of origin after that tryout?
- What is the performance schedule?
- What are the important holidays that could affect schedule or ticket sales?

Once these basic decisions are made, the stage manager will work with the designers and production manager to flesh out the calendar to include the following:

- Design deadlines that allow for the approval, drafting, bidding, and building of the set, costumes, lighting, and sound
- Build schedules or shop schedules for all technical elements
- Delivery deadlines for all technical elements
- Rehearsal schedule
- Load-in schedule
- Tech schedule

And since everyone is usually working on more than one production at a time, availabilities for all key personnel should be included on this calendar.

These calendars can become quite intricate, but they are always based on the initial decisions made by the producer and general manager. Each new piece of information should be added to the production calendar and regular distribution of the calendar is essential. Figure 4.1 is an example of the production calendar done in Calendar Creator for a recent show with all the personal details removed.

OUT-OF-TOWN TRYOUT

Billy Rose—that fabulous producer, showman, and lyricist—famously quipped, "I wouldn't open a can of tuna fish without taking it out of town first."

The challenges of "tryout" in town with New York's predatory press and demanding audience in daily attendance are well documented. Previews of *Spider-Man Turn Off the Dark* were extensively reviewed, commented upon, and shared well before this technically complex production had a chance to work out its kinks.

Even though the constant glare of social media makes it hard to try anything out "under the radar," there are still certain venues and cities that are great places to try out. Chicago and Seattle are two cities that come immediately to mind. However the costs of an out of town tryout can be prohibitive, especially on a large musical. The current rule of thumb is that going out-of-town will add $2 million to the capitalization of a musical and

$1 million to the capitalization of a play. That said, there are ways to lower these costs.

Out-of-town theatres are usually one of three types:

- A Broadway-sized rental theatre in which the producer makes a four-wall deal: renting the theatre, selling the show from scratch, paying all expenses, and taking all responsibility for everything that takes place within those four walls
- A smaller League of Regional Theatres (LORT) theatre, like the Old Globe, or La Jolla Playhouse in San Diego, where the host theatre produces the show, often with enhancement money from the commercial producer. The show is usually part of the LORT theatre's subscription season
- A larger subscription house, like the Fifth Avenue Theatre in Seattle, where the tryout production becomes part of that theatre's season

LORT theatres and larger civic theatres usually have a sizable subscription base, which eases the ticket-selling burden. Both the out-of-town press and audiences tend to be more forgiving than their New York counterparts, so changes to a show may be done in relative peace and anonymity. Unless the commercial producer is doing a four-wall deal, it is the host theatre that becomes the producer during the show's try out. Since LORT budgets are usually less than a Broadway budget, commercial producers often enhance the local budget to create a higher quality, Broadway-ready show and to test out complex design elements.

Generally, the better out-of-town theatres have good local shops that can build a portion of the set, props, and costumes at less than New York rates.

It is the producer who makes the final decision about an out-of-town tryout with recommendations and input from the general manager. Here are some questions and considerations for the production stage manager:

- Do the conditions at the out-of-town theatre match those of the New York theatre? Consider off-stage space, fly space, dressing rooms, sightlines.
- If the production is not being built at or near the out-of-town venue, how long does trucking take from the scene shop to the out-of-town theatre?
- What's the cost of trucking? Not just the initial trucking, but also that of any set pieces that may be added or changed.
- Are there local scene, lighting, prop, and sound shops?
- Will the dry tech in the theatre keep the stage manager away from the rehearsal studio too long? On *Shrek The Musical,* we rehearsed the final two weeks at a studio near the out-of-town theatre so that I could attend some rehearsals while dry teching at the theatre. Also, the director could then attend dry tech each night after rehearsals.
- Will the first assistant stage manager also have to be at dry tech? Who runs rehearsals?
- What is the reputation of crew at the out-of-town theatre?
- If there are children in the production, could some of them be hired locally?
- Is there adequate housing for the traveling company within walking distance of the theatre?

- How long will the production have to be shut down while transporting the production elements back to New York City?
- Will there be rehearsals during this shutdown?
- Should the shutdown be long enough to allow for recasting?
- Is the local orchestra pit approximately the same size as in New York?
- Does the out-of-town theatre have the right "feel" for the show? *Phantom of the Opera*, for example, doesn't work as well in a modern, unadorned theatre as it does in a more traditional, ornate proscenium house.

Another Story

When Emanuel Azenberg was producing Neil Simon's *Broadway Bound*, he assembled the team in his office for the initial production meeting: Gene Saks, the director, David Mitchell, the scenic designer, Joseph Aulisi, the costume designer, Tharon Musser, the lighting designer, Tom Morse, the sound designer, and me, the production stage manager. He opened with, "Let's design the national tour first." We all laughed, but took his point—pare the show down to its essentials now. Azenberg even asked Neil Simon to rewrite some of the stage directions to make the set simpler. We had our marching orders from the producer and scaled the show accordingly.

Design Meetings

The Idea

After the producer, author, and director have approved the idea of the scenic design, there is a period of wonderful collaboration among the various designers, the production manager, the production stage manager, and the director. Design meetings work out the specifics of all design elements. If all the creative artists have worked together before, this pre-production period can sharpen and enhance each of the designs with respectful input from each participant.

In addition to the practical considerations, all the designers must agree during pre-production on the color palette for the show. This may seem obvious, but we've all done shows where the lighting designer was surprised by the color of the set or costumes.

The production stage manager tends to be the most practical person at the table, but it is very important not to stunt creative ideas—even if you know ultimately the idea on the table won't work. Bad ideas often lead to good ideas, and they must be nurtured.

In my view it is imperative for the production stage manager to attend pre-production design meetings. You have to understand the genesis of the design idea, how all the design elements are meant to work together, and to give appropriate input.

Most importantly, as described in detail below, you will be the arbitrator in the inevitable battle for space—on the deck, in the wings, and overhead—that will ensue between the various departments. The production stage manager must see the big picture and know how to prioritize everyone's needs.

A Story

On *Spamalot*, scenic designer Tim Hatley had originally designed wooden wings that would pivot shut to form a solid wall on each side of the stage. I held off giving my point of view until late in the process, waiting to see where this idea would lead. When it looked as if that idea was going to be carried forward, I pointed out that approximately 10 seconds before the end of each scene, those walls would have to begin their pivot in order to allow scenery and actors to come on and off stage, tipping the end of the scene. Hatley instantly agreed and the design was changed to wider, non-pivoting wings.

Scenic Design

The Idea

Full-on animations are usually cost- or time-prohibitive, but computer savvy designers frequently have a studio assistant who can put together a simple animatic. If an animatic or animation is not an option, the pre-production team must either work with a model, drawings, or renderings while talking through each scenic change in the show. But regardless of how these transitions are visualized, the timing, which scenic pieces are being moved, and storage must be agreed upon in pre-productions where changes are relatively inexpensive. Changes made in the theatre with actors, stagehands, and musicians on payroll can break a show financially.

A Story

On both *Spamalot* and *Shrek The Musical*, scenic designer Tim Hatley made animations of the scene changes. Although they were rough, all the designers, the production manager, and I could see how many pieces were moving at a time, how many pieces were coming on or going off stage as well as the intended speed of each change. The director and choreographer could see what staging challenges presented themselves and how long they had for actor crossovers and costume changes. The composer and musical director could gauge how much incidental music needed to be written.

PRODUCTION STAGE MANAGER'S INVOLVEMENT

The decision about what to automate and what to move manually is really up to the designer, the general manager, and the production manager. That team decides about relative cost of man vs. machine. However, because it involves coordination, the stage manager is crucial to these decisions. If two pieces of scenery must move together in harmony and match, they must both be automated. If exact timing of a set piece movement is necessary (to match a dance move, for instance) then automation is necessary. Knowing what kinds of scenic coordination will be need is essential to decisions about automation.

Once again, the stage manager needs to be involved at the earliest stages of the design to participate in the discussions, and some considerations include:

- What kind of dancing is there in the show and what kind of deck is required?
- Is there an upstage crossover?
- Will there be flying, pyro, or other special effects that can necessitate special, additional manpower?
- Are there elevators that would require one or more additional stage managers?
- How much time will it take to tech the individual elements?

THE CALENDAR

In design pre-production, the scenic design process needs to be quantified. How much time does the designer need to complete the conceptual designs? How much time and how many assistants are needed to draft the design? And since the construction bids are usually more than the budget allows, you have to factor in how much time will be needed after the bid session to redesign and redraft to come in on budget.

At this point, the production manager should weigh in with how long it will take to build the show and how long to load it into the theatre. Both the build and the load-in should be figured so that you do not incur overtime charges.

Then the production stage manager can work backwards, laying out in the calendar dry tech time, load-in, scenic build, bid and redrafting time, drafting time, and design time to arrive at a calendar date for the approval of the conceptual design by the producer, director, and author. This is sometimes a cruel reality check for the producer and general manager. When time is not accurately accounted, overtime or missed performances can easily result.

Lighting Design and Special Effects

The Idea

During the scenic drafting process, the lighting designer works very closely with the scenic designer to divvy up space, both on the deck and in the air. Both designers will need as much space as they can get and both will try to cram as much equipment into the available space as possible. And if there are special effects, many of which are electrified, these will also require space, either overhead or on the deck.

In this struggle for space, it's important to be generous. Moving pieces must not pass impractically close to each other. As Artie Siccardi, a great production manager, says, "In the theatre, there's no such thing as a straight line." Air currents, bent pipes, humidity, and speed all affect moving scenery. Insist on enough room in the air and on the deck to keep scenic pieces from colliding.

It's essential that the stage manager and production manager keep a close eye on how tightly scenery, lighting, and special effects equipment is hung in the air and placed in the wings—actors need space to move and might also require quick-change booths for wardrobe.

Within the realm of lighting design are a host of other design professionals. These might include the moving light programmers and the special effects designer. Depending the lighting designer's personal working style or the complexity of the production, the lighting designer might also serve as the projection or video designer.

LIGHT LADDERS AND BOOMS

Flying light ladders, fixed light ladders, and fixed booms in the wings greatly impact both movement backstage and productions costs. Flying light ladders are immensely practical because they can hold more lighting instruments than conventional booms. Since they can be flown in and out, they can be positioned to take up an entire wing when required and then flown out, leaving space for deck-mounted scenery or actors.

However, flying light ladders require a powerful winch, which is expensive. And they are time-consuming since each movement of each light ladder must be programmed and teched. Fixed booms are less expensive but hold fewer lighting instruments and take up valuable wing space, decreasing the width available for other elements. Fixed light ladders are usually hung just higher than the tallest piece of scenery entering from that wing and are the width of the wing. They are inexpensive and can hold a great number of lighting instruments, but none of the lighting positions can be low. Fixed light ladders are useful for high sidelight positions, but not for more dramatic low sidelight.

It's very important that you be involved with these lighting location decisions. Only the production stage manager can understand the potential traffic problems with actors, required wing space for maneuvering scenery, and need for quick-change booths. Compromise among the departments is essential and the stage manager should broker these compromises.

MOVING LIGHTS

Moving lights are practical in many ways. They are faster to program than conventional lights are to focus. They decrease the number of conventional focusing instruments necessary, cut down on focus time, and are much more flexible as the needs of the show change. However, each moving light is much more expensive than a conventional instrument.

You will also need a moving light programmer (an additional salary) and a moving light console available each day of tech. Because moving lights give the designer more flexibility and are faster to program, they actually speed up tech. And on the road, they are even more valuable: just hang the lamps, find their "zero," and run the show. No focus required.

While there are different generations of moving lights in rental inventory, we still figure that we need 10% spares in moving lights. As moving lights break down during the run of the show they will need to be replaced by the spares and repairs. So you will need to allocate space for the moving light "hospital" in house to repair the instruments.

Lighting styles and equipment fashions come and go. Some shows are all moving lights. Others mix moving lights with conventional. Others—frequently revivals—decide to use only conventional instruments—for that certain period look. If they fit the design style of your show, moving lights are worth the effort and expense.

FOLLOW SPOTS

Most musicals and many plays use follow spots—also called front lights by many old-timers. The follow spots should not be confused with front of house lights in various positions in the house—balcony rail, box booms, or ceiling mounted. Those are the purview of the lighting designer not the production stage manager.

The PSM is concerned with helping the GM budget for the time and cost implications of the lighting designer's decisions. If the spots are not in the traditional follow spot booth, where will they be? Do follow spot towers need to be built? At what cost? Will any seats be lost?

SPECIAL EFFECTS

Special effects cannot be an afterthought. Usually, there is a special effects designer who should take part in the initial production design meetings. For the most part, the special effects designer works within the lighting department, and electricians service the special effects needs. Special effects may include fog, mist and rain (water), smoke and haze (fog machines), even fire and explosions. Depending on the production there may be other show-specific special effects that fall within other departments. Each of these standard special effects function under specific rules laid down by both the local fire departments and by various unions. Many effects, especially fire and explosions, require a separate, licensed operator to be present at every performance.

As previously mentioned, special effects require space, overhead and/or on the deck. And many must be electrified, either on a temporary basis by trailing a cable on the deck or permanently by wiring overhead. The scenic, lighting, and sound departments must all be involved in solving the needs of special effects.

PRODUCTION STAGE MANAGER'S INVOLVEMENT

The amount and kind of lighting equipment directly affects everything on the production—from the calendar to the tech. I suggest doing some research on the lighting designer by talking to other stage managers. Is this designer fast or slow? Are there any quirks you should know about? Below are several details relating to lighting and special effects that the production stage manager must consider during the pre-production period.

Moving Lights

The more moving lights on the show, the shorter the load-in and tech time. Moving lights cut down the number of instruments to be hung, thus shortening the focus time. Moving lights mean that a special light can be focused remotely—no need for a man on a ladder.

Follow Spots

How many follow spots are being used? The fewer the follow spots, the longer the tech. For example if you have only two follow spots and more that two featured actors, the lighting plot fixtures will have to cover some of them. That's extra cues and time.

Special Effects

Discuss how much haze and smoke will be used in the show. Both AEA and OSHA have very strict guidelines about smoke and haze. Equity requires a chart of how many minutes each machine will run. Some actors—usually singers—won't work with either smoke or haze. My experience is that the best low-hanging fog for these effects uses a combination of dry ice and liquid nitrogen. The stage manager and the electricians need to be in close communication about the volume and keep the stage from getting too slick. But if it does, I don't hesitate to send an actor (or if necessary, a stage hand) on stage with a towel to wipe up. It's a good idea to stage dance numbers away from the haze source.

THE CALENDAR

Using our "working backwards" system, figure how much focus time in the theatre a lighting designer will need before dry tech (technical rehearsal without actors) begins. Then figure how much time the electrics load-in requires. Remember that lighting is usually hung before any scenery is loaded into the building. Trucking time to the theatre (more if it's an out-of-town theatre) and rental shop preparation time must then be back-counted in order to figure how much design time the lighting designer will have before a bid session. And like the scenery, the lighting rig will probably come in over budget and need to be rethought.

Focus time will be greater with a conventional lighting rig. It decreases as more moving lights are used in the design—but the more moving lights in the design the more time the programmer needs in the house during set up. Generally, front-of-house focus can be accomplished once the downstage-most piece of scenery—usually the false proscenium —is installed. Focus time should be worked out with both the lighting designer and the production electrician. Of course, like every other element of the calendar, there has to be agreement that everyone works to the schedule.

Sound Design

The Idea

The range of equipment used in sound design is probably the largest of any department. It can stretch from absolutely none—no mics, no recorded sound—to a rig that is larger and more expensive than the lighting equipment. And more than any other department, sound design is geek heaven. There is a tendency for the designer to want the newest, most technologically advanced, and most expensive equipment available. Depending on the type and amount of equipment, the sound designer may also be fighting for some of the overhead and deck space.

PRODUCTION STAGE MANAGER'S INVOLVEMENT

As the PSM, there is very little you can or should do to influence the sound design. The size of the sound rig depends on the creative team—especially the composer—and the budget.

If radio (wireless) mics are being used in the show, there must be at least one backstage sound person to check and swap mics. Use of radio mics also means that positions must be allocated for the antennae (one per mic) and an area for the backstage sound person to work and repair mics must be designated.

Most headset communication systems are fairly simple. The stage manager wants to be able to speak to and hear from selected departments—and not from others. That is, you should be able to program certain departments into your channel and to cut out others. You *do* want to be able to speak to your assistants, electric board operator, winch control operator, and certain department heads, probably carpentry and props. You *do not* want to tune into follow spot operators and lighting designers; however, they should be able to speak or listen to you when necessary.

Many headset systems now have a "privacy channel." This allows the ASMs and selected crew to speak to one another when they need to discuss an unfolding event (or gossip) during a show without the calling stage manager overhearing. I never want to hear extraneous chatter when calling a show.

A Story

My headset system on one musical was so complicated it couldn't be repaired in the theatre, or indeed by anyone in New York City. A tech had to be flown in from California to repair it. After it failed twice, I replaced it with a simpler, repairable headset system. The show didn't need this fancy a system; the sound designer wanted to try it out and no one said "no."

BACKSTAGE VIDEO

The sound department is also responsible for communications and safety backstage video. You should give the sound designer a list of all the video shots you need to run the show. It should include a high definition master shot in color and an infrared master shot to see in the dark. Additional shots and monitors may be necessary to clearly oversee safe operation of trap doors and moving scenery. All backstage video (considered by the unions to be "monitoring") are the province of the sound department. This also includes pit video, off-stage audio and video, and dressing room audio and video.

SOUND DESK AND MIXING CONSOLE

The sound desk and mixing console is normally placed in the center-rear of the orchestra section of the house and usually requires the removal of seats. Since this reduces the seating capacity of the house, the general manager must be a part of the discussion. Very few shows mix from a box seat position or from backstage because the sound mixer cannot hear the true balance of the show's mix. In newly designed and built houses you will usually find that the location of the sound desk and mixing console has already been accounted for.

The choice of who to hire to mix the sound is the sole province of the sound designer. I believe the mixer is an artist. No matter how good the design, the show will only sound as good as the operator who mixes. If your show has a star or perhaps a difficult actor, it is important that the sound mixer be actor-friendly.

Some mixers are very good at training other mixers to replace them and also in setting up future companies. And some are prima donnas who are unwilling to pass along the tricks and idiosyncrasies of the mix. A little research (once again, call people who have worked with them) on the mixer can make for a harmonious show, and if all goes well, for many a happy tour.

PIT LAYOUT

In a musical, it's important for the sound designer and the musical director to lay out the pit early in pre-production. The composer, musical director, and general manager determine the number of musicians. Then the pit should be laid out to ensure that all the players and their instruments fit in the orchestra pit of the intended theatres. If the pit is too small, the orchestra can be divided among several other locations: in the house, in the basement, and occasionally, in extreme cases, off site. I've done a number of shows this way. It does however require a more complicated sound and video design. Once identified, these additional spaces may require expensive modifications. A budget item to keep in mind.

Figure 4.2 is a sample pit layout for the revival of *Annie*. This layout in Broadway's Palace Theatre is simple and clean. The most important thing to note is the acoustical isolation of the drum kit. The effect of constant "drumming" is a growing OSHA concern that sometimes sends a show's percussion-heavy section to the basement or perhaps off site. In addition, drums need to be isolated so that their sound doesn't bleed through to other orchestra mics and muddy the sound quality.

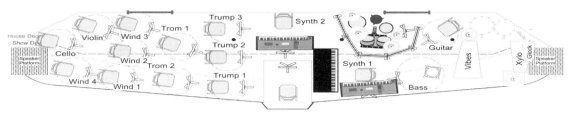

Figure 4.2: Pit layout 2012 revival of *Annie,* Palace Theatre, New York

THE CALENDAR

In addition to the normal items like design time, bid dates, shop work dates, and load-in, several other items for the sound department are important for the calendar.

Orchestra Sessions

How many orchestra sessions (of three hours each) are necessary to properly rehearse the players? Where will these rehearsals take place? Orchestra rehearsals are almost always held away from the theatre for two reasons. First, other than the orchestra pit there is rarely a large enough space in the theatre for such rehearsals. Second, even if there were a large enough space, the sound would certainly interfere with onstage work and vice versa. Often, to minimize the amount of turn-around time between orchestra studio rehearsals and the theatre pit rehearsals with the cast, large instruments are rented separately for each venue. Typically these would be pianos, drums, percussion, harp, xylophone or vibraphone. If the drummer wants to play his own kit in the show, his drums would be loaded into the pit early and the drummer would use a rented (but identical) kit for the studio rehearsals.

SIM Sessions

Balancing the theatre's speakers to get the best and most even sound for all the audience requires absolute quiet and is usually done late at night when no work or rehearsal is in progress. This Source Independent Measurement (SIM) session should be scheduled and put on the calendar.

Sitzprobe and Wandelprobe

These are two German rehearsal terms that have been adopted by American opera and musical theatre. They are rehearsals that bring cast and orchestra together for the first time. The Sitzprobe is done in a studio (usually where the orchestra has been rehearsing), and the Wandelprobe is done onstage with the orchestra in the pit. I prefer a Sitzprobe to a Wandelprobe because the purpose of this rehearsal is for the cast to hear the exact instrument that gives them their pitch and to hear the orchestrations for the first time—with both the orchestra and cast in close proximity in the same room, the cast can easily hear the subtleties of the orchestrations and the individual instruments.

Orchestra Seating

Orchestra seating is usually done in one three-hour session in the theatre after the Sitzprobe and before the beginning of orchestra tech. It's important to check that each orchestra member feels comfortable in the pit, that there is enough room to play each instrument, and that each instrument has a proper amplification setup.

Sound Check

The sound check is usually one three-hour session in the theatre after the orchestra seating and before the beginning of orchestra tech. This allows the sound department to check each player for the quality of the amplified sound, to adjust mic positions if necessary, and to get preliminary balances for the whole orchestra.

Mic Use and Maintenance

At the beginning of a tech rehearsal, the sound department will usually need 30 minutes to get actors into their mics. At the end of a tech session, at least 15 minutes should be allowed for the sound department to gather the mics. Before the next tech session, the sound department will need to re-battery the mics—this is usually a 30-minute job. When an actor is teching a scene that includes a costume with wigs or hats, they should be worn—wigs and hats make a great impact on the quality of the sound.

Costume Design

The Idea

In costume design, the first thing to be worked out is the style. Is the show to be realistic? Fantasy? Heavily detailed? Period? What is the clothing meant to convey? On a fantasy show like *Shrek The Musical*, this basic design decision was difficult and time-consuming. The director, choreographer, scenic designer, author, producer, and general manager all have to agree on the overall look of the show. Then you can move on to the practical considerations, such as how many costumes there are to be in the show, how many changes per actor, how many dressers, and what the budget is.

Once the basic design decision is made, the costume designer will work with the scenic and lighting designers to agree on the color palette.

PRODUCTION STAGE MANAGER'S INVOLVEMENT

There are several costume design decisions that involve the PSM:
- Is there strenuous dancing or acrobatics in the show?
- How do the costumes reflect these needs in terms of materials and construction?
- Are there hats and headpieces that the sound designer needs to consider?
- Will there be "special" costumes—overly heavy and needing ventilation, skimpy or nude, or involving stilts or platform shoes?

General managers are often unwilling to build understudy and swing costumes until the show is in previews. This is entirely practical. Costume designs have been known to change during rehearsal and previews, so don't spend the money on costumes that will never be worn. However, it is your job to be sure the swings and understudies can perform in costume when necessary. Wardrobe supervisors are a very good resource here. They can tell you which costumes must be built to get an understudy or swing onstage, and which costumes the principal performer and their cover can share. Swing and understudy costumes is another negotiation with the general manager. Interestingly, the costume designer usually does not participate. I always come to an early agreement with the general manager and wardrobe supervisor on the swings' and understudies' costuming.

It's important to check out the wardrobe facilities at your intended venues. *Shrek The Musical*, was the perfect example of a show that needed a large wardrobe room with multiple washers and dryers. The heavier the show's wardrobe, the more space and machines the wardrobe department needs. In a try-out house, roadhouse, or sit-down house, you will often have to find a creative way to carve out all the space needed for running wardrobe. And don't forget you need storage for those extra costumes for understudies, swings, and replacements.

THE CALENDAR

The design and bidding of the costumes will almost always come after the scenery has been designed, and it will be done in consultation with the scenic designer. Often the scenic and costume designers are the same person, especially if the scenic designer is British.

A basic decision for the production is whether or not to tech the show in costume. The British nearly always do it this way, the Americans generally do not. I am in favor of teching in costume for a host of reasons. It gives the lighting designer the true color palette onstage. It forces traffic decisions about quick-change booths and backstage choreography to be made early in tech. It allows time to tech and time quick changes. And it forces the costume shops to have the clothes completed early. General managers often do not like teching in costumes because the wardrobe staff and dressers must be on salary earlier. If you are not teching in costume, then you have to schedule a separate costume tech of at least one day, usually two days on a musical. This costume tech will usually happen after the full show is teched and before the Sitzprobe.

Several wardrobe items should be included on the calendar:
- Design time, including number of assistants for how many weeks
- Bid due date
- Award bid date
- Pre-rehearsal measurements for cast
- Delivery dates for costumes

Hair and Wig Design

The Idea

Like sound design, hair and wig design has a great range of complexity. Some shows have no hair and wig department at all. Other large musicals may have a department of five or six people and hundreds of wigs. The scope of work and staffing of this department depends largely on how many characters any one actor plays, the period of the show, and the budget.

Because the hair design is such an integral part of the costume design, the costume designer usually chooses the hair and wig designer. The hair designer and the costume designer work out the number of wigs and hairstyles they believe necessary for the show, and then submit designs and requests to the general manager for budgeting.

PRODUCTION STAGE MANAGER'S INVOLVEMENT

The production stage manager coordinates time and space needs with the hair design team. Consider the following:

- During pre-rehearsal and rehearsal, there are usually at least three wig fittings per actor, more if there are a lot of wigs. Your schedule needs to include time for wig, costume, and makeup fittings. Fitting can be scheduled daily depending on that day's rehearsal schedule.
- Hair departments can have from one to five members. The hair room should be easily accessible, have running water, and have adequate power for wig ovens. Each hairdresser needs a station with a mirror, good lighting, and room to work.
- Once the number of wigs—several hundred on a musical—has been determined for a show, it's important to work with the hair supervisor to discuss adequate racks and wig blocks, storage for both active wigs and understudy wigs.

A Caution

The hair room can be the most fun of any room in the theatre when a show is running. However, the combination of ensemble singers and dancers along with hairdressers can often make for a gossipy room. When selecting the head of the hair department and the hairdressers, do some research (again, I recommend calling colleagues for background information). Some hairdressers can keep a room light-hearted and easy, while others can encourage a rumor-filled atmosphere.

THE CALENDAR

Hair, wigs and wardrobe are usually needed at the same time. Make a note in the calendar about the date the hair department should begin operation. Don't assume that the hair supervisor knows this.

Makeup Design

The Idea

On contemporary straight plays, makeup is almost an afterthought, something the actors generally do themselves with their own makeup kit. However, in period dramas or musicals, the makeup design and execution can be as complicated as wardrobe or hair.

A Story

On *Shrek The Musical*, I made a huge mistake with the makeup department. I had accounted for the enormous time and expense of the Shrek character makeup and prosthetics. But I hadn't counted on the time and expense for the other characters in the show. There were fairytale creatures, a donkey, and a female ogre, all of whom also had very complicated makeup designs, and some had prosthetics. I needed to find time for makeup design sessions, similar to hair and wardrobe fittings, for each character, often two or three sessions per actor, plus extensive makeup consultations during both tech and previews. Prosthetics were built in the theatre on a regular basis; this meant finding a dedicated, well-ventilated space for a workshop. There was also a makeup/prosthetics department of three people working the show; this meant another room with stations for three makeup artists, close to the stage with mirrors and lights. I simply hadn't accounted for the size, scope, and needs of the *Shrek* makeup department and did a lot of quick rearranging of dressing rooms out-of-town and in New York to accommodate this very necessary department.

PRODUCTION STAGE MANAGER'S INVOLVEMENT

As with costumes, hair, and makeup, the production stage manger has to plan for physical space as well as time to accommodate the show's makeup. Often a makeup consultant will work with the actors during tech and previews, and then leave the actors to apply their own makeup for the run of the show. But some shows have bigger demands.

Makeup Room
If you need makeup crew for the run of the show, then you usually set aside a room for them. Sometimes a solo makeup artist will go from dressing room to dressing room to do the work, needing no home base. Think about whether or not the makeup department could share space with hair or with wardrobe.

Unusual Makeup
Actors are required to supply their own makeup and brushes, unless those materials would not normally be in their personal kit. Make sure you have early discussions

with the makeup designer about what management will supply and what the actor will supply—it will prevent later misunderstandings.

Prosthetics

If there are prosthetics on a show, determine early in the process who, how, and where to build them. If built in the theatre, then a dedicated, ventilated room must be found. If they're built off site, then you'll need to arrange delivery. Some prosthetic materials eventually wear out. Double check how frequently a piece might need to be remade for both your calendar and the budget. While the materials used in making prosthetics might be toxic in their "raw" state, the final product worn by the actor must not be. Check with the prosthetics builder to be sure.

Fittings

If makeup or prosthetic sessions or fittings are done before moving into the theatre, you need to find a site for these fittings. As in the makeup room, there should be adequate mirrors, lights, and running water. Again, because of the changing needs of the rehearsal process, makeup sessions, like hair and wig fittings, can only be scheduled day by day.

THE CALENDAR

If there is a complicated makeup design, or if there are prosthetics involved in a show, makeup fittings must be scheduled in addition to costume and hair fittings. The number of costume, hair, and makeup fittings prior to rehearsals is limited and varies from contract to contract. It's advisable to get as many fittings as possible in before rehearsals begin, but keep close track these fittings to avoid overtime costs.

Video and Projection Design

The Idea

Projections and projection design used to be primarily handled by the lighting design team. But in recent years all aspects of video and projection design—with their own programmers and their own in-house control systems—has expanded exponentially. Keep a close eye on the fast emerging technology of LED screens and pixel mapping—it will impact the budget and every other aspect of the design and your production.

Before this recent explosion, projection equipment could be as simple as a shadow puppet or a 35mm slide projector. Equipment placement was either front of house, overhead onstage, from behind a projection surface, or all three. Images were contained on glass or film slides, motion picture film, or video and projected onto virtually any surface: traditional screens, scenery, architectural elements of the theatre like the back wall, moving objects—even actors. Important note here: if LED screens are in play in your production, those screens are not projection surfaces but are quite literally the projector themselves, with each LED broadcasting a pixel (or more) of the image. Thus they are both the projector (controlled by a media server and its programmer) as well as the scenic projection surface. Media technology style, equipment, and techniques are crossing over from the world of rock concert tours, dance clubs, and electronic dance festivals. How and whether these contemporary media techniques are used will depend on the director, designer, and budget of your show. I recommend that if you are not really up to date with the technology, find someone who is to help you out.

There are cost implications to keep in mind. Most projection designers work with multiple assistants for finding or creating images, programming, and cueing. The more extensive the projection design, the more expensive the projection system and the greater the tech time required. Also, the greater the throw distance, the more it will cost to get a high-quality image onto the stage.

VIDEO DESIGNER INTERACTION

Video Designers will work closely with many of the creative team to form the plan for projection.

Director

The director will decide whether or not projection is necessary for the production, how detailed the projection must be, and the idea of the content. Generally, the projection designer will offer samples of content to the director, and together they will decide on the specific sequence of images for the production.

Scenic Designer

The scenic designer will determine projection surfaces and color. Since the images must be projected onto some surface, the projection and scenic designers will determine the size and reflective qualities of the projection surface as well as how hidden these surfaces will be when not being used for projection. And if LED surfaces are being used, there are myriad other decisions to be made. Also, both designers must decide whether the projections are meant to be part of the scenery or a separate design that tells its own story. For instance, in a show like *Woman in White*, the projections really were the scenery and the scenic design was a number of highly reflective surfaces for delivery of video projection images. In *The People in the Picture*, the video images commented upon and enhanced the action onstage but were not a part of the scenery. For *Spamalot*, the video was projected onto existing scenery to give it different looks and to provide visual gags. In each case, the idea of the projection design was worked out well in advance of the scenery being finalized.

Lighting Designer

The lighting designer must be consulted for color, how the lighting and projection interact, and for space, dividing up hanging positions. Make sure that the lighting and projection designer are working within the same color palette. Schedule and monitor meetings between these designers so there are no surprises in dry tech. Design coordination is also needed if the projection is to aid the lighting by outlining pieces of scenery, providing a short color punch, creating effects like rain or lightning, or animating scenery. Be sure to consider that projectors take up space where lighting instruments are often hung, they can be noisy and may require cooling and/or noise-proof housing, and they require dark time to focus. The lighting designer/projection designer relationship is competitive and complementary at the same time.

General Manager

The general manager must approve projection rental cost, assistant time and cost, and additional dry tech time. Projectors are usually rented, and multiple, high-intensity projectors can cost as much in weekly rental as sound equipment.

THE CALENDAR

In laying out time requirements, think of the video and projection department just like the lighting department. Allow the same amount of time for production meetings, design time, bidding, and load-in for video and projection as for lighting—depending, of course, on the size of the show's projection design and rig. If part of your design, extra time needs to be allowed for the video mapping process that registers the video to its targets and for cueing in dry tech and in tech. And dark time will be needed for video and projection that is not shared with dark time for lighting.

The video and projection designer will want as complete and detailed a design look as possible by the beginning of tech for two very simple reasons: they seldom get enough dedicated stage time; and because projections are so visible, they are highly subject to notes. Everyone seems to think they can judge projections.

Production Manager or Technical Supervisor

The Idea

The relationship between the production stage manager and the production manager is one of the most critical in the theatre process. The duties of each overlap, so great care and planning must go into how they work together. From the production stage manager's point of view, you certainly do not want to step on the production manager's toes. Failing to think out crucial details can derail a project or, at the very least, make your working relationship with the PM unpleasant.

An Editorial

Until recently, there was a production triumvirate: the general manager was in charge of all things financial; the production manager was in charge of devising the mechanical operation of the scenery and scheduling the shops and crew; and the production stage manager was in charge of organizing the overall calendar and running rehearsals, whether in the studio or in the theatre.

Beginning in the early 1990s, exactly who was in charge of which part of the budget began to change. General managers made production managers responsible for the budgeting of load-in, as well as the hiring of crew. Production managers began to work with shops to negotiate scenery costs and recommend cuts. In other words, the production manager became responsible for the money and became a de facto adjunct general manager.

I often hear production managers say, "We can't afford that." This puts the production stage manager in the awkward position of being the only production team member who speaks for the cast and crew, the artistic and technical needs of the show, and the calendar—without regard to cost. I must say that I liked the triumvirate better—each of the three production arms represented a specific area. Compromise could be reached without one arm having more weight than another. The money should be only one—not the only—consideration.

PRODUCTION STAGE MANAGER'S INVOLVEMENT

Crew size is a joint decision by the PSM and the PM. The production stage manager and the production manager go through each piece of flown scenery and note which pieces will move at the same time to determine how many flymen are needed. Motorizing several pieces of scenery rather than adding flymen is often more economical. The same is done with deck scenery and with props. The stage manager and production manager together should be able to accurately predict crew size, including deck electricians and sound techs, thus avoiding surprises for the general manager that impact the weekly operating costs.

On a Broadway production or national tour, the pink contract crew and size are chosen by the production manager and general manager. The pink contract (named for the color of IATSE contracts) crew heads direct the work of their individual departments during the load-in, as well as direct the running of the show in performance.

The choice of pink contract crew is as crucial to the success of a production as the casting of actors. Each crew head must have specific skills, both technical and personal. The hiring decision is entirely up to the production manager, but consultation with the stage manager is usually welcome. Certain pink contract crew members work only with specific production managers, so the final choices may be built around whom the PM usually works with.

The production stage manager and production manager are often involved in the choice of theatre, especially if there is an out-of-town tryout. The production stage manager is usually involved with dressing rooms and offices, crossovers and access to the stage, size of the orchestra pit (if it's a musical), and wing space. The production manager considers the reputation of the house and local crew, condition of the backstage, load-in ease, and availability of supplies. The production stage manager and the production manager should always do a joint theatre survey to go over individual concerns.

THE CALENDAR

Constructing the calendar is the most important collaboration between production stage manager and production manager. Both parties must agree on design, bidding, build, load-in, dry tech, and tech schedules. Some production managers are better at scheduling than others, just as are some production stage managers. Play to the strengths of each. Collaboration is the key—if the stage manager and the production manager do not agree on the detailed calendar (no matter who actually writes it up), the production schedule cannot work.

Casting

The Idea

Casting, along with design concept, are the earliest artistic collaborations in a new play or musical. Before casting, the casting director meets with the director (and choreographer, if it's a musical) to discuss what sort of actor is required for each character and what particular skills are required. The general manager will often weigh in with the intended salary range for each part.

The casting director then begins the long process of narrowing down the thousands of available actors to a much smaller group, that will be shown to the director. The director will then narrow that actor group down to "final callbacks." Final callbacks usually include the producers and authors in the selection of the perfect available actor for each role. Casting may also be held in multiple cities, and often multiple countries.

Actors' Equity Association (AEA) requires that Equity principal auditions be held during a set period of time for every show, and the casting director will see any AEA actor who wants to be seen, within the time constraints set by AEA.

Casting directors will also organize "open dance calls" so that every available dancer has the opportunity to dance a short combination of steps for the choreographer. Often hundreds of dancers come to an open call and are taught an audition routine in groups of 30 to 50. Like the actors, the dancers are then narrowed down by type and skill to be called back for the director and producers. Open dance calls are another AEA requirement.

Open singer calls will be organized in the same way as dance calls. Every AEA singer who wants to be seen during a specified time period must be seen. This is also an AEA requirement. Singers who are called back will be asked to dance, and dancers will be asked to sing.

"Typing out" both singers and dancers is a good idea. If an actor has no chance of getting a part in this show, it is better not to waste their time or yours. Spend more time vetting the real possibilities.

The production stage manager should attend all casting sessions. It is no secret that directors absorb many ideas about approaches to a character during auditions. Good actors will show a range of possibilities from which a director chooses. Since you, the PSM, will be involved in casting, directing, and giving notes to the cast after a show opens, it's very important to know what the director's essential vision is for each character. Who the director rejects in casting is often as important as who is selected.

Casting is integral to the evolution of a show—be it new or revival. If you are not present for these basic decisions, you will not be fully informed about the needs of the show for the future. And if a commercial show is a hit, the production stage manager will be making casting decisions long after the director and authors have lost interest and moved on to other projects. The PSM is there from the beginning to the end of casting. Even if you've ended your involvement in the day-to-day running of the show, you might be involved in its on-going maintenance. To maintain the director's vision, you must know what that vision is and where it came from. This begins with casting.

THE AUDITION ROOM

If you are asked to find an audition room, a couple of things should be kept in mind.

Cost
Find a selection of venues at differing prices. Tell the general manager the pros and cons of each room and let the general manager make the decision.

Sound Proofing
Be sure that the room you've chosen is isolated from street noise and from the rooms around it. You don't want singers in the next room competing with your audition.

Mirrors
If you're auditioning dancers, there must be mirrors covering one entire wall.

Size of Room
Be sure the room is big enough for an actor to stand at a reasonable distance from the artistic staff's table.

Considerations for Dance

Take into account how many dancers will be dancing in that room and how much space is needed for the choreographed dance numbers. Consider the condition of the floor. How easily can the heat or air conditioning be adjusted? How well is the room ventilated? Dancers sweat and generate a lot of heat when they dance, and you want them to be comfortable in the room.

PRODUCTION STAGE MANAGER'S NOTES

Keep your own notes on casting. You should include not only your own opinion, but also the opinions of the director, choreographer, and musical director. Figure 4.3 shows a sample of my casting notes. My shortcuts need explanation.

Acting Notes

Always include height. A question mark means I'm guessing. Include some physical characteristics and quirks that make you remember this actor. If the actor read, then give them a grade, yours or the director's. Include personal feelings about the actor, whether positive or negative.

Vocal Notes

Note what song they sang and what the musical director's grade is.

Dance

This will vary from show to show. In this case, D means dance and P means personality. Some shows may have grades for tap or ballet or acrobatics.

Role

What role in the show is the actor right for? Often it is multiple roles. I also keep two different categories. Those in the top category have been approved by the artistic staff and can be hired from the sheet. Those in the "bank" are second choice and must be seen again.

RECASTING

The director, choreographer, musical director, and producers have casting approval for the life of the show. But they may be scattered all over the planet when a role is recast. As the PSM you should be able to remind the artistic staff of the approved actors, along with their physical characteristics and how they performed in the audition, to prevent recasting problems.

Although your own note-taking system may vary significantly from the one included, the notes should be compact (so you don't have to shuffle through stacks of papers), email-able, and highly detailed.

PRODUCTION STAGE MANAGER'S INVOLVEMENT

In addition to taking detailed casting notes, the production will be well served by the PSM's input and conduct.

Ask Questions

On a break, ask questions about why a particular actor was kept or rejected if that choice is confusing to you. It will not only clarify your thinking, but may help clarify the director's thinking, too.

Speak Up

If you know that an actor is particularly helpful in rehearsal or, conversely, is disruptive to the process, tell the artistic staff. Actors who serve the process should work, and those who don't should not.

Make Suggestions

This is tricky. Some casting directors hate suggestions, some welcome them. Don't try to do a favor for a friend; only recommend actors for the audition who would really serve the play. Otherwise you'll look like an idiot. Also, never tell an actor that you'll get them an audition. And then if your suggestion was successful, don't tell them that you got them the audition.

Keep It in the Room

Never speak about casting outside the audition room. Theatre is a gossipy business, and actors deserve respect. An inadvertent comment about an audition might be devastating to a career. Telling an actor they're going to be hired and then having the artistic staff change their minds can lose you a lot of friends.

Guard Confidentiality of Files

The notes you've taken in casting sessions will contain many off-hand comments, sometimes cruel to outside eyes. Keep your raw files away from prying eyes (especially if stored at the theatre) and be sure that your emailed casting notes are kept confidential to a small group in the artistic staff.

5
Production Meetings

Production meetings are where commitments are made—where money is allocated, concepts are approved, and details worked out about how and where the production will move forward. And it's where the players get to know each other. It's obvious that production meetings are crucial, but producers, general managers, or members of the creative team often resist them.

It is possible to have too many production meetings—film companies are notorious for this—or too few. The right number of meetings depends on the availability of the personnel and the level of detail in the show. A one-set play with no stars, a non-involved author, and no out-of-town tryout needs far fewer production meetings than a big new musical with an out-of-town tryout.

Production meetings should be live and in person. Email cannot convey tone. Phone conferencing is faceless. Even video conferencing stifles sharing. Each of these communication methods is fine for relaying facts; but group decisions, especially artistic ones, are better handled face-to-face.

Talk is cheap. Scenery is not. Artistic details and budget must be decided in concept before committing to any building, buying, or renting. Adding or cutting scenery, changing the lighting design, altering the costume concept, hanging a sound cluster where there wasn't one, or cancelling previews can throw a production into chaos. It's very important not to generalize in production meetings. Changes made in a production meeting discussion are inexpensive and private. Changes that affect cost, size, time, and quality of scenery, lighting, costumes, sound, casting, and schedule that happen near performance time are very expensive. They are also embarrassing if they were caused by a lack of detailed production meetings. Production meetings create the blueprint for the production, and they are indispensable to a successful show.

Remember the Cameron Mackintosh rule: There should be 52 weeks from the time the producers commit money to opening night. This 52-week rule allows enough time to properly consider design, do the casting, draw the set, bid out the technical elements, and then build these technical elements without overtime. It allows a production to proceed without hysteria.

Early, Conceptual Production Meetings

The Idea

Early meetings include the producers, general manager, designers, production manager, and production stage manager. The production stage manager's goal here is to develop a production calendar. The producers' targeted opening night, the general manager's overall the production timetable, and the director's rehearsal schedule are your building blocks. This preliminary calendar will almost certainly be wrong in many aspects, but it does provide a framework for discussion for what will eventually become the actual production schedule.

All budgets will be created or modified according to this calendar, so specific agreement from both management and creative is important here. A week of rehearsal in a studio can cost over $50,000 in New York; a day of tech can cost $25,000. The PSM should not allow anyone to generalize here.

AVAILABILITY OF THE CREATIVE TEAM

Nearly all members of the creative team will work other jobs during the long production period before rehearsals begin. Dates when key members of the team are not available need to be included on the calendar to make sure there are no misunderstandings.

SET DESIGN, DRAWING, BID AND CONSTRUCTION TIME

You'll need to work this out with the designer and the production manager. Note that scenic shops are much busier at certain times of year than at others, so make your preliminary schedule accordingly.

REHEARSAL/TECH/PREVIEW SCHEDULE

How many weeks of rehearsal in the studio, how much tech time, and how many previews are necessary for this production? Rehearsals will continue daily during previews. Will you be performing eight shows a week throughout preview? Should there be a schedule change between tech and previews or during previews leading up to opening night? The GM will be heavily involved here.

CASTING SCHEDULE

When will casting happen and who will be involved? Often the authors, producers, and general manager want to be a part of final casting.

Conceptual production meetings may go on for many weeks—sometimes months. Usually the production stage manager or production manager sets the agenda and organizes the meetings. Again, it's important to be as detailed as possible.

More Highly Detailed Production Meetings

These meetings usually happen after the conceptual work on the production is finished. They should include all the earlier personnel plus the rest of the team: crew heads, casting director, design assistants, music director, and perhaps the musical coordinator.

This is when you discuss specific numbers of casting sessions, orchestra rehearsal sessions, and delivery dates for all designs. Designers usually make their presentations during these meetings so that the crew heads, as well as the creative and management teams, can be introduced to the design idea and the scope of the production.

Crew heads will weigh in on the required number and skills of the members of their crews, as well as space requirements in the theatre. How large a wardrobe room is required for this show? Can wardrobe share with hair? With makeup? Will the basement be taken up with machinery? With costumes? How many seats will be lost for a sound console?

No matter how accurately the designers, general managers, and stage managers estimate these needs in early production meetings, when the working crew comes aboard, these space requirements will change. It's very important to listen to the crew members who will be actually working in the space. You must give them what they need to do their jobs.

The specifics help the GM determine future cost and revenue. If there is ever a time to scale back a production, this is it.

Production Meetings Just Prior To Rehearsals

Nearing the start of rehearsals, production meetings become smaller and more specific. The meetings are no longer conceptual—they are practical and will generally focus on rehearsal requirements.

REHEARSAL SCHEDULES

The Actors' Equity maximum rehearsal schedule for musicals is either seven hours in eight or seven hours in eight and one-half per day. The rehearsal hours are usually 10:00 a.m. to 6:00 p.m. or 6:30 p.m.

Plays will often rehearse the same hours as a musical, but many directors find that actors' energies are best when rehearsing five continuous hours with no lunch break, and then calling it a day.

Schedule the lunch break. Everyone involved will want to book this time ahead for personal or show-related activities.

Setting the Rehearsal Start Dates

Actors go on payroll from the first day of rehearsal, so general managers will often want to phase in calling the cast to rehearse. For example, in a complicated dance show, the ensemble may be called a week earlier than the principals. This is standard procedure, but needs to be agreed upon by the whole creative team.

Calling the understudies and/or swings later than the rest of the cast is counterproductive. Basic character decisions are made early in the rehearsal process and the understudies should not miss these details. In musicals, the intention of a dance as well as the steps are taught in detail at the beginning of the choreographic process. In complicated dance shows, swings can never catch up if they miss those initial rehearsals.

A Story

Musicals tend to be taught and plays tend to be discovered. Because musicals have so many interlocking parts—book, choreography, complicated scenery, musical numbers and transitions—the parts are often worked out in pre-production by the creative team and then taught to the cast. Plays, however, are usually more linear —they unfold during rehearsals, incorporating input from the actors. The director of a play is like a guide. The director of a musical is more like a military general.

When Mike Nichols directs a play, he prefers to rehearse five days a week, not six. For five hours a day with no lunch break. He believes this allows the work to "percolate" in the actors' brains, giving the actors' time to dream about the work rather than making quick, objective decisions. Nichols trusts his actors as contributing artists and does not use them as mouthpieces. This process can be scary—often leading down blind alleys. But the result is a depth and ownership of the character that is seldom achieved by any other director.

REHEARSAL POLICIES

Some authors, directors, and choreographers like an open rehearsal room where producers, managers, and designers free to come and go at will. Others want a closed rehearsal room, with specific "visiting hours" for those not involved in the daily rehearsal process. The creative team and producers should set the policy before rehearsals begin—otherwise, feelings get hurt.

REHEARSAL REPORTS

The stage manager should issue a report at the end of each day's rehearsal as well as a weekly summary. These reports may include sensitive information, so you need to decide who gets them. The entire creative team and management, certainly. But all the producers? All the investors?

Take note that rehearsal reports are legal documents. They could be used in disputes, firings, and even lawsuits. You must be sure that they are accurate, concise, and free of gossip.

Check out the sample daily rehearsal report, Figure 5.1. Each report should include a list of technical additions or deletions, such as props and wardrobe, that evolved that day. You should also note who was absent, what was rehearsed, and any problems encountered.

REHEARSAL NEEDS IN DETAIL

You'll need a list from the director and choreographer of all required rehearsal props and rehearsal wardrobe. Once the GM approves the budget for these items, the stage manager assembles the props, unless they're custom-designed. The stage manager also buys off-the-rack wardrobe when possible, but the costume designer should provide any complicated pieces.

Rehearsal scenery is becoming more and more common—especially for musicals, but it depends on the visual imagination of the director and choreographer. The range of rehearsal scenery is huge—from foam-core cutouts to working turntables. Cost, timing, and need must all be considered, so discuss each item with the creative team and with management.

Production Meetings During Rehearsals

Most of the creative team is already in the rehearsal hall, so a production meeting either before or after rehearsal should be easy to organize. The lead producer, general manager, company manager, musical director, technical director, and all designers should attend these meetings in person.

The production stage manager should organize and run these production meetings once or twice per week. This is the time to resolve all accumulated questions. Then include the resolutions in your daily report. Also, now is the right time to discuss issues that cannot be put into your stage manager's report. Personnel and disciplinary issues, rehearsal progress, and other sensitive items are often easier to discuss in person and in a small group than by email.

This is also the time to focus on specific design details. Because the director and choreographer are no longer working from scaled designs, issues with sets and props can be easily discussed and demonstrated in the rehearsal hall. Distances between set pieces, ease of movement, size and weight of props, and sightlines can be shown and discussed in full scale with the entire creative team present.

Production Meetings During Load-In

The frequency and place of these meetings depends on a couple of things. Is the load-in taking place in the same city as the rehearsals? Are there specific load-in versus rehearsal issues that need to be discussed? If rehearsals and load-in are in different locations, a few digital photos or a Skype conference may be enough to keep the crew and the rehearsal team in sync.

The production manager sets the agenda and frequency of the production meetings during load-in. It is very important that everyone adhere to the calendar agreed upon by the production stage manager and the production manager. The entire production staff needs to know about any delays in the load-in or scenic delivery, or any changes that happen in the rehearsal hall that affect the load-in. The production stage manager and the production manager need to make sure that the load-in site does not become autonomous—a job site divorced both from the calendar and from the ever-changing needs of the rehearsal hall.

Production Meetings During Tech

These are often the most crucial meetings of the entire production period, since so many masters must be served. They should be scheduled daily, either at the theatre, or in the stage managers' office.

The production stage manager and production manager together will set the agenda. The stage manager will lay out the goals for each day of tech and make sure the tech is on schedule. I always do an entire day-by-day tech schedule and distribute it to the creative and technical teams.

Typical tech schedules for both a play and a musical are discussed in depth in Chapter 9, Technical Rehearsals. It is important to hold a production meeting at the end of each tech day. That meeting should include the creative team, the stage managerial staff, the production manager, crew heads, and company or general managers. Discuss the needs and structure of the next day's tech—which crew has priority onstage at which hours, what the tech goal is for the day, and what scenic, lighting, prop, sound, video, and wardrobe elements are crucial for the next day's tech.

Additional scenery and other money items may also be discussed. It's crucial that a representative of management, who can approve expenditures, be active in these talks.

Production Meetings During Previews

Many conflicting needs must be addressed at production meetings during previews. The director controls these meetings, laying out a rehearsal schedule for the next day and prioritizing which production elements need attention—script, set, music, choreography, or performance. All departments follow the director's lead, no matter what their individual needs may be.

The stage manager is very useful at these meetings—you can estimate the time needed to solve each of the director's items, and then create the next day's work schedule to actualize these items.

As the stage manager, you represent the actors and the crew in these meetings. The cast and crew will be exhausted as the preview period comes to an end. Their energy and ability to absorb new information may not be what it was at the start of the process. You need to judge whether the wishes of the creative team and management are possible given the backstage realities—you are the only person who will know this.

Authors, producers, and the director meet in the mornings and may come into rehearsal with a new agenda. Keep crew and actor calls as flexible as possible, and always be ready to adapt to new information.

A Story

During out-of-town previews of *Spamalot*, we worked for two days to fix a huge dance number. New scenery was built, new orchestrations were done, new lyrics were written, and the number was completely rechoreographed. At the end of the second day, we ran the number and were very pleased that everything worked—it was smooth and all the new elements seemed to click. With 15 minutes left of rehearsal time, director Mike Nichols came to me and said, "Can we cut the whole number tonight?" "We can't go back to the old number now!" I said. The old scenery was out in the alley. "No, I want to cut the entire sequence and go from the end of the previous number directly to the following number," said Nichols. My initial reaction was that we had just spent two days working out this new number—we were owed a payoff for all that hard work. But my job is to do what the director wants.

There was no time to rehearse the cut. I called a quick meeting with the musical director, designers, crew heads, and my stage management team to explain how I thought this could be done. We decided to make the cut on paper and run it that night. I then met with the cast to explain the cut. The two meetings together took the remaining 15 minutes of rehearsal. I then told Nichols I thought we could do it—it might look a little rough, but we could get through it.

My team and I spent the hours between rehearsal and performance going over the cut in detail. We put the exact changes on paper for each department—what fly, automation, lighting, and sound cues would be cut. We mapped changes to wardrobe and follow-spot pickups. Everyone had to change their mindset about the number we'd been working on for two days. And we had to perform something in front of a paying audience that we'd never tried before. My job was to show all departments how to do this, and to be positive about it.

The cut worked well in the show that night, and that number never made a reappearance. Had we resisted this last-minute change from Nichols, the show might never have achieved the streamlined flow that made it a hit.

6
Choosing Your Management Team

The Idea

Choosing your stage management team is harder—and more crucial—than you may think. The temptation to hire your friends is a serious threat to your team. Don't do it. Your team should be organized to meet specific needs.

A Story

My first stage manager gig on Broadway was a play, and the producer gave me an assistant. This producer didn't want me on the show. I was forced on her by the director and star—we'd done the show in stock together. The assistant was planted as a spy, meant to report my shortcomings back to the producer so she could get rid of me. Instead, my assistant stage manager and I became good friends and colleagues, and he never reported anything back to the producer.

My next big show was the national tour of a huge musical, and I was determined to hire my own assistants who were good at the things that I was not—props and wardrobe. I hired Jim Woolley as my first assistant; at that time Jim had done more Broadway work than I had. He handled props, wardrobe fittings, and deck organization. I handled everything else. Jim and I are complete opposites—he's good at what I'm poor at, and vice versa. We also trust each other. I have worked with Jim for 33 years and have continued to hire assistants and production assistants who have talents that I do not. They cover me and I cover them.

A Few Tips on Hiring Assistants

I've learned a lot over the years about putting together balanced and proficient stage management teams. This list covers many of those things.

MIX UP YOUR TEAM

Everyone in the cast and crew should feel connected with someone on the SM staff. Be sure there is a mix of men and women, gay and straight, older and younger. If your show has young girls, be sure there is a motherly figure on your team, and for young boys, a fatherly figure.

DON'T HIRE YOUR FRIENDS

I know I said this before, but it needs to be said twice.

HIRE SKILLS

Determine what specific skills your show will need and hire your staff to satisfy those needs. Some shows need a dancer's mentality, some need great attention to props, some need extraordinary computer skills, and some need a musician's ear. Each show is different. Be sure you're covered.

INSIST THAT YOU PICK YOUR OWN TEAM

This is part of your contract negotiation. Producers or general managers will often ask you to use someone whom they've worked with. My advice is to say that you'd be happy to meet with this person, but that the final choice has to be yours.

DO YOUR RESEARCH

You will often hire stage managers or production assistants who are new to you. Always interview them first to see if their personality meshes well with yours and if they have the skills needed for your show. Get recommendations from people you trust who've worked on shows with them. And be sure to get them approved by the creative team and management—you don't want to tell someone they have a job only to be told by a member of the production team that they cannot work with that person.

CAN YOU HAVE DINNER WITH THEM?

You will be spending more time with your team than with your significant other and it is crucial that you get along. Can you have an easy conversation with your assistants? Are their politics offensive to you?

Some Tips on Hiring Production Assistants

The number of PAs you request and have approved on a show will depend on the needs of that show. On a complicated musical, there are often four PAs. On a play, there may be only one.

The PAs should perform the functions your SM team doesn't have time for—script printing, rehearsal prop shopping, moving rehearsal scenery, running errands. PAs should be hired and available from the time the rehearsal hall is set up.

GO THROUGH THE SAME VETTING PROCESS AS FOR ASSISTANTS

Your PAs will function as stage managers from the first day of rehearsal through the press opening of the show. All the same rules apply.

HIRE OVER-QUALIFIED PAs

If you're doing a Broadway show, off-Broadway stage managers make terrific PAs. Be sure your hires are not favors to someone—get real stage managers who are looking to break into the Broadway scene. If you're doing an off-Broadway show, find PAs who have been working in stock or on workshops. You don't want to spend your time training someone who doesn't yet know the basics.

MIX IT UP

If your Actors' Equity stage management staff is missing a gender or sexual orientation, use your production assistant selections to round out your staff.

GET AS MUCH MONEY FOR THE PAs AS YOU CAN

The general manager may ask you how much is the proper amount to pay PAs. Check with similar shows and get the highest amount you can. Your PAs will have done that same homework. You want them to feel valued.

LOYALTY AND REWARD

If you're happy with your PAs on a show, hire them on your next show. Use your PAs as substitute stage managers—they already know the show, the cast, crew, and management. They're an easy fit.

AEA stage managers have continued employment on the show, PAs don't. And PAs are woefully underpaid. I always try to hire my former PAs as stage managers on another show where they can earn real money. Moving the PA on to stage manager on the national tour of a Broadway show they've already worked on is a perfect fit—and an idea that can be easily sold to a GM. I also recommend my production assistants to other stage managers. My motives are partially selfish—I'll get a much higher quality PA if they know there will be a reward in the future.

Organizing Your Team

Here's the breakdown I've developed over the years of who's who and what their job functions are.

THE PRODUCTION STAGE MANAGER

As I explained earlier, Actors' Equity does not yet recognize the term "production stage manager." For AEA, there are only stage managers and assistants. However, it is now traditional on virtually all professional shows for the lead stage manager to be called the production stage manager or PSM. Following is a summary of the PSM's responsibilities.

Hire and Lead the Team

The PSM hires the AEA stage managers and the PAs. He or she speaks for the team—all ASMs and PAs should bring questions and problems to the PSM to handle. The PSM is the funnel for all information.

Tech the Show

The PSMs should always tech the show. They are responsible for the style and content of the calling and for way that the calling script is laid out. The PSM maintains the calling script and the blocking script, both of which should be digitized for backup.

Do the Paperwork

The PSM creates the templates for all reports and calls—rehearsal, performance, and weekly—and is responsible for their content. This correspondence should go out with the PSM's signature.

Handle the Politics

The PSM is responsible for the politics of the team. All disputes, policies, and recommendations must come from the PSM after careful consultation with the team. Also, all dealings with Actors' Equity should be handled by the PSM.

Manage Script Changes

Before computers, most New York theatre scripts were processed by a company called Studio Duplicating. They would type a stencil of the script in a format of your choosing, and then print any number of copies and bind them in a leatherette folder with little brass screws. Script changes were made in pencil by the actors, and if scenes were re-arranged, the actors would re-arrange the pages themselves. If the script changes became too complicated to be done by hand, a new stencil was typed by Studio Duplicating and new scripts were distributed. This was expensive and time-consuming, and usually required several days.

Computers have changed all this. Stage managers routinely make changes to the script and distribute them. Here are a few suggestions to help everyone keep track:

- Date each changed page.
- Keep a copy of each "cut" page in a separate folder so that it can be re-instated, if needed.
- Any time a script is changed, date that day's script as the current script and archive the old script. You may have an archive with a different script for each day of rehearsal and previews.
- Each time it is changed, email the entire new script to the whole creative team— everyone needs to be working with the latest script.

Follow the Director
In the American theatre system, the PSM becomes the de facto director after the show opens, and they must be the director's confidante during production. Wherever the director is, the PSM should be there, too. It's important for you to understand the director's intentions on script interpretation, staging, and point of view.

THE FIRST ASSISTANT STAGE MANAGER

The first assistant plays first mate to the PSM's role of captain. The first assistant will probably call most of the shows after the production opens, so calling skills are crucial. During tech, the first assistant must have a personality that works well with the crew and must possess a thorough technical knowledge of what the PSM is trying to achieve. The PSM may assign any number of duties to the first assistant stage manager, but the most common and most useful duties are as follows.

Organize the Deck
Since the PSM will usually tech the show from the front of house, the first assistant will run the stage deck. They will work out the placement and spiking of all props on the deck and, with crew heads, work out the backstage storage of all props and set pieces.

Coordinate with Automated Pieces
Since the PSM is working out the timing of all automated deck and flying pieces, as well as manually flown pieces of scenery, the first assistant must coordinate the arrival of actors, props, and manually set scenery with those pieces under the control of the PSM.

Backstage Choreography
There are usually more crew on a show than there are actors, most of them in the very limited backstage space—which must be shared with scenery and actors. The first assistant will work out the order and placement of events backstage such as actor entrances, scenic prep, prop hand-offs, and quick wardrobe changes.

Do the Paperwork
Up-to-date running sheets for the deck crew are essential. Substitute stagehands may come into a show at a moment's notice with no rehearsal, and the first ASM must be

able to hand a sheet of paper or a stack of index cards to a new stagehand with each step of their duties for the night. This begins on the first day of tech and is updated daily.

THE SECOND ASSISTANT STAGE MANAGER

All production contract musicals and most large LORT and Off-Broadway musicals are required by Actors' Equity Association to employ a second ASM position from the first day of rehearsal. Plays do not require this position unless they are unusually large and complicated. In addition to the responsibilities outlined below, the second ASM will assist the first ASM on props. On musicals or plays that don't have a second assistant stage manager, the first assistant and the PAs must take over these duties.

Coordinate Wardrobe Fittings

A new Broadway musical may require dozens of wardrobe fittings per actor during rehearsal and tech. Each fitting usually lasts an hour and may require travel away from the rehearsal hall. This means that a swing or understudy must fill in for the actor being fitted. The wardrobe department will request certain fittings, usually the day before the fitting. The second ASM will review the requests with the PSM, who will say which fittings can happen during the rehearsal day, depending on the schedule. The second ASM will then contact the wardrobe department to confirm, contact each actor to be fitted, and then arrange transportation (if needed) for the actor. Then of course there are the last-minute changes. It is a foolish PSM who tries to do this job himself.

Create Wardrobe Chart

The second assistant will also make the chart. I recommend using the French Scene Breakdown. This chart shows clearly how each group of actors on stage is organized and changes to the next scene—which actors are in each scene, what character they play, which entrance they use, which exit they use, and how long they are off-stage between scenes. The wardrobe department needs this chart to work out where wardrobe changes can happen—onstage for a quick change, in the dressing room for a slower change—and how dressers are to be deployed. The second ASM is invaluable to the PSM in assigning dressing rooms and in determining the needs of the wardrobe room. Figure 6.1 is a sample wardrobe breakdown.

Organize Hair Needs

Everything that applies to wardrobe applies to hair. The second ASM will organize fittings in the same way and with the same restrictions. The second ASM will also recommend to the PSM location and size of the hair room.

Maintain Computer Records

The second assistant will usually handle most of the computerized paperwork on a show—sign-in sheets, dressing room signs, directional signs backstage, opening night good wishes to people or shows. The second ASM may also keep computerized cast histories, a record of absences, late arrivals, vacations, personal days, and disciplinary issues, which are compiled weekly from the daily reports.

A Tip

I've had very good luck using former dancers as second ASMs. They are highly disciplined, know how a backstage operates, and understand music. I often have these dancer ASMs work closely with the choreographer on a musical to lay out the dance numbers in eight counts, with visual references for each eight count. Since I'm always with the director and laying out dance numbers comes so naturally to former dancers, this is a perfect fit.

PRODUCTION ASSISTANTS

I view working with PAs as growing stage managers for the future. The guidelines I included above are very important to follow in hiring. If you've got good people who are capable and whom you trust, assign them the following duties.

Distribute Script Changes
One of your PAs should be assigned to copy and distribute script changes. This is a bigger job than it seems. Once the PSM has made the script changes as described above, the script PA will make the needed number of copies and then distribute them either by hand or in mailboxes to the actors and creative team. If everyone in the cast and creative team is not working from exactly the same script, confusion reigns.

Maintain Cut Pages Book
The script PA should also keep a cut pages book that contains each of the PSM's discarded pages, dated on the day it was cut and kept in page number order. When authors or directors suddenly find they liked a former scene rather than the current scene, the old scene can be quickly found and restored.

Maintain Mailboxes
A PA should set up and maintain mailboxes (usually portable file boxes) for the cast and creative team. Script changes, announcements, forms to be filled out, photos, bios to be approved, and individual fitting schedules are put into the mailboxes.

Provide Services
PAs should handle coffee and tea machines and be available to fetch food for the creative team. Picking up birthday cards and cakes, finding rehearsal props, and restocking first aid, and office supplies are all part of normal PA duties.

Act as Crew in Rehearsals

In the theatre there will of course be adequate crew to move scenery, set props, assist in wardrobe changes, and run sound. But in the rehearsal studio, these duties often fall to PAs, which make them invaluable as substitute stage managers.

7

Before Rehearsals Begin

This pre-production period is a great time to take care of many very important bits of business that should be in place before rehearsals begin.

A Story

Early in my career, I was setting up an off-Broadway production of a new musical. The director and choreographer were very insistent that for pre-production I should bring in certain dancers, that I have certain rehearsal props available, and that we use the off-off-Broadway theatre of the director's choice. I had spoken with the general manager in vague terms about pre-production, but had never gotten specific. I set everything up the way the creative team wanted, called the dancers, and used the hall. But because I was rushed, I didn't clear the specific payments with the GM. I told him after I had made the commitments—but without knowing exactly what everything would cost.

He called me into his office raked me over the coals. He shouted that I was not in charge, that it was the GM's job to approve and allocate money, to hire personnel, and to book rehearsal space. I was to run the show, not to approve its management. I had gotten arrogant in my haste. He was right and I was wrong.

Production Stage Manager
Pre-Production

The Idea

Once rehearsals begin you'll want to concentrate only on the director and the progress of rehearsals. So getting all your organizational busywork done in pre-production will allow you a distraction-free rehearsal period.

MEET WITH YOUR TEAM

Chances are that some members of your team have not worked with each other before. Getting together before creative team pre-production begins is a great way to be sure you have a relaxed team at the outset. Holding this meeting at your apartment with some wine and snacks makes the process friendly and collegial.

Let each member of your team know what their specific responsibility will be and, if necessary, show them paperwork from previous productions for them to use as a template.

ORGANIZE YOUR EMAIL AND TEXTING CONTACTS

Even though it takes some time and effort, making contact groups of actors, creative team, stage management, and management on your phone and computer will save a lot of time later on in the process when time is much more precious. With one click you can email an entire group in production with daily rehearsal calls, rehearsal reports, changes in schedule, or questions. You also won't have to sort through your contact sheet when the director wants an actor's phone number.

Choreographic Pre-Production

The Idea

Speak with the choreographer early in pre-production meetings about how much time will be needed in a rehearsal studio before the first day of rehearsal. You also need to determine if pre-production is contiguous with the rehearsal period. Or are there days—perhaps weeks—between pre-production and the first day of rehearsal? The earlier you figure this out, the better the chances are that you'll get a desirable rehearsal hall at a good price. If possible, the choreographic pre-production should be scheduled in the same room as the dance rehearsals.

THE PRE-PRODUCTION REHEARSAL HALL

This space should be as wide and as deep as the playing area of the stage as designed. If there is tap dancing in the show, you may need a special surface installed in the hall. Do you need sound in the hall? If sound equipment is not already installed, determine how much it will cost to install and who will operate this equipment.

PRE-PRODUCTION STAFF

Will the choreographer be working with an assistant? More than one? If the choreographer needs dancers to work out numbers, who will these dancers be and how will they be paid? The dancers used in pre-production are often not the same as those used in the show. They are paid on a day rate rather than on an AEA contract. Will you need a piano player or will the choreographer use taped music? Should a stage manager be present?

The Production Rehearsal Hall

The Idea

Finding the right space for a rehearsal hall is a trickier than you might think. In most major cities, there just aren't that many desirable spaces. Book your rehearsal hall as far in advance as possible. Many people are involved in the decision—the director, the choreographer, the musical director, the general manager, and the authors (if it's a new play) all need to sign off on the rehearsal space. And each will have unique requirements.

FINDING THE RIGHT SPACE

Here are some important considerations when looking for a production rehearsal hall.

Size and Configuration
The room must be large enough to lay out the complete stage with enough space left for the director or choreographer to stand back to view the show. There should be at least eight feet from the wall to the taped stage edge. You also need enough room outside the taped wings to store props and rehearsal wardrobe. Consider where the actors will sit while waiting for their scenes.

Privacy
Does anyone outside your company need to pass through the rehearsal hall? Can passersby see into the rehearsal room? Is the room soundproofed—will you disturb others or will they disturb you? Is the room yours 24/7? Or do you have to clear away your gear after each use? These are all important considerations.

Mirrors
If the show is a musical, you'll need adequate mirrors. These mirrors must be easily covered when they're not wanted.

Location

Is your rehearsal hall near public transportation? Does it have adequate parking? Is it close to restaurants, to the theatre, to shops, to the GM's office? Try to find the most accessible space.

Other items

Make sure the rehearsal hall has adequate toilets. Coffee machines, microwave ovens, a green room, outside access, and a PA system are all important. Find out if the director wants windows to allow natural light into the room.

Cost

This is always the biggest consideration: Can the show afford the rehearsal hall that's best for the show? The creative team and stage managers often must bow to the budget on this one. Get the best you can for the money you have.

Figuring Your Rehearsal Hall Requirements

Not surprisingly, plays and muscials have very different rehearsal space requirements. For a play the requirements are fairly simple. Generally, you will need only one rehearsal room and an office. As I've already mentioned, the rehearsal room should be deeper and wider than your playing area in the theatre. This allows room for prop storage and for the director's area downstage of the playing area.

The office should have enough room for all the stage managers and PAs to work, plus room for the director and assistant director to make calls and do some work. The room should be private and relatively soundproofed so that sensitive conversations can take place. Of course, adequate power, phone lines, Internet access, and lighting are essential.

REHEARSAL HALL REQUIREMENTS FOR A MUSICAL

For a musical things are more complicated. Here is a breakdown of the way rooms on a musical are generally configured, along with requirements for each.

Room 1

This is usually the "put-together" room, the place where all the elements of the musical come together. All major props and rehearsal scenery are stored here. It should be bigger than your stage. Space offstage of the taped wings should allow for running exits and for prop storage.

In the downstage area, against the mirrors, there should be tables for each department—one each for director, dance department, authors, stage managers, and swings. All tables will need power for computers. Additionally the stage managers' table needs power for a printer. On musicals with extensive floor taping and a fair amount of rehearsal scenery and props, this room may be required a week before rehearsals begin.

For the music department, there needs to be adequate space for the rehearsal instruments (usually piano and drums) as well as a table for the music director. If new material is being added on a regular basis, then another table with a computer setup and printer will be required. Arrange to have the piano tuned at least once a week.

Requirements for tap dancing, sound playback, and soundproofing in the pre-production rehearsal hall are the same for in the production rehearsal hall.

Room 2

This is usually the choreography room. Here the dance team works out the dance numbers. Props and rehearsal costumes specific to the dance numbers are usually stored in this room. Mirrors are, of course, essential.

Again, this room should be bigger than the performance area to allow space downstage for the choreographer to view the dances at some distance, allow for running exits, and allow for prop storage. The same requirements for musicians' space, piano tuning, soundproofing, number of tables, and power for these tables apply to this space as Room 1.

The choreographer will tell you how far in advance of rehearsals the room will be needed and how extensively the set should be taped out.

Room 3

This is usually the piano/vocal room. Here individual or small group vocals are worked out. No props or rehearsal scenery are stored in this room. It should be a private space without a lot of foot traffic. It can be quite small and no mirrors are required.

When this room is not in use for rehearsing vocals, it can be quite useful for pianists to rehearse, for composers to work on new material, or for the occasional costume fitting.

The Office

The first question is, "How many people will be using this space?" On a play, it can be as few as two in the SM department, the director, and the author, so the smallest office a show would ever need would have to hold four people, each with a place to sit and work. On a musical, that number could swell to as many as eleven or twelve.

There also needs to be room for the office supplies and machinery:
- Internet router
- Fax machine
- Multiple phone lines
- Copier
- File cabinets
- Computers
- Printers
- Safe (if necessary)
- Laminator
- Storage for paper and supplies

OTHER SPACES

Depending on the production, you may require additional spaces.

Classroom

If there are minor children in the show, you'll need one or more classrooms for daily classes during rehearsal. The number of hours of class per day varies by state.

Fitting Room

The best use of the actor's time is to arrange for costumes to be fitted at the rehearsal hall. This will require a dedicated space, or part of a space, for the private fitting of costumes and for costume storage.

Author Room

On many new shows, the authors prefer to work at the rehearsal hall rather than go home or to an office to do rewrites. One or more separate offices often need to be rented for the authors. Ask about this before renting the rehearsal hall—a displaced author is not a pretty sight.

A Story

For the main, five-week workshop of *Shrek The Musical*, there were two areas of the show that required their own dedicated space. The dragon number required a full-scale dragon puppet—it did not fit into the regular rehearsal hall. It was an enormous expense and interrupted run-throughs, but it could not be avoided. Secondly, we needed a separate prop-building room at the rehearsal hall—which was also used for prosthetics. Most producers would have balked at the expense of these two additional spaces, but DreamWorks insisted that the needs of the show be served first.

Taping the Floor

The first thing to decide (with the director and choreographer) is how to orient the room. If there are permanent mirrors, the "audience" will probably be the mirrors. Let the director and choreographer know how much wing space and how much viewing space will be left once the room is taped out.

THE TAPE

Always use a good quality ½- or ¾-inch cloth tape. The director and choreographer should approve the colors you use—there are color blindness issues and color prejudices to consider. All tape should be covered with a clear packing tape to keep it from fraying.

HOW AND WHAT TO TAPE OUT

Most ground plans are in ½-inch scale, which means that ½ inch on the ground plan equals 1 foot on the stage. The most important tape lines in the rehearsal hall are the center line and the downstage edge of the stage. All measurements are from these two lines, which also appear on the ground plan.

Clearly outline the downstage edge, the proscenium, the wings, and any permanent obstructions on the set, all in the same color. Mark the center line. In multiple scene shows, each scene should have it's own color for that scene's spike marks, and the piece of scenery or prop being spiked should be written on the tape itself. Use as few marks as possible to keep the actor's confusion level down.

Measure the outline points for scenic pieces on the ground plan, transferring those points to the rehearsal hall floor, and then connecting those points to create the outline of the object. Outline circular pieces by finding the center point and then drawing a radius from that center.

Don't cheat by measuring from one scenic piece to the next. Always measure from both the center line and downstage edge for each new object. Otherwise, one bad measurement could throw off the entire taping.

Always tape out all winch tracks, elevators, fog vents, and floor lights. This helps dancers and choreographers in the transfer from rehearsal hall to theatre.

When any one scenic piece has multiple locations, like a wagon, it becomes confusing to fully tape out these locations. If the budget allows, build rehearsal scenery for these pieces. Or a cheaper alternative is to cut carpet scraps and tape out the piece on carpet and then move the carpet.

NUMBER LINES

On all musicals and many plays, there must be numbers or colors on the downstage taped edge of the set to facilitate spacing for the director and choreographer. Numbers are generally marked in 2-foot increments, beginning with 0 at center and spaced out right and left. So a 36-foot proscenium opening would be marked: 18 16 14 12 10 8 6 4 2 0 2 4 6 8 10 12 14 16 18. This number spacing must be repeated exactly when the show moves into the theatre.

Many designers detest the look of numbers across the front of the stage and request either painted colors or small LED lights counter-sunk into the deck. The pattern of colors may be anything decided upon by the creative team, but must repeat exactly right and left from center. Colors take some getting used to and are not recommended for short rehearsal periods.

CREATIVE TEAM SPACE

The creative team will set up between the downstage taped edge of the stage and the wall or mirrors. Input from all members of the creative team is important here so that you know how much space and equipment each person needs.

You'll want to have your table near the director and near the door to the rehearsal hall. Decide early who needs to be sitting at your table, how much equipment you'll need on this table, and what rules you have about your table regarding eating, drinking, talking, and use of the computer or printer.

Scripts

The printing and distribution of an accurate rehearsal script—whether for a revival, original play, or musical—is the sole responsibility of the production stage manager.

DELIVERY

The authors should deliver to the production stage manager a complete script in editable format in plenty of time to have the script printed. Authors will often format the script heavily in order to make their initial writing quicker; and just as often, this formatting will make it nearly impossible to change the script as needed or to make it into a format suitable for cuing. Be sure you can add cues to the script quickly and in a form you wish to use.

FORMAT

The script may have to be reformatted, or in some cases completely retyped, to allow for quick and reliable editing. Take the following into consideration when reformatting or retyping:

- *Hard page breaks.* Authors usually allow automatic page breaks, which means that any time material is added or deleted, the pagination is changed. Before printing the script, add hard page breaks.
- *Hard page numbers.* Automatic page numbers are easier for authors to work with, but don't allow "A" or "B" pages, or the combining of pages, which will happen with extensive cuts. Add hard page numbers before printing.
- *Large margins.* Be sure there are margins at the top, bottom, and sides that are large enough for the actors to include their own penciled blocking and character notes.
- *Emailing copies.* If the script is to be emailed, this should be done in PDF, non-editable form. Because creative teams are usually very careful about who can read a new script, be sure to get approval before emailing a script.

BINDERS

Each script for cast, crew, and creative team should be printed single-sided and assembled in three-ring notebooks, not in bound or clamped binders. This makes the addition or deletion of material much easier and faster. The binders should be big enough to hold the script, score, calendars, and contact sheets. But not so large as to be unwieldy.

Be sure that all scripts are approved not only by the authors, but also by the producers, director, and general manager. Pay particular attention to the title page that outlines everyone's role. Remember, billing is everything.

Scores

Scores should be delivered in PDF format by the musical director or composer and printed double-sided for the cast and creative team. They can be included in the three-ring binder with the script and given to the actors.

Since singing assignments often change during a rehearsal process, I think each actor should have a complete score. However, this decision is really up to the musical director.

Rehearsal Props

The Idea

Substitute props or rehearsal props are usually used in rehearsal before the real props arrive. These rehearsal props help in figuring out what the real props should be. Some directors will make a list of rehearsal props for the stage manager. More often, the stage manager will go through the script and guess at what props are necessary for the staging of the show and then have the director edit that list.

BUDGET

Since rehearsal props are mostly disposable and will not be used in the final production, the general manager should approve a separate budget for these items. No matter how demanding or insistent the director or choreographer becomes, be careful not to spend more than the approved budget, or it may come from your own pocket.

A Story

My longtime assistant, Jim Woolley, is a genius at building scenic mock-ups from foam core. While this is not dimensional rehearsal scenery, it does allow the creative team to see the stage picture accurately. And Jim is very witty. In *Spamalot*, during the Knights of Ni scene, King Arthur calls the trees "very expensive." As a gag, Jim drew dollar signs all over the trees, which got a good laugh from everyone in rehearsal. The designer liked the idea so much, he put it into the show—getting one of the biggest and most consistent laughs in the show.

PROP ASM

Assign one of your ASMs or PAs to organize and track all props in the show. This person will be responsible for estimating the rehearsal prop budget, being sure the required props get to rehearsal on time, organizing the props so they are reliably accessible for the actors, tracking the movement of the props, and making the prop running sheets for the crew in the theatre. See figure 7.1 for an example of a prop list for the revival of *Annie*. The budgeting of rehearsal props was done from this list.

SHOW PROP PERSON

On most commercial productions, the prop person for the show is available to the designer and the stage manager from pre-production through the press opening of the show. This person is an expert in shopping and building all the show props and works with the designer on a daily basis. The prop ASM should make the prop person their best friend.

RACKS AND TABLES

You may need to have storage racks or additional tables built, rented, or bought for rehearsal in order to properly organize the props.

Rehearsal Scenery

The Idea

Producers and general managers often think rehearsal scenery is a waste of money, since these pieces won't be used after rehearsals. However, large props or scenic pieces often cannot be designed without less-expensive prototypes being created for rehearsal.

A Story

In one scene of *Shrek The Musical*, Lord Farquaad is taking a bath while singing a song. At one point in the song, the bathtub splits and Farquaad emerges fully dressed. The look of the bath had to be credible and the transformation instantaneous. We had the shop built a mock-up of the tub. During rehearsal we made constant adjustments to the mock-up: where the props go, where the costume pieces go, how the unit split apart, what the water and bubbles look like, how quickly each piece of stage business had to happen. The prototype was expensive. But more importantly the extremely expensive final prop piece only had to be made once because we had rehearsed with the prototype.

Another Story

In *The Goodbye Girl*, a spinning kitchen unit that had to do a number of tricks on its turntable figured prominently in the design. The rehearsal mock-up allowed us to choreograph to the spinning unit (pushed by stage managers). It also allowed us to figure out where and how the props could be built in and to determine the necessary speed of the turntable to allow the actors to work out their business. This rehearsal unit also saved us an untold amount of tech time.

VISUALLY CHALLENGED DIRECTORS

The unspoken value of rehearsal scenery is that it allows directors and choreographers to see how the volume of the stage space looks. It allows them to balance stage pictures before they get into the theatre. Some directors and choreographers are very good at reading designs or looking at a model or reading spike marks, but most are not. Rehearsal scenery becomes a terrific visual aid.

Union Notification

The production stage manager is responsible for notifying Actors' Equity Association of the first day of rehearsal and arranging for the AEA representative to speak with the cast alone at the beginning of this first day in rehearsal. The AEA representative is there to be sure that all actors and stage managers have properly signed contracts and are fully informed of the rights and benefits of union membership.

    The production stage manager will also get the stage manager's packet and the deputy kit from the AEA offices. Every show elects an Equity deputy (more on this in Chapter 13, Running the Show) to be the voice of the cast, the liaison between cast and management and between cast and Equity. The stage manager's packet contains notices to be posted on the callboard, forms to be filled out and returned to the union, and rule books.

8
Rehearsals

The Idea

It is the job of the production stage manager to create a safe, calm, well-organized, and respectful room in which the actors and creative team can do their work—in the agreed-upon amount of time. Everyone should feel they are in good hands and that the rehearsal process has been carefully thought out.

Notification

Well in advance of the first day of rehearsal, everyone on the production team needs to know what the rehearsal plan will be.

CAST NOTIFICATION: FIRST DAY OF REHEARSAL

Here's what each cast member should know:
- When is the first day of rehearsal?
- What are the hours and where will rehearsal be held?
- Will the press be there?
- Will photographs or video taken then?
- Will there be a reading of the script and who will be there for this reading?
- Will there be an Actors' Equity representative there?
- Will there be a Meet & Greet?
- Will food be provided?

It's good to include information in this notice about the standard rehearsal schedule: the hours, the standard day off, and the standard lunch breaks.

CREATIVE TEAM NOTIFICATION: FIRST DAY OF REHEARSAL

Here's what the creative team should know:
- When is the first day of rehearsal?
- Where is it and when should they be there?
- If there is to be a reading (and singing) of the show, who may and who may not stay for this reading?
- Will the creative team be involved in photos or interviews?
- Will they be asked to speak?
- Will food be provided?

NOTIFICATION FOR MANAGEMENT, PRODUCERS, AND INVESTORS: FIRST DAY OF REHEARSAL

And here's what management and producers should know:
- Who is invited to the first day of rehearsal?
- Where is the rehearsal hall and what time should they be there?
- May they stay for the reading/singing?
- Will food be provided?

The First Day Of Rehearsal

This would be the schedule for normal first day of rehearsal for either a play or musical:

10 a.m.–11 a.m.	AEA Cast meets with the Union representative
11 a.m.–12 p.m.	Meet & Greet
12 noon–2:30 p.m.	Read/Sing through the show
2:30 p.m.–3:30 p.m.	Lunch
3:30 p.m.–6 p.m.	Learn Music/Table discussion of the script

AEA CAST MEETS WITH UNION REPRESENTATIVE

Only Actors' Equity members may attend this meeting. This means no management and no PAs. AEA deputies are often elected at this meeting, and a vote is taken about the length of the lunch hour either one or one and one-half hours.

MEET & GREET WITH CAST, CREW, CREATIVE TEAM, PRODUCERS, AND MANAGEMENT

Producers will often ask investors to attend a Meet & Greet as a way of making them feel a part of the production. Determine in advance who will speak at this gathering—you don't want it to go on for too long.

READ/SING THROUGH THE SHOW

The actors may be nervous—many will get their new scripts just as they begin to read. The composer, lyricist, or musical director will often sing the songs.

LEARN MUSIC/TABLE DISCUSSION

For a musical, the company may be broken down into groups to learn the music, often utilizing all three rehearsal rooms. For a play, the director will often want to sit at the table and read slowly through the script, discussing each scene with the cast.

Typical Rehearsal Schedules

For a new play, four to six weeks in the rehearsal studio is typical. Plus appropriate tech time in the theatre. For a new musical, four to seven weeks in the studio is typical. Plus appropriate tech time in the theatre.

NORMAL REHEARSAL DAY

On any professional production, rehearsals are usually held six days a week for seven out of eight and one-half hours a day. If the cast votes for a one-hour lunch, the length of the day is reduced to seven out of eight hours. The shorter day is much preferable.

9 a.m.–10 a.m. Stage management and the creative team prepare for the day—cleaning up the rehearsal hall taping, dealing with rehearsal scenery and props, and distributing information to the production mailboxes. Often the creative team will meet to discuss the specific plan for the day.

10 a.m.–2 p.m. This is the most creative part of the day and the ideal time to work on new scenes, new music, or new choreography. A longer morning and shorter afternoon tends to maximize everyone's energies.

2 p.m.–3 p.m. Lunch. Stage management and the creative team should meet to discuss the next day's rehearsal calls, keeping conflicts and fittings in mind. This gives the stage manager the rest of the afternoon to work out the specifics of the rehearsal call.

3 p.m.–6 p.m. This time is best used for review or for learning new material that is not too taxing. Energies are lower after lunch for both actors and the creative team. Don't push during this period—most accidents and arguments happen during this time.

6 p.m.–7 p.m. Stage management will put out the rehearsal calls for the next day, send out the daily report for that day's rehearsal, and meet with the creative team about the next day's needs.

TYPICAL WEEKLY SCHEDULES FOR A MUSICAL

Of course, there is no "normal." But just as a general manager would go about budgeting a show by using a similar musical as a guide, the stage manager is well-served to have a template for rehearsing a new or revised musical and adjust from there.

Six weeks in the rehearsal studio is a normal rehearsal period for a new musical. Tech time will be discussed later. I've done revivals in four weeks and very complicated new musicals in seven weeks, but start with six weeks and add or subtract from there.

Musical Rehearsal Week 1

This usually begins with events outlined for the first rehearsal: a mandatory Actors' Equity meeting with the cast and stage managers and the Meet & Greet.

For the director, the primary goal of the week is to set the tone of the show for the actors, to read through the script with the cast to make sure the casting is correct, and to allow the authors (if present) to be satisfied that the structure of the show is right. This week the director unites the company—often using theatre games and stories.

For the musical director, the primary goal is for the ensemble to learn their music so that the choreographer can begin work, and to work with the principals on setting musical keys.

For the choreographer, basic dance vocabulary for the show is often taught, and the individual dancers' strengths and weaknesses are assessed.

Musical Rehearsal Weeks 2 and 3

These weeks are mainly choreographic. Dance arrangements must be finalized in order for orchestration to be done later in the process. It will take at least two weeks on most large musicals to work out the choreography for the ensemble and principals and to set the dance arrangements.

For the director, these weeks are about approving the choreography and dance arrangements, and working with the principals in private on the book scenes.

The musical director will work with the principals on their individual numbers, and begin to work with the understudies on their principal vocal assignments.

These two weeks are usually the hardest of the process. They can feel like a slog. However, it's important that all the basic work for all acts is completed—there's a tendency to work on and polish only the first act and leave the second act (often the harder of the two) to languish until the end of the rehearsal period. Try not to let that happen.

Musical Rehearsal Week 4

This is when the book scenes, the music, and the choreography begin to mesh together. It's not time yet for a run-through, but principals are added to choreographic numbers and choral singing is often added to principal vocals.

For the director, this is the week when various elements of the show are combined. It's also the time the director figures out transitions from one scene to the next and makes sure that the book scenes and the choreography have a similar tone.

The choreographer responds to the needs of the musical director—can the singers accomplish what they need to do in the choreography? And to the needs of the director—are the book scenes and the dances seamlessly integrated storytelling?

For the musical director, this is the time to insist on the harmonies and phrasing—they were initially taught in music rehearsals, but may have been pulled apart in the staging. It is also the time to get agreement on tempo.

The fourth week is usually when the musical numbers start to be given to the orchestrator. The orchestra and the musical director determine how rapidly these numbers are handed over.

Musical Rehearsal Week 5

Full acts are put together and then run for the authors, designers, and key crew. The run-through of each act usually takes a day followed by notes and fixes. The first run-through of each act will probably be a mess.

Stage managers, please be sure you have enough PAs to run the props and any rehearsal scenery. If additional seating needs to be added to the rehearsal studio, it should be delivered and set up long before the seats are needed for a run-through audience—the actors must know what the room will look and feel like.

For the lighting designer, these early act run-throughs are crucial. It is here that the show is initially cued and here that lighting problems are solved in the conceptual stage. The scenic designer will see exactly how the set is being used and spot problems in the design or the staging so they can be solved before the cast gets onstage. The costume designer can the time the quick-changes and make sure the clothes accommodate the staging and the dances.

This week is very stressful for the director and choreographer—designers, authors, and management are now violating the privacy of the rehearsal. The director and choreographer will feel judged—rightly so.

Musical Rehearsal Week 6

There should be at least three complete run-throughs of the entire show for the creative team, all crew heads, follow-spot operators, dressers, sound operators, and producers.

The show is completely public now—for all those hired by the production. These run-throughs are to get the right timing for all the show elements, to be sure that the authors and creative team have signed-off on the production, and to allow the director and choreographer to look at the flow and storytelling of their work. The producers will surely have "helpful" suggestions.

A video of the run-through is often taken for the lighting designer; this allows staging to be checked during dry tech. If possible, a complete set of light cues should be given to the production stage manager early in this week in prep for dry tech.

The set designer, technical director, and stage manager must have worked out the exact movement of all set pieces by the beginning of this week. The stage manager can then estimate timings of scenery movement during these run-throughs.

A gypsy run of the show may occur during this week. This is when friends of the cast and the creative team, who are not associated with the show, may view a run-through. This is very useful in assessing laughs, emotional moments, and clarity of storytelling.

If the production is going to open out of town, the PSM and first assistant may very well be absent during this sixth week in the studio. If it's a big show, they may be conducting dry tech at the out-of-town theatre. If the show is opening in the same city as the rehearsal hall, then the rehearsal day should be staggered to allow all stage managers to participate in the run-throughs. But in either case, PAs may need to be added.

9

Technical Rehearsals

The Idea

Technical rehearsals marry the technical elements of the show to the cast. All the rehearsal hall guesswork stops and the actors and creative team must adjust to the realities of the stage space, scenery, lighting, costumes, props, and sound. It is an intensely creative period—fast and expensive, too. It is the production stage manager's job to make the process safe, repeatable, and respectful.

Tech rehearsals are divided into four distinct sections, each with its own priorities:
- Dry tech
- Actor tech
- Orchestra tech
- Orchestra dress rehearsals

Preparing the Theatre For Tech

This is a period of intense work for the stage manager, and the better prepared you are, the more successful the rehearsals will be. There are several things to consider and to do.

WHAT ARE YOUR CREW NUMBERS?

The number of crew in each department will determine how quickly flown scenery, deck scenery, and props can be moved and rearranged. If you have six pieces of manually flown scenery moving during a transition and only three flymen, you'll have to figure out how to stage the order of pieces since they can't all fly at once.

HOW DOES THE SCENERY WORK?

Before deciding how much dry tech time to allot for your show, be sure you understand how each piece of scenery works and how it interacts with every other piece. Do masking tabs need to fly before a scenic piece can move? If there are stage elevators, how are they masked? Do sections of the stage deck need to retract? How much time does this take? What are the speed capabilities of each piece of automated and manual scenery?

MEET WITH DESIGNERS, DIRECTOR, AND CHOREOGRAPHER

It's important that all affected members of the creative team sign off on how the set moves. The production stage manager should get a description of the scenic designer's intent, then work out with the designer what's possible given the crew numbers. Describe the movement of the scenery and approximate timing to the director and choreographer. Even though things will change throughout tech, the fewer the surprises for the creative team, the better.

MAKE A SPIKE MAP

Every spike mark from the rehearsal hall—set by the director and choreographer—must be carefully measured and transferred to the theatre. Placement of mechanized deck scenery, manually placed scenery, and props must be exact. In essence, stage pictures of the rehearsal hall are being recreated onstage in the theatre.

CUE YOUR CALLING SCRIPT

You've already worked out with the scenic designer, director, and choreographer how the scenery is meant to look in each move—now you can break these moves down into specific cues for each department. The lighting designer will have attended several rehearsals and will probably already have cue placements assigned. Get all this into your calling script—it will save you valuable writing time during dry tech.

Chapter 10 and figure 10.1 depict what a finished calling script should look like. Discuss with the automation operators, the flyman, the sound mixer, and the light board operator how you intend to number and call cues.

Auto Fly Cues
How will the cues be numbered? You may want to start deck automation at cue 100 and flying automation at cue 500 to avoid calling the same number for both deck and flying automation. This can confuse the operators.

Will cue lights be used? How many colors and in what order? Check the automation control and system you are using. How many cues may be added between each whole numbered cue? Usually 10 cues may be added as "point cues" between each whole number, e.g. 100.1, 100.2, etc. Some systems allow 100 cues between each whole number, e.g. 100.11, 100.12, 100.13, etc.

It is important to avoid renumbering during tech and preview. Be sure you know how flexible the automation systems are.

Manual Fly Cues

Will cues be numbered or lettered? Lettering is most common for manual fly cues. How will inserting of additional cues be numbered or lettered? Cue lights are almost always used for manual fly. How many colors are needed and in what order?

Lighting Cues

It is standard for commercial productions that "standbys" are not given for lighting cues—the cue is simply called with a slight pause between the cue number and the "Go." Be sure this is what the electrician is expecting.

How are the cues to be numbered? This is most often up to the lighting designer and not the electrician. Does the stage manager call follow-spot cues? Most often the head follow–spot operator calls the cues on a separate channel from the stage manager. Follow–spot operators must be able to hear the stage manager's calling of the show in order to take certain cues from lighting board cues or automation cues, such as blackout cues or "button" cues.

Sound Cues

The person mixing the sound does not wear a headset—it interferes with them actually being able to hear the show—crucial when mixing. Sound cues from the stage manager are always done with a cue light. Are any sound-effect cues to be called by the stage manager? Is more than one cue light needed at the sound console?

Email your preliminary calling script to the lighting designer and scenic designer. This puts you all on the same page and provides a common document to which you may all refer.

WHO GETS GOD MICS

God mics are handheld microphones used to broadcast the user's voice throughout the auditorium and backstage. A god mic allows the speaker to quickly talk to everyone involved in the tech—knowing they will be heard. If a tech has to be stopped quickly because of a potential scenic problem, if a choreographic adjustment needs to be made, or if some staging needs to be altered, the god mic is the easiest way to speak to everyone at once.

Usually, the director, choreographer (if there is one), and production stage manager are the only members of the team with god mics. It's a danger to have too many people with the ability to make themselves heard.

CHECK STAGE ACCESS

Be sure there are house steps with railings from the house aisles onto the stage.

Tech Tables

The Idea

This may seem like a minor item, but it is not. Artists and technicians are equally sensitive to proper respect being shown. Just like the billing on a contact sheet, the location and size of tech tables can make or break a tech rehearsal. If the director's table is in a slightly worse position than the choreographer's, you'll hear about it and soon be making adjustments. You must be sensitive to pecking order when laying out the tech tables.

Figure 9.1 shows a tech table layout for the revival of *Annie*. Because New York's Palace Theatre, where *Annie* was to play, had a center aisle, the tech table placements had to be adjusted.

INTERNET, PHONES, AND ELECTRIC POWER

A wireless Internet system that is reserved for the creative team is essential during the entire dry tech, actor tech, and preview period. A separate wireless Internet system should be in place for the actors and a third for the crew. The creative team and the crew will be uploading and downloading and sending huge files often; too many users slow a system down miserably. Scripts, light plots, sound plots, music files and scores, photos, and daily reports will all be emailed daily. A slow Internet connection will get the blame for information not being transmitted or received.

Phones are not really an issue in the era of cell phones, but it's always good to ask if anyone on the creative team requires a phone at the tech table.

Be sure there are adequate outlets with plenty of power at each tech table.

LOCATING THE TECH TABLES

Once again, pecking order should be considered when laying out the tech tables, but you also need to consider the work to be done at each.

Director's Table
The director should be in the center, and in front of all other tech tables. There should be room for the director's assistants and associates. There should be no one else in the Director's aisle, allowing easy access to the stage.

Choreographer's Table
The choreographer should be just behind and off to the side of the director so that both have an unobstructed view of the stage. Choreographers usually like to be right on an aisle, since they go up onto the stage so often. Again, allow room at the tech table for all the assistants and associates.

Production Stage Manager's Table

I like to be on the opposite side of the house from the choreographer and on the outside aisle, usually in line with the director. This way I have easy access to the aisle, and I'm not in anyone's way in the center section of the house. The stage manager needs exactly the same communication, video feeds, cue lights, and announce mics that have been requested for the run of the show backstage.

Lighting Designer's Table

Normally the lighting designer will require an entire row in the center section. Because of the enormous number of computers, screens, printers, and other equipment needed, be very conscious of the number of power outlets and the available power. The lighting designer usually has two or three assistants.

Sound Designer's Table

The sound designer usually likes to be at the rear of the house, off-center, and very near the mixing console, which will probably be center and at the rear of the house. There should be easy access from the sound designer's table to the mixing console.

Musical Director's Table

The music department will need a tech table near the rehearsal piano to lay out music. And power for the computer they will be using.

Prop Master's Table

The prop master will probably want a large tech table with good light for doing paperwork, displaying alternate props, and repairing items. It should be located somewhere in the house.

Swing and Dance Captain Table

Once again, remember these are very valuable folks. Take good care of them. They will need to take copious notes and store their notebooks during tech. Give them a table large enough for all of them to work comfortably, with good light and power. If you take care of them, they'll take care of you.

Tech Supervisor, Set Designer, Costume Designer, Authors, Producers, and General Manager Tables

Each of these players will need tech tables, especially if this is to be a long tech. The costume designer, authors, producers, and general manager may not need or use a tech table, but they should be offered one that is properly outfitted.

Backstage Rooms

In addition to the dressing rooms, a number of backstage rooms need to be set aside for specific functions. Broadway and road houses will usually have rooms already assigned to the various departments. But many shows have specific requirements outside the range of normal theatre operations. For instance, *Shrek The Musical* required a prosthetics workshop with running water, abundant electrical power, and good ventilation to the outside.

STAGE MANAGER'S OFFICE

This room will house not only the stage managers during the run of the show, but also the PAs and often the creative team during technical rehearsals and previews. There should be at least one landline phone (just in case someone forgets their cell phone) with voice mail, computers, printers, scanners, and copy machine—with the power to support them all at once. A dressing room page system, a full stage video monitor, and headset extension—all identical to the one at the stage manager's desk—should also be installed in the office. Since many impromptu meetings will be held in this space, it should be large enough to hold at least 10 people.

The stage managers will need to get quickly to the stage, so the office should be as close as possible to the stage. The stage managers' office should also be easily accessible from the dressing rooms—you want actors to feel free to come into the office to discuss problems.

I find it very useful to have a spot for the dance captain in the stage manager's office, and to encourage the dance captain to store their staging charts there. In an emergency, when the show needs to be cut quickly and roles reassigned, the stage manager and dance captain can have all their material, plus computers and printers for distribution of information, in one place. This arrangement also makes the dance captain feel more a part of the management of the show.

WARDROBE ROOM

The size of the show and specific needs of the production again dictate the needs of the wardrobe department. However, no matter what the size of the show, every wardrobe room needs at least one washer and dryer, sinks for dyeing and hand-washing, steamers, sewing machines, and work tables. Be sure the wardrobe supervisor approves of the space you're assigning them.

Size of the Wardrobe Crew
The wardrobe staff will be working in the room constantly, and the dressers will be using the room to pick up and drop off costumes. Day workers will be doing repairs, washing, and ironing. Be sure the wardrobe room is big enough for the staff.

Storage of Extra Costumes
Since every musical or play has understudies, standbys, and/or swings, their costumes need to be stored and readily accessible. They are usually stored in the wardrobe room.

Fittings
It's useful to have a private area or curtained-off section of the wardrobe room for fittings.

Building a Wardrobe Room

On many large shows, whether musicals or plays, the basement of the theatre becomes the wardrobe room. This requires considerable planning, since there may be machinery, or musicians, and a clear crossover in the basement.

HAIR ROOM

The hair department often consists of three or four people, and has many specific requirements. Each person in the hair department needs a workstation with a comfortable chair, mirror, good lighting, and plenty of power outlets for curling irons and blow dryers.

If the show has wigs, there will have to be a wig oven and running water. On many large plays and musicals, considerable space in the hair room is taken up by storing wigs—each understudy, standby, or swing often has a separate wig for each character they cover. On shows like *Sunset Boulevard* or *Shrek The Musical*, there are over 150 wigs.

As with wardrobe, always consult with the head of the hair department before assigning the hair room.

MAKEUP/PROSTHETICS ROOM

On smaller and/or contemporary shows, actors usually do their own makeup in the dressing room after an initial consultation with the makeup designer. Or if there is minimal specialty makeup, that department may share with the hair department. However, on big shows with specialty makeup, a separate room for makeup and prosthetics is essential and has the same requirements as the hair room, except that because of quick changes, the makeup room should be very close to the stage.

PROPS ROOM

The prop department will need an area backstage with good light and a table for repairing props. If there are firearms, knives, or any other potentially dangerous props on the show, a secure lock-up area needs to be provided.

MOVING LIGHT HOSPITAL

Moving lights, which almost every commercial show now uses, break down with alarming frequency. Most shows keep at least 10% spares on hand, which must be stored somewhere until they are needed—and they are always needed quickly. Then the newly broken fixture must be repaired. A lock-up (usually a cage) with worktable and tools is necessary on most shows. The head electrician will tell you how much space is required.

DECK SOUND STATION

The A2, that sound person responsible for all the wireless mics, needs a place to work. Mic batteries must be changed each day, repairs must be done, equipment to check the mics must be handy, and spare mics and parts must be stored. This area is usually in the basement and easily accessible to the actors for emergency mic swaps. There needs to be a lock-up for valuable equipment.

Optional Rooms

If space allows, it's nice to have additional rooms available backstage.

DIRECTOR/CHOREOGRAPHER/AUTHOR ROOM

This is a place for the creative team to hang their coats, store their books, and have quiet, private meetings. If this space is not available, they'll be in the stage manager's office.

COMPANY MANAGER'S ROOM

The company manager will usually work from the general manager's office, away from the theatre. But box office reports must still be sent each night and files must be kept at the theatre. If there is not a separate room for the company manager, they too will work out of the stage manager's office.

GREEN ROOM

There is almost never a meeting room for the actors, musicians, and crew. This is a great but welcome luxury, especially on long-running shows. Cast meetings, birthdays, meals between shows, and just hanging out before an entrance are all activities yearning for a green room. If the space for such a room can be carved out, it should be made available to everyone working backstage, not just the actors.

The PSM's Calling Desk

The Idea

Your calling desk is your home. It not only houses all the gear needed to run the show —communications, video, announce mics, cue light switches—but the desk also communicates solidity and seriousness of purpose. I've had many desks built over the years—some for touring, some that were never intended to move, some for specific shows. None of these desks were utilitarian; they all looked designed, classy, and comfortable and suited some very specific needs. And I always felt at home standing in front of them running a show.

LOCATION

The calling desk can be located almost anywhere backstage—on either side of the stage, on a platform above the wings, upstage, or downstage. Placement of the calling desk usually depends on scenic storage and movement offstage and the stage manager's need for clear sightlines.

My preference is *not* to call a show from a booth in the back of the house. I like to be backstage with the actors and crew so I can be in direct contact with the company. I also like to be on the side of the stage closest to the dressing rooms—that way I can easily see if actors are on time for their entrances. I dislike calling a show from a "jump"—a platform above the wings accessible by ladder. I want to be able to move around backstage easily and to speak to cast and crew in case there's a problem.

There are no rules about the location of the calling desk. A site survey of the theatre and study of the ground plan will reveal the ideal location from which to call the show. Letting the production manager and production carpenter know where you want the desk even before the show loads into the theatre will ensure that you get your preferred placement and are not shoved into a convenient corner.

STORAGE

You'll probably be locking up valuables in this desk, as well as storing sensitive materials, emergency medical supplies and some office supplies. Your desk should have a large lockable drawer for valuables, as well as a top drawer for office supplies, and a lower area for medical supplies (especially instant ice). The calling surface of the desk should be angled to allow you to see the calling script clearly, with a sill at the bottom to prevent the script from sliding off the desk. I like to have a large enough surface to hold the calling script and

Photo: Jeremy Davis

Figure 9.2: My ideal layout of the PSM's calling desk

a three-ring notebook for daily reports. This calling surface should be hinged and flip up to allow storage of at least three calling scripts underneath (since on musicals, you will probably have three calling stage managers).

CUE LIGHT SWITCHES

Cue lights are used for a variety of purposes, but most often to cue automation and manual fly moves instead of using the verbal "Go." The sequence of the cue lights for each department should be the same. I prefer red, white, blue (it's patriotic and easy to remember) and then green if a fourth is needed. This makes calling the show more logical. In professional shows there is no "standby" cue. Cue light on means "warning." Cue light off means "Go!" Cues should be warned verbally at the same time the appropriate switch is turned on.

Normally, lighting cues are all called verbally. Auto-deck, auto-fly, and manual fly cues are called with cue lights. Other cue lights are only to cue an actor onto the stage or to attract someone's attention.

Above and behind the calling surface, there should be room for cue light switches. These switches may be mounted either vertically along the outside edge of this upper area of the desk, or horizontally just above and behind the calling surface. There should be at least twelve switches—some shows may require more. Cue lights will be needed on a musical for:

- auto deck
- auto fly
- manual fly
- house curtain
- musical director
- sound
- electrics (as a back up)
- actor cues

The number of cue lights you will need for each department will depend on the anticipated number of cues in any sequence. More than four lights for any department can be confusing. Some stage managers work with master switches or programmable cue lights. Personally, I am not a fan.

Mastering Switches
This means the assigning of a number of individual cue lights to a separate master switch. Throwing this master switch turns off or on all the cue lights assigned to that master. Some stage managers like mastering switches when more than three individual cue lights must be thrown at once.

My personal preference is not to master any cue lights. Mastering works fine during the normal operation of a show, but in emergencies it becomes difficult to pull apart a sequence to skip over or delay some cues.

Programmable Cue Lights

There are some very fancy cue light systems on the market. They are enormous fun to play with and look great on your desk. And during the normal operation of a show, they work wonderfully. However, the same problem exists as with mastering of mechanical switches—how to get out of emergency situations. When you warn with an individual switch, the stage manager is always aware of exactly what pieces of scenery are being cued. With programmable cue lights, you are simply advancing from one cue packet to the next with no reminder of what is actually being cued. Complacency can easily set in. Always remember—you're there to run the show, not simply to push buttons.

VIDEO MONITORS

Video monitors sit on the stage manager's desk just above and behind the calling surface. The monitors should be as close to the eye line of the calling script as possible, so the stage manager can see the monitors while looking at the calling script. Live show video is supplied and maintained by the sound department. The number of monitors and type of shots will vary from show to show.

Master Shot

Usually a color shot of the full stage opening, this is most often the largest monitor and with the highest definition.

Infra-Red Shot

Same as the master shot, but this one can be seen in a blackout.

Conductor Shot

This is a close-up of the conductor for taking musical cues. This shot is also used for monitors on the balcony rail for the singers.

Overhead Shot

An overhead shot is used when a piece of scenery blocks the master shot and you need to see upstage of that piece of scenery. This shot is also useful for monitoring onstage elevators.

Individual Close-up Shots

You may need site-specific cameras and monitors for a variety of show needs such as flying, elevators, treadmills, or off-stage scenic moves.

Movable Cameras

Sometimes there are so many different and specific camera shots on a production that a remote zoom with tilt and pan is needed to see individual moments of cueing. This camera movement should be programmable so that you can hit a preset button for the needed shot, rather than having to manually zoom and pan.

This video feed should go to the stage manager's office and to crew operation points if they cannot see the stage.

AUDIO MONITORS

It may seem counterintuitive to ask for audio monitors on the calling desk when the stage manager is standing several feet from the stage, but the stage manager requires an audio feed from the sound desk if it is noisy off-stage on a musical or the actors are speaking quietly in a play. The exact mix is usually controlled by the sound desk and adjusted to suit the stage manager during tech. However, on some musicals, it's useful to have separate vocal and orchestra mixes controlled by the stage manager.

This same monitor mix should be available in the stage manager's office, as well in the dressing rooms and at the various operation points for the show (fly floor, auto deck, auto fly, and lighting board).

HEADSET SYSTEM

This is how the stage manager speaks to all departments who need to hear called cues. The number of stations will vary tremendously from one show to the next, but the master station must be on the stage manager's desk.

Programmable System
The system must be programmable from the stage manager's desk so that you don't speak to all departments all the time. A separate "private" channel for the assistant stage managers is a great convenience so that discussions of potential problems or solutions may be had in private.

Simple System
Many different stage managers will be using the same system during the run of the show. The operation of the system should be easily taught and understood.

Repairable System
There are gorgeous, flexible headset systems on the market that require servicing by the company that built it—that is, it cannot be repaired by the crew in the theatre. No matter how wonderful these systems seem to be, I suggest you avoid them. If your crew cannot repair the system and if replacement parts are not available locally, don't use it.

Line Switch
This is a surface-mounted push switch for turning your headset mic on and off. It will save you a lot of reaching.

Wired and Wireless Headsets
Since the calling stage manager will be stationery at the desk, that headset will be wired and will not require batteries. The same is true for the other stationary opera-

tors—electrics, auto deck, auto fly, and sound. Those who are mobile will need wireless headsets—carpenters, props, ASMs. The batteries on these headsets must be recharged before each show.

PAGING SYSTEM

All backstage areas—dressing rooms, crew rooms, and hallways—must be able to be paged from the calling desk and from the stage manager's office.

GOD MIC

During dry tech and actor tech, there must a live mic at the calling desk or front-of-house tech station that reaches the house and onstage areas. This will be used to make announcements, give instructions, or stop a rehearsal. The director and choreographer will also have god mics—theirs should be wireless; the stage manager's may be wired.

HOUSE ANNOUNCE MIC

Once the show is up and running, this mic makes emergency announcements to the house. It should always be kept "on" at the sound console and controlled by a switch at the calling desk.

Dry Tech

The Idea

After all the technical elements have been loaded into the theatre and are up and working, but before the actors come onstage, these elements are rehearsed in what's called a dry tech. The control and organization of the technical elements are now under the direction of the production stage manager. The dry tech period may be as short as a half-day for some plays or as long as two weeks for complicated musicals. During this period, the calling stage manager writes the calling script and the deck stage manager organizes what each deck crew member does throughout the show. The lighting designer sets all the basic looks for each cue and the sound designer sets playback levels. Wardrobe and hair are not involved.

After consultation with the director and choreographer, you should go into dry tech knowing the overall look of the scenic movement. The idea is for the stage manager and crew to have complete control over the movement and timing of the scenery and lighting *before* the actors ever set foot onstage. Adjustments will be made during actor tech, but running a dry tech allows the actor tech to move along more quickly.

Cue sheets (all of which will change mightily during dry tech and actor tech) are given to each department before the dry tech begins. This ensures that each technical department has a roadmap for the production; it also gives the crew confidence that the stage manager has done the homework and is in control. See figures 9.3, 9.4 and 9.5 for examples of auto and manual fly cues.

DRY TECH TIMING

Because the crew will still be completing load-in, you need to make the best use of time in dry tech. Here's a workable schedule:

8 a.m.–1 p.m.	Crew Work Onstage
1 p.m.–2 p.m.	Crew Lunch
2 p.m.–6 p.m.	Dry Tech
6 p.m.–7 p.m.	Crew Dinner
7 p.m.–12 a.m.	Dry Tech

This schedule allows maximum crew work time during the morning session. Set the stage for the beginning of that day's dry tech when the crew breaks for lunch. This schedule also allows the stage manager to be in the rehearsal studio with the actors during the morning session.

The number of days allotted to dry tech comes from negotiation—usually between designers, production manager, and PSM—when the production calendar was being laid out. The production stage manager must have confidence that at the end of dry tech, the scenery and lighting moves are sufficiently prepared so that actor tech can proceed safely and without wasting actor time.

DRY TECH PARTICIPANTS

The full running crew, with the exception of follow spots, wardrobe, hair, and makeup should be involved in dry tech. Since you're working out the backstage choreography, timing, and storage, it's important that the show's running crew—not subs—do the dry tech.

The scenic designer and lighting designer are the primary designers involved in dry tech. The stage manager has already worked out the idea of each scenic move with the designer and the director—the dry tech gives physical dimension to the theory of scenic movement. The speed and/or order of scenic moves may change during dry tech as the theory evolves into the reality of the scenic movement. Allow time for experimentation—the scenic designer is entitled to this.

The lighting designer will be working along with the stage manager to set basic looks for each scene, to focus lights on specific pieces of scenery, and to work out lighting timing to coincide with scenic timing.

DRY TECH GOALS

It's important to set daily goals for dry tech. This is a good way of keeping everyone on track, especially yourself. Most importantly, dry tech is the time for the stage manager to work out scenery and prop movement and storage before the actors arrive. The schedule is the stage manager's and everyone else must keep to that schedule.

At the end of each dry tech day, invite the director and choreographer to see what has been worked out during that day's session. This way, adjustments can be made before the actors arrive. You want to be sure the whole creative team is in agreement about the look of the movement of scenery, the placement of props and scenic pieces, and the overall look of the lighting. You may be able to move faster by not including the director and choreographer, but eventually it will be their choice—getting their input early avoids friction later. See figure 9.6 for a sample list of dry tech goals for *Annie*. I also create a personal version of cue sheets for distribution—see figures 9.3 and 9.4.

Actor Tech Rehearsal

The Idea

Safety and repeatability are the goals of any tech. A theatre is inherently unsafe—many people are frequently working quickly in a small space with drastically changing lighting conditions and large pieces of scenery moving at high speeds. Coordinating people with the scenic and prop pieces requires patience and respect.

There should be very few, if any, script rewrites during tech. The creative team has had at least four weeks in the rehearsal studio to work out the script. Rewrites in tech are very cumbersome because of the number of scripts to replace and departments to update.

Finally, it's your duty to keep the whole process as relaxed as possible. If the stage manager is tense, everyone is tense.

ACTOR TECH SCHEDULE

Here is a sample two-week actor tech schedule for a musical. Some shows require more time and some less, but this is a good average schedule.

Days 1 through 6	First pass through show with all tech elements, including wardrobe
Day 7	Day Off
Day 8	Afternoon–Sitzprobe in Studio
	Evening–Piano Dress
Day 9	Morning–Orchestra Seating
	Afternoon–Piano Dress
	Evening–Piano Dress
Day 10	Morning–Orchestra Sound Check
	Afternoon–Orchestra Tech
	Evening–Orchestra Tech
Day 11	Afternoon– Orchestra Dress with Photos
	Evening–Orchestra Dress with Photos

Day 12	Afternoon–Orchestra Dress or Working Rehearsal
	Evening–Invited Dress
Day 13	Afternoon–Working Rehearsal
	First Preview
Day 14	Day Off

Let the actors know that they are on call every day of tech and that they will get their daily call the night before each tech day. You don't want to have actors sitting around the theatre if you know they won't be used. However, you also want to have the actors available to tech a particular scene if you've moved along more quickly than you'd anticipated during the day.

THE DAILY SCHEDULE

The schedule for each actor will vary daily. Again, it's counterproductive to have actors sitting idly in the theatre. The goal for the following day should be worked out with the director and choreographer and posted and/or emailed before the end of each rehearsal day.

Until the final week before previews begin, the actors will work seven out of eight and one-half hours each day of tech rehearsal. The daily schedule should look like this.

8 a.m.–1 p.m.	Crew Work Onstage–No Actors Called
1 p.m.–2 p.m.	Crew Lunch
2 p.m.–6 p.m.	Onstage Tech with Actors
6 p.m.–7 p.m.	Crew Dinner
6 p.m.–7:30 p.m.	Cast Dinner
7 p.m.–7:30 p.m.	Crew Re-Set Stage & Re-Battery Mics
7:30 p.m.–10:30 p.m.	Onstage Tech with Actors
10:30 p.m.–11:30 p.m.	Production Meeting–No Actors Called

This schedule gives maximum work time for the crew in the morning and maximum tech time with the actors.

During the final week before previews, the actors may work 10 out of 12 hours each day. The daily schedule might look like this.

8 a.m.–12 p.m.	Crew Work Onstage–No Actors Called
12 p.m.–1 p.m.	Crew Lunch (except Sound–overtime is involved here)
12:30 p.m.–1 p.m.	Cast into Costumes & Mics
1 p.m.–6 p.m.	Onstage Tech with Actors
6 p.m.–7 p.m.	Crew Dinner
6 p.m.–7:30 p.m.	Cast Dinner
7 p.m.–7:30 p.m.	Crew Re-Set Stage & Re-Battery Mics
7:30 p.m.–12 a.m.	Onstage Tech with Actors

The final three days of the actor tech period will be taken up with orchestra tech rehearsals and final dress rehearsals.

BEFORE ACTOR TECH BEGINS

There are some specific things to do and to consider before bringing actors in for their tech rehearsals.

Tour the Stage with the Actors

Spend some time walking the actors around the set and backstage areas. Show them the crossovers, the entrances, the winch tracks and elevators, and how you've marked the stage for safety. Let them know that glow tape or white tape will be added anywhere they need it. Show them potential danger points and how they are marked for safety, especially if there are flying light ladders. Show them the quick-change booths.

Introduce the Crew

It is very important that the cast and crew work in harmony and with the same goals. Introduce the cast not only to the crew heads, but to the entire crew. This will pay dividends of respect for the whole run of the show.

Plan to Tech in Costume

I've learned from the British to always tech a show in costume. This allows the choreographer to make stage pictures more accurately, the lighting designer to judge color properly, and the actors to test the costumes for ease of movement and the off-stage choreography of quick changes.

A Lesson from the Sound Designer

Nearly all musicals and many straight plays use wireless mics. Some actors have never handled these very delicate, very expensive pieces of equipment. The sound designer should speak to the full company about how to treat the mics.

Show the Actors All Moving Scenery

Even if the scenery moves overhead and doesn't come near the actors, show them the scenery before you move it. The actors must be able to trust that anything moving anywhere near them is intended and fully teched.

Some Basic Rules for Actors

- There can be no eating or drinking onstage or in costume.
- Respect your costume—don't sit around in costume and always hang it up when done.
- Any notes the actors have should go to a stage manager and never to the crew. This includes wardrobe and prop notes.
- Don't leave the building without permission of the PSM.

See figure 9.7 for an example of notes to actors from the first tech day of a small musical.

RESPONSIBILITIES TO ACTORS DURING THE TECH

Actor tech will be most productive and least dramatic if you follow a few basic guidelines.

Keep the Cast Informed

Surprises are the enemy during tech. There will be days during tech when a particular piece of scenery is not working properly, some props are missing, or certain wardrobe pieces are not ready. Before the tech day begins, let the cast know. If a piece of scenery malfunctions with the actors onstage, stop the rehearsal for a moment, go onstage, and explain to the cast what happened and what is being done to correct it. Before rehearsals or during breaks, drop by the dressing rooms and chat with the actors. Useful information and concerns will often be voiced in casual situations.

Honor All Breaks

The AEA rulebook specifies the breaks for each type of contract. Honor these breaks to the letter; otherwise, you can't legitimately require your actors to honor call times.

Post Daily Tech Calls

As you did during studio rehearsals, send out daily emails with the next day's tech schedule and each actor's call. Since the end of a tech day is late at night, announcing the next day's schedule over the dressing room page and onstage is also helpful.

Moving Scenery with Actors

When the stage manager comes to a scenic move, ask the actors to step downstage, out of the way of any scenery. Turn on the work lights and have the actors watch the entire scenic move, imagining where they would be onstage during the move. When the actors feel safe and confident, have them move back into their positions onstage and run the scenic change again with bright work lights. Finally, run the scenic change again in stage light.

Repeat the scenic move as many times as necessary until the creative team and the cast are satisfied. Remind the cast that they must always be in the positions worked out in tech and move in the same patterns. After a scenic shift has been teched, it will always be run at the same speed in the future and the cast must not vary from what has been rehearsed.

RESPONSIBILITIES TO CREW DURING THE TECH

The stage manager also has responsibilities to the creative team and crew heads during technical rehearsals.

Publish a Tech Schedule

Giving the creative team and crew a piece of paper with the overall tech schedule gives everyone a sense of confidence and purpose. This schedule may have to be adjusted and republished. Include the general goals of each day, along with the Sitzprobe, orchestra rehearsals, dress rehearsals, and preview schedule.

It is not necessary to give the actors the daily tech goals, but they should have all the other information. Two separate calendars may be a good idea—a detailed one for the creative team and crew, and a more general one for the cast. Be sure the theatre's house manager has these schedules, because the theatre may be used for something else when the show is not working there.

Figure 9.8 shows a sample tech rehearsal goals sheet used by the creative team and crew.

Gather and Distribute Information

It's good to have a brief meeting before each tech day starts to let the creative team know what's missing or not working properly for that day. The director or choreographer may have specific needs to be addressed. Encourage the crew heads to voice concerns or give information during these meetings.

And, of course, a production meeting at the end of the day is essential to discuss the next day's morning work call needs and to set priorities for the next day's actor tech. This may all seem obvious, but in the rush and exhaustion of each day these meetings can be forgotten, which leads to confusion and a sense of being leaderless. The production stage manager is the leader.

Give Breaks

The lighting designer, especially, will want to use cast breaks to get ahead in writing cues. Be sure the crew gets humane breaks. They'll work more intelligently if they are treated with value. The crew also needs time to collect mics at the end of each session and to clear the stage for mopping and resetting before the next actor session.

Get a Computer Printout

Auto deck and auto fly computers can print out a hard copy of all cues and the target positions for each winch. Since computers can crash and lose information, a hard copy of the cues could prevent some sleepless nights.

The Sitzprobe

Sitzprobe means, literally, to sit and explore the music. It's my favorite day of rehearsal, filled with enormous pleasure for everyone in the cast. It's the first time the cast hears the orchestrations and it tends to be a very emotional day. The cast uses this rehearsal to identify specific musical instruments they need to hear for rhythm or pitch. The composer, director, choreographer, and producers will also check the orchestrations to be sure they are appropriate to the material.

This rehearsal ideally happens in the same studio where the musicians have been rehearsing without the cast. After the orchestra has been sufficiently rehearsed, the cast goes to the music studio and sings through the show with the orchestra. Mics should be provided, so the actors don't have to try to sing over the orchestra.

The Sitzprobe is usually timed to happen after the show is fully teched. After the Sitzprobe, very little time elapses until the cast is rehearsing onstage with the full orchestra.

Thank Everyone for the Day

10
The Calling Script

The Idea

> A calling script must be as clear, readable, and flexible a document as possible. Every-thing that moves in every cue should be included, but in such a way as not to distract from the quick identification of cue numbers. It should be email-able and able to be opened in standard word processing programs. If you can read, you should be able to call the show from this script.

In the pre-computer era, there were only handwritten calling scripts. The stage manager would write the cues into a book in pencil, and every time there was a script change, that page had to be re-cued. My greatest fear during these techs was that I would lose my call-ing script, or someone would spill coffee on it, or it would be destroyed. There was only one up-to-date copy—you couldn't photocopy fast enough to keep back-up copies.

During long runs, each new stage manager would make a new handwritten copy of the calling script in a style they preferred. This would almost always lead to writing errors.

For any show, whether play or musical, for any size theatre, and for any length of run, a stage manager today would have to be an idiot to handwrite the calling script. It must be done on a computer. It is just as fast to enter cues in a computer as to handwrite. The script can (and should) be backed up at the end of each session. A digital calling script can be emailed to the designers and there will be no writing errors for subsequent stage managers. Figure 10.1 is a calling-script excerpt from the 2012 Broadway revival of *Annie*.

The Computer Software

You will be emailing the calling script to many different people with many different levels of computer sophistication. You may also need to call up a script of yours many years after you've written it and many generations of software later.

For these reasons, I like using plain old Microsoft Word, with no fancy formatting. Anyone can open it and it can be easily manipulated. The only trick I use is to create a small left margin and a large right one. I then set a tab outside the right margin and use that large margin for writing my cues. The cues are picked out easily from the text.

Calling Dance Numbers

I personally do not use a score for calling a musical. Calling from a score means writing penciled cues in the small margins of a printed score—and I don't read music. It's also difficult to email because it must be scanned first. I create a dance calling script.

Laying out the dances in dancers' counts—usually in eights—is the simplest, clearest way to cue dance numbers. Using the same counts that the choreographer and dancers use means you're counting with them—you can discuss the dance in their terms. If sections of the dance are cut, you can cut them cleanly in the calling script without having to scratch out sections of the score.

With each eight-count—or whatever the count is for that dance phrase—I include a description of what is happening in the dance. This way, if I get lost in the counting, I can reference the movement onstage and pick up the counts again.

Figure 10.2 shows my calling script of a twelve-minute dance number.

Some Calling Script Tips

The script doesn't have to be beautiful in tech, or even in previews. Since you will be teching and calling from a printed script, make your corrections on this calling script in pencil. At the end of the day, go back through your hard copy script and enter all penciled corrections into the computer and print clean pages. Your pencil corrections will be easy to find, and you can take notes from the director, choreographer, and designers quickly. It's important to make the corrections each day—otherwise, you won't know what are new notes and what are old notes.

Many stage managers like to make color notations in the calling script, matching the color in the script with the color of the light warning a cue. Or designating one color for electric cues and another for sound. If you want to do this after the show opens, then do so. However, during tech and previews, you must work faster than this coloring will allow. It also means you'll have to use a color printer, which is slower than a black and white laser.

Back up your script at the end of each session. This can be done on a jump drive, or by emailing the script to yourself and your assistants (my preferred method), or using a dedicated, wireless backup system like Time Capsule. There are also a number of Web-based ways to store information in the Cloud. Dropbox is currently the most popular of these. Whatever method you use, be diligent about backing up.

11
Previews

The Idea

The commercial theatre is a handcrafted industry. It is one of the few art forms in which an unfinished work is put before a paying audience and adjusted performance by performance in response to the audience—either out of town or in New York City. Jokes that seemed really funny in rehearsal may not work in front of an audience; exposition that seemed essential may be irrelevant; characters may be built up or written out—all in response to what the audience tells the creative team at each performance.

At one time, previews were called "low-priced previews," and the idea was that the audiences would pay less money to be guinea pigs for the improvement of the show. "Low-priced" has long since disappeared, with preview box office prices being the same as post-opening prices. And previews grew from a week to ten days to the now-common three to five weeks.

A Story

David Merrick famously extended the preview period of the original *42nd Street* —indefinitely—claiming he was waiting for a "signal from God." He refused to let any critics in to see the show. And then, suddenly, Merrick announced it would open the next day. Director Gower Champion died the night *42nd Street* opened. There were many in the Broadway community who claimed that this was the signal from God that Merrick had been waiting for.

The Preview Schedule

Preview period is the most exciting and exhausting phase of the production process. During the early weeks of previews, there are generally no mid-week matinees. This is to allow more daily rehearsal time.

Here is a sample of a normal preview day.

8 a.m.–12 p.m.	Crew Work Onstage
	SMs meet with Elecs/Sound to get all cuing changes
1 p.m.–5 p.m.	Cast Working Rehearsal Onstage with Crew
5:30 p.m.–6:30 p.m.	Crew Dinner
5 p.m.–7 p.m.	Cast Dinner
6:30 p.m.–7:30 p.m.	Cast Called for Notes
7:30 p.m.	Half-Hour Call for Preview
8 p.m.	Curtain
Following Preview	Cast Notes in House
	Production Meeting

Tech During Previews

In the four hours of onstage rehearsal during previews, changes will be made quickly and often without a proper technical rehearsal. Lines may be cut in a note session without ever being rehearsed; scenes may be shortened without ever reteching scenic changes or wardrobe quick-changes; entrances and exits may be changed without ever rehearsing them for the follow spots or lighting designer.

The stage manager must be able to estimate for the crew and for wardrobe how much time has been taken out of any scene to be sure there is still enough time to accomplish the necessary off-stage business. If there is any doubt about timing, you must insist upon a rehearsal with all technical elements.

Rehearsals During Previews

Nothing sucks energy out of actors like sitting around doing nothing. When laying out the changes for the next day at the evening's production meeting, identify for the creative team those actors who will be called. And then be sure to use them in rehearsal.

If possible, let the actors know before they leave the building after the performance whether they are called the next day or not.

LIST CHANGES MADE DURING REHEARSALS

At the end of the afternoon's rehearsal and before the evening's performance, all changes must be written up and distributed to all departments and posted on the callboard for the actors. The follow spots may not be called for the rehearsal and must be brought up to date on the day's changes. It's helpful to post or distribute a list of all dialog changes for that day, as a reminder to the cast and to the sound operator.

RUN ALL AUTOMATION CHANGES MADE DURING REHEARSALS

You may think that automation changes can be made with notes, but any automation change—the slowing of a turntable, the speeding up of an auto fly cue—must be run with the cast. Unintended consequences are common with these changes, and they should be tested before being presented to an audience—not only for safety, but to avoid potential embarrassment for actor.

KEEP REHEARSAL GOALS REALISTIC

Remember, the cast and crew (and you) are tired and not functioning as quickly as you were early in the rehearsal period. When planning the day's rehearsal, don't cram too much work into too little time. There will be mistakes by both cast and crew, and the creative team may change their minds about the effectiveness of a change.

The production stage manager's job above all is to provide for the safety and protection of cast and crew. Don't allow yourself or the cast and crew to be rushed. Be sure all changes are thoroughly discussed, approved, and rehearsed—not just thrown onto the stage in a panic.

Stage Manager Rotation

Like backing up the calling script, the production stage manager must back up the performances of the entire stage management team. Rehearsals during previews are the perfect time to rotate your team. The PSM usually will have been calling all shows during early previews, since that's who teched the show. Put your first assistant into calling the show as early as possible, and move the deck stage managers around so they all know all positions. Preview rehearsals are a perfect time to give the assistants rehearsal in their backup assignments. It also allows the PSM to spend time in the house with the creative team.

Freezing the Show

Any production is a living, evolving experience. The idea is to keep it similar, but not identical from performance to performance. Freshness and the appearance of spontaneity is the goal—otherwise, shows become reanimated corpses lurching about the stage.

However, during the preview process, there must come a time when the creative tinkering stops. Then the cast and crew are permitted to make the show their own, to repeat their performances without trying to incorporate large changes. This doesn't mean that notes and small line changes won't continue, but it does mean that the creative team steps back and allows the cast and crew to hone their work.

This "freezing" should happen at least two or three performances before the start of the critics' period. Forge an agreement with the creative team about when the show is to be "frozen" and then make sure it happens—this protects the cast and crew. It's often hard for the creative team to let go, to turn the show over to the cast, crew, and stage managers, but it has to be done in time for those who will perform the show each night to be confident in their own work. Otherwise, you risk a shaky opening night performance.

12

Opening Night and the Critics

Critics no longer attend opening night in the commercial theatre—that practice stopped decades ago. The sight of critics running up the aisles to make their deadlines after the final curtain but before the curtain call is just a distant memory.

A Story

I once did a musical with a book written by a then-prominent television critic. He had been very forthcoming during rehearsals about his view of his job as a critic—his job was to entertain his viewer audience. A few days before opening night he came into my SM office, closed the door, and broke down in tears. "These bastards can close our show," he sobbed. He had never understood the relationship between reviews and employment until he was on the receiving end of a review. We got poor reviews and closed three weeks later. He never wrote another show.

Critics and Reviews

Critics now begin coming to a show during the final week before the official opening night. The exact timing of which critics come on which night is up to the press agent. Since the press agent works for the show and not for the media, the press performances are set by the production. The benefit of this is that one terrible performance cannot ruin an entire production—the critics are spread out.

Review Quirks and Tips

- Don't ever tell the cast which critics are coming to a particular performance. As professionals, they are entitled to know what the critics' period is, but not the performance-by-performance specifics.
- Keep nervous producers and investors away from backstage during the critics' period. They'll blab about who's there.
- The PSM should call all critics' performances; do not let an assistant call the show at this time. If anyone is going to screw something up, it should be the person in charge.
- Never post or talk about reviews. If you're going to believe a good review, you have to believe the bad reviews, too. And there will be both.
- A good review can be just as destructive as a bad one. If an actor is praised for a particular moment or line reading, they will be forever self-conscious about that moment.
- Reviews, like awards, are business concerns. They cannot and must not affect the feelings of those backstage about their colleagues.
- Encourage the actors not to read the reviews. Good luck with this one!

Opening Night Gifts

The Idea

If you're going to give gifts—and you don't have to—give them to everyone. Not just the cast, but the crew, creative team, management, and orchestra are entitled to your thanks and largesse. Personal cards to each person involved with the show are warmer and more appreciated than any purchased gift.

A Story

In years past, giving liquor and wine was common on opening nights. Often, I would get so much booze that it would serve me until the next opening. Booze is no longer cool, I'm sorry to say.

GIFTS IN GENERAL

Charitable giving in someone's name is appreciated by most everyone on a production. I would stay away from donations to controversial organizations. Look for a charity that mirrors the concerns of the show. *Annie,* for instance, is ideal for giving to animal shelters.

GIFTS TO YOUR SM TEAM

If you are the PSM, your gifts and cards must be personal and reflect how grateful you are for the support and tireless effort of all on your team. A friend of mine always gives engraved, high-intensity flashlights. Another gives gift certificates for massages. But the note is the most important thing. Plan ahead—specially monogrammed gifts must be order far in advance.

DISTRIBUTION OF GIFTS

Not just your own gifts, but all the gifts in the theatre must be distributed. Figure out who is going to be responsible for flowers and other gifts dropped off at the stage door. You'll also need to figure out how to handle the gifts for those without dressing rooms, like the creative team and management.

Opening Night Curtain

A holdover from the days of all critics attending the opening night performance is the early curtain. It used to be that critics had to make their 11 p.m. deadline at the paper—now, everyone just wants to get to the party earlier.

Opening night curtain time will have been established by the producers long before the show ever goes into previews. Generally, 6:30 p.m., 6:45 p.m. or 7:00 p.m. is the announced time. However, the producer, press agent, or general manager will control when the curtain actually goes up, depending on the seating of all the important investors, perhaps a television critic or two, and the celebrities.

As production stage manager, be sure you have a system for the producer to let you know it's okay to start the performance. It can be disaster to go too early—or too late.

Gypsy Robe

This Broadway tradition dates from 1950 when a chorus member from *Gentlemen Prefer Blondes* gave a dressing gown to a chorus member in *Call Me Madam*. That robe was then passed on to *Guys and Dolls*, but with a rose from Ethel Merman attached.

This tradition has been passed down ever since—the chorus member in the new production who has been in the chorus of the most Broadway shows receives the Gypsy Robe from a similar chorus member in the most recent Broadway show to open. It's a swell tradition, complete with the recipient moving around inside a circle of cast, crew, and management, touching their hands, and then visiting each dressing room. Retired robes are kept at Lincoln Center, the Smithsonian, and the Actors' Equity Association office.

You must allow time for this great tradition and be sure everyone associated with the production knows when the Gypsy Robe will be presented. It is usually presented onstage an hour before curtain on opening night. Since the ceremony is frequently a publicity event as well, inform all who will attend that they may be photographed and videoed.

Speeches

The director and the lead producer will usually want to say something to the whole production team. As much as the cast and crew want to hear what their leaders have to say, they also want to do their normal preparation for the performance. Always allow enough time for the Gypsy Robe and speeches before the half-hour call, and encourage those making speeches to be aware of the half-hour call, too. The whole company will appreciate you watching out for them.

A Story

My first show with Mike Nichols was *Hurlyburly*. It was a difficult show to put together, with a long tryout period and a starry cast. On opening night, Mike asked me to assemble the company onstage at the places call. He kept us waiting. When he walked onstage he said, "Just remember, everything depends upon tonight!" And left the stage. We all had a good laugh—Mike said the unsayable, and the tension was broken.

13
Running a Show

Directorial and Managerial Duties

Once the show is up and running, the production stage manager's duties become directorial and managerial. Assistants will call most performances, and the creative team will be addressed through daily and weekly reports.

DIRECTORIAL DUTIES

Even if there is a resident or associate director on the show, most of the daily notes will be given by the stage manager. Be sure the director has told the cast that the stage manager will be giving the director's notes—with the director's full confidence. Otherwise actors, especially English and European actors, may find it unusual for a stage manager to be giving them notes.

Actor notes may include staging corrections, line notes, and adjustments to character intentions. If an actor challenges a note, or if a note might change the director's original intention, then the note must be approved by the director. Only the stage manager should give notes to the crew—never the actors.

Watching the Show

Don't over-watch the show. If you watch the show more than three times per week, you soon won't know what you're looking at. You may need to go out to the front of house to watch a specific scene to look for a noted problem, but two or three complete shows a week is about all anyone can watch with clarity.

Who Gives Notes

It's important that no one except the director, choreographer, dance captain, associate director, associate choreographer, and stage manager give notes to the actors.

Actors should not give notes to other actors. Producers, general managers, press agents, and casting directors should never give notes directly to actors. That way lies madness. Ask them to give the notes to you so you can check with the director and pass them along if they are appropriate.

Understudy Rehearsals

After opening night, understudy rehearsals should be held twice a week until all understudies are fully rehearsed in their roles. If the show is complicated or dangerous technically, a full dress rehearsal put-in may be necessary. Because of the expense of such a rehearsal, it's important to clear it with management. The director and choreographer may very well want to attend a complete run-through for each set of understudies to give notes and make performance adjustments.

Casting Sessions

The production stage manager should attend all post-opening casting sessions. If the show is a long run, eventually the production stage manager will be making casting recommendations or actually doing the casting.

Keep good notes! After opening, many in the creative team will not remember specifics about various actors. And since casting decisions must often be made from notes and not with everyone present in the audition room, the stage manager's notes may be needed to remind everyone what they thought. See figure 4.3 in chapter 4 for a sample of my casting notes.

MANAGERIAL DUTIES

The PSM runs the backstage. Setting a professional tone, openly distributing information, consulting with the house staff, and the respecting the crew—especially the house crew— will make for a harmonious run at the theatre.

Involve the House Staff

The house manager, doormen, and house crew know a lot about their theatre and can either help or hinder the stage manager's running of a show. If there are problems with heat, air conditioning, personnel, cleanliness, or any issue relating to the theatre itself, discuss it will the appropriate house person before going to management with the issue. House staff should feel involved in solving the show's problems —they should not get a call from the theatre owner about a problem they didn't know existed.

Tipping

The production should tip all doormen every week. The stage manager should work out the amount with the general manager and give the cash in an envelope.

Since many actors will not know that it's customary to tip their dressers weekly, the stage manager should tell the actors about tipping and suggest an appropriate amount—the amount should be discussed with the wardrobe supervisor.

Reports

The Idea

The daily and weekly stage manager's reports, along with the weekly theatre schedule, should convey to all who receive them an accurate picture of what is going on with the show artistically, technically, and personally with the actors and crew. They should not be gossipy or speculative, but neither should problems or praise be glossed over.

DAILY REPORTS

A daily report is written after each performance and emailed or faxed to the producers, management, and creative team. It does not go to the actors and only selected producers. It should include the following information:

- Day and date of performance, matinee or evening
- Performance number
- Number from opening night (include any out-of-town and preview performances separately)
- Running time
- Start and end times of each act
- Intermission
- Playing time—the total of both acts
- Running Time—the total of both acts plus intermission
- Personnel for that performance
    Calling stage manager
    Deck stage managers
    Sound mixer
    Conductor
    Observers of record—director, PSM, conductor, etc.
- Cast changes
    Who is absent, who is the replacement actor, in what role, reason for actor's absence
    Late arrivals of actors
- Injuries
- Overtime
- Rehearsals for that day, including who was called
- Crew Calls for that day, including how many in each department were called
- Performance notes

I often like to include the number of sub musicians in the pit that night. This is especially useful for the music contractor if there are complaints about the quality of the playing.

Check out Figure 13.1 for a sample of a daily performance report.

WEEKLY REPORTS

A weekly report is written following the final performance of the week. It is from this summary report that the company manager will pay overtime or deduct pay, check crew payrolls, note accidents, etc. Like the daily report, the PSM should always write this report, since you are responsible for its content.

This report will go to fewer people than the daily report, since it will often contain reprimands for actors or crew and may give sensitive information about cast members. Recommendations for the future are often included in weekly reports. The weekly report should include:

- A daily summary of who was out and who was on at performances, with explanations
- A daily summary of lateness
- Accidents
- Who conducted which performances
- Rehearsal calls
- Crew Calls
- Additional payments
- Press events
- Technical issues
- Management notes
- General backstage notes and recommendations

The producer and general manager should decide who gets these reports. Every investor and design assistant does not need to know the intimate details of the show. See figure 13.2 for a sample weekly report.

WEEKLY SCHEDULE

This schedule is usually published on the last performance day of the week and it gives a detailed preview of the next week's activities. The house manager and house crew should receive this schedule, as well as the show's management and creative team.

The schedule for the use of the theatre will change from week to week. If the show is not using the theatre, the theatre is sometimes booked for outside events. But the show always has first call on the theatre, not only for performances, but also for rehearsals and crew calls. So by publishing the schedule the show is claiming use of the theatre and the necessary house personnel.

The weekly schedule should be broken down into days of the week and include the following information:

- Performance times for each day of the week
- All rehearsal and crew calls
- Vacations with replacements
- Personal days with replacements
- Press Events

Figure 13.3 is an example of a weekly schedule.

CAST HISTORY

A cast history should be kept from the first day of rehearsal for each actor and stage manager. I prefer to keep this history on the computer, with a file for each actor and stage manager, but it may be kept in a binder as well.

These cast histories should be kept private and added to at the end of each rehearsal or performance week. They are especially useful for quickly checking how many personal days, sick days, or vacation days an actor has had. They may also be used for disciplinary action.

The cast histories should include all of the following pertinent information for each actor and stage manager:

- Name
- Phone number
- Date of birth
- Email address
- Home address
- Social Security Number
- Emergency contact
- Pertinent medical information
- First rehearsal
- First performance
- Final performance
- Costume or wig fittings outside rehearsal
- Injuries
- Lateness
- Vacations
- Personal days
- Warnings or reprimands

Figure 13.4 is an example of a cast history.

The Stage Management Team

The Idea

Once a show has opened, the stage management team should settle into a predicable routine. The calling SM and musical conductor rotation, the distribution of reports, the giving of notes, the understudy rehearsals, and the performance schedule should all assume a shape the cast and crew can count on.

ORGANIZING THE TEAM AFTER OPENING

Once a show has opened, the PAs' jobs are finished. The stage management team is reduced in size to the number of SMs employed on the AEA contract. For plays, two stage managers are required—for musicals it's three. This number may be increased in complex shows.

There should be one extra stage manager on each team. That is, if it takes two stage managers to run a show—one calling and one running the deck—then the team needs three stage managers. This is often a difficult concept for management to understand. But if the PSM is to watch and note the show three times a week, as well as needing the final performance of the week to do all the necessary weekly paperwork, then for four performances a week the PSM is not available to call the show or run the deck. Also, emergencies happen during a show—stage managers get sick, an accident happens that requires a stage manager to give medical attention, or a show must be cut and reorganized quickly because an actor has become ill. If each stage manager is locked into a position for each performance, unusual situations cannot be handled.

The number of stage managers depends on the show itself. Many shows have four stage managers, and some may have six or more depending on the complexity of the scenic moves. I have turned down shows because the management did not think it necessary to have the number of SMs I thought were required for safety.

In any potentially dangerous situation, a stage manager's eyes must be on the safety of the actor. If there is an elevator, a "Clear" from a stage manager must be given before the elevator moves; same with flying. No matter how good the crew is, safety is the stage manager's responsibility and must be handled by that department.

STAGE MANAGER SUBS

All shows need substitute stage managers for personal days, vacations, or illnesses of the regular SM team. There should be at least two trained subs on any show available at any time. This may mean the constant training of new subs when the old subs get permanent jobs somewhere else.

I already mentioned, but it bears repeating: Since the PAs were poorly paid during the production period and because they already know the general operation of the show, they make the perfect subs. The subs should be trained as deck stage managers, but not necessarily to call the show—especially not on complicated musicals.

ROTATING STAGE MANAGERS

If every stage manager does the same job each night, boredom can set in quickly and it will be felt throughout the company. Rotating the calling and deck duties of the stage managers keeps everyone fresh and interested. Some PSMs do not like to call the show after it has opened. I think this is a mistake, since calling the show keeps the PSM in touch with the crew and gives credibility to technical notes.

If there are three stage managers on a team, the PSM should call at least two shows per week, with the other two stage managers calling three shows apiece. The two ASMs should switch sides of the stage every other show if there are two deck stage managers. On a play that does not require a deck stage manager, the PSM should call three shows per week and the ASM should call five.

REPLACING A PRODUCTION STAGE MANAGER OR ASSISTANT STAGE MANAGER

The amount of training time necessary to replace a stage manager depends upon the complexity of the show and on whether or not the replacement has been a sub on the show. Since backstage is a private place, introduce any new stage managers to the cast, crew, and musicians immediately. Let everyone know what this person is doing in the building.

Production Stage Manager
Since the PSM is responsible for artistic maintenance of the show, as well as technical maintenance and running of the show, more time is required to replace this position. For a new lead SM, two weeks is the minimum amount of time for training. Remember that technically the Production Stage Manager is that one stage manager who took the show from the idea through opening. Thus there is not really a replacement for the PSM even if that is the title that is given to the new lead stage manager.

Assistant Stage Manager
At least one week is the required to put a new ASM into a show.

Learning the Show
Before stage managers can become involved in learning the technical aspects of a musical, they must understand the book and the music. Allow time for the new stage manager to watch the show, see the staging, see the audience reaction, and understand the music before putting them into a backstage track. For new calling stage managers, a recording of the music is invaluable.

For plays, a thorough grounding in the literature of the play, the background of each character, the idea of the design elements, and the needs of the actors are essential. Everyone backstage needs to know that the new stage manager fully understands the show. A calling tape that records the PSM calling the cues live, complete with dialogue and music, should be provided to each new calling stage manager.

Defining the Duties
This may seem so basic as to not need mentioning, but letting a new stage manager know what are their exact duties takes a lot of anxiety out of the training. Tell them what you expect and how it needs to be done. Will this person be calling the show? Working both sides of the deck? Doing paperwork? Dealing with management?

Provide all Technical Information
The new stage manger will want to take paperwork, music recordings, and the calling script home to study. And since each person learns differently, providing all the necessary information immediately allows new people to work at their own speed.

Standbys, Understudies, and Swings

The Idea

Swings, standbys, and understudies can be great assets to a stage manager. Their preparedness and willingness to sometimes perform split tracks—playing more than one role in an emergency—can make the difference between a performance looking ragged or looking crisp and seamless. Be sure their dressing room accommodations are thoughtful, that during tech they have well-lighted tables to take notes, and that they are always kept informed about the health of the actors they are covering. Make them feel important and well taken care of and they will keep your show looking fresh.

Be sure all the swings, standbys, and understudies feel adequately rehearsed— they should participate in technical rehearsals. Allow these covers to bring their own artistic sensibilities to the roles they cover. Their performance must be similar enough to that of the regular performer so as not to throw off the rest of the cast, but they should have the freedom to feel like artists and not like utility robots.

A Story

Emanuel Azenberg, longtime Broadway Producer and good friend, always says that understudies and swings are the cheapest form of insurance available in the theatre. You can think of it like this—if a Broadway musical is grossing $1 million per week, then each performance is worth $125,000. The cost of an understudy or swing is less than $100,000 per year. So, if an understudy saves one cancellation of a show in a year, they have more than paid for their salary for that year. These are very good gamblers' odds.

STANDBYS

A standby is a principal actor who does not have regular role in the production, performing only when one of the principal actors they cover is absent. A standby generally covers a star, not a featured player. Standbys must have their own dressing rooms (or may share with another standby) but when they go on they use the dressing room of the person they are replacing.

A standby is not necessarily in the theatre at every performance and may call in at half-hour to be sure no one is out or feeling ill. The standby must be reachable by phone and within a short distance of the theatre for the entire performance. I'm a believer in not requiring the standby to be in the theatre at all times—it could drive them insane. However, if the standby is not in the theatre every night, they should be required to watch a certain number of shows per week, just to keep up with incremental changes. Two shows a week is a good number.

UNDERSTUDIES

Every principal role in a production must have at least one understudy—this is an AEA rule. In most commercial productions, two understudies cover each principal role—one of whom may very well be a standby. Unlike standbys, understudies have another role in the production, either as principal or chorus.

Be very careful of the "domino effect," which occurs when one absence from a performance causes the switching of many tracks in a show. One other thing—it's not a good idea to actually designate a first and second cover for each role. This will always make the second cover feel lesser than the first.

SWINGS

In musicals, a swing is a chorus performer who does not have a regular role in the production—they only go on when a performer they cover is absent. Generally, a swing may not cover more than six chorus or principal parts, but AEA reserves the right to make this determination. The swing needs to be in the theatre during all performances, since accidents involving singers and dancers can happen suddenly.

VACATION SWINGS

Vacation swings are temporary swings hired to fill in for vacations, leaves of absence, or emergencies. Their contracts are for a specific period of time and they have all the duties and perks of a regular swing during their employment. Those hired must fit the costumes of the person they're replacing, since there won't be time or money to build new costumes.

Since vacation swings often get other employment as soon as their temporary contract with your show is finished, put together as many continuous weeks of employment for them as possible. Although you'll want to rehire this trained vacation swing as often as possible, they're usually not available when you try to reemploy them.

Reward vacation swings with more permanent employment as replacements on the show or on tours. If it becomes known that your show rewards temporary employees, you'll get better ones and they'll try to make themselves available in the future.

DANCE CAPTAIN AS SWING

Dance captain is one of the most important jobs on a musical and you should make this person your partner and friend. The dance captain is responsible for the daily maintenance of the dances on a musical. They are hired by the choreographer and responsible to the choreographer.

It's important that the dance captain also be a swing on the show, and therefore free to watch any performance without having to replace their track onstage. Also, since dance captains know so many tracks in a production, they have instant credibility with the rest of the ensemble.

If there is an assistant dance captain, it's a good idea for this person to be of the opposite sex from the dance captain.

COSTUMES AND HAIR FOR UNDERSTUDIES AND SWINGS

Although the production is not required to provide understudies and swings with their own costumes and wigs (except for underwear and tights) it is to the benefit of the show that you do provide them. In an emergency, the understudy or swing can quickly change into their own costumes without having to take them off the person being replaced. The costumes and wigs will also fit properly if they've been made for the understudy or swing. There is also the "ick" factor—imagine having to climb into someone else's wet, warm clothes when you have to go on in an emergency.

Because costume designs change during previews, managements often don't like to make the costumes for the understudies and swings until after the show has opened. Although this is standard procedure, the wardrobe supervisor must be sure that the cover can go on at any time. This may mean that a cover doesn't have a full set of costumes but has only one costume for the entire show. Just be sure that the cover can go on in some fashion, and then let the management and the creative teams know what to expect.

PERKS FOR UNDERSTUDIES AND SWINGS

Swings are usually paid more than the regular ensemble. Swings get additional weekly money for each small role they cover; this amount is the sum of all the ensemble parts payments.

Allow the swings and understudies to observe the show from backstage or the house anytime they wish. Make them feel welcome and included. Management is not required to include swings in cast recordings, Tony Award production numbers, TV performances of show numbers, or the shooting of television commercials. And it costs more to include them since they must be paid. However, the benefits in good will are tremendous. Happy swings stay with a show, resentful swings leave. It costs a lot of money to rehearse and costume a new swing.

The Production Stage Manager and Notes

The Idea

Production stage managers have varying levels of directorial training. But the thing that all PSMs have in common is that they were in the rehearsal room with the director—they know the director's (and author's) intention for the production. It the stage manager's job to remind the actors of that intention, to keep the running time of the show approximately what it was on opening night, and to solve any interpersonal problems among the actors.

Audiences spend just the same (or more) for tickets in the second year of the run of a show as they did for opening night. The stage manager's job is to help the director keep the show as fresh as it was when it opened, to give the illusion of the first time to every performance.

A Story

Mike Nichols says, "It is the job of the director to give an actor back their original impulse." This means that the reason an actor was hired in the first place was that they brought something to the role that was unique—don't direct it out of them. For stage managers, the job is to remind the actors of the rehearsal spark struck during the early work. Never allow the actors to "set it and forget it."

THE PRODUCTION STAGE MANAGER IS NOT THE DIRECTOR

On many shows, the director returns to the production very infrequently to give notes. And so, the PSM is the main note-giver. Your job is to maintain the director's vision, not to establish one of your own. The production stage manager is not the director and must never alter the director's vision without permission of the director.

Be clear with the actors that you are in touch with the director and acting with the director's permission, especially when changing staging or intention. Some directors will encourage minor changes in staging or intention to keep a show fresh, especially when new actors come into a cast as replacements. Others require exact replication of performances every night. It's important to know which kind of director you are serving and to give notes accordingly. Quoting notes from the director is a great way for the stage manager to channel the director.

NOTES BEGIN AFTER OPENING

Many directors will tell the cast that the production stage manager will be giving notes, especially if you encourage them to do so. As soon as the show opens, begin giving small notes to individual cast members—this will establish the principle that notes will be coming from you. It's a good idea to have a full company note session within a month of opening night, whether it is conducted by the production stage manager or by the director. This lets the company know they are being regularly observed.

NOTES ON STAGING

If the show is a musical, work with the dance captain to keep the staging and choreography as clean and accurate as it was when the director and choreographer left the show. Staging tends to drift as a result of laziness or spontaneous "improvements." This makes it especially hard for swings and understudies, who learned the staging during rehearsal.

Once again, changes in staging can be dangerous. A piece of scenery will always go to the same place at the same speed—so must the actors. And since lighting is so specific, any drift in staging will often take an actor or dancer out of their intended light. This is always a good note to give an actor: You are no longer in your light.

PRANKS AND JOKES

Just don't allow them. Shows can fall apart quickly if the audience believes that the actors are sharing in private jokes to which they aren't privileged. British actors, especially, are given to elaborate stage pranks. They often feel it is their right.

Actors or crew sometimes like to comment on holidays by adding decorations to the set or costumes, or adding a line to the show. Remember that some theatre patrons go to the theatre on holidays to get away from the loneliness or religiosity of a particular holiday. Just because the cast or crew wants to celebrate a holiday does not mean that the audience wants to.

Final performances seem to bring out the prankishness in everyone. Having a ritual for a departing cast or crew member usually is a good replacement for onstage fooling around. A goodbye cake, the signing of the back of a piece of scenery, or a party are much better than an onstage joke, which can ruin an audience's enjoyment of the play.

Cutting up in the wings is meant to distract the actors onstage and so is just as bad an idea as onstage pranks.

All rules have exceptions, and I do believe that sometimes a cast needs a boost, something to wake them up. So I have sometimes allowed small pranks—of which the audience is unaware—just to delight a company.

Vacations, Personal Days, and Leaves of Absence

The Idea

Vacations and personal days are to refresh actors and crew. They take time to relax, to change their routine, or to attend to personal matters—weddings, funerals, or graduations.

AEA has strict rules with minimum standards for time off. But more personal days and longer vacations are also possible and sometimes desirable. If the goal on a long-running show is to keep good cast members and crew with the show as long as possible, then don't make them feel like they are in jail. Management and stage management need to be flexible and grant additional personal days or even vacations, as long as it does not adversely affect the production. The principles for granting vacation and personal days must be worked out with the management before the first request is granted. Consistency is the key.

This loose principal about vacations and personal days is often a hard one for management and creative teams. But for a stage manager, predictability is the key to running a show—you must know what to expect from the actors and to make the actors responsible for their own behavior. If an actor knows that they are likely to be granted a personal day—whether or not it conforms to AEA rules—the actor will apply for it. Then the stage manager knows the actor will be out and knows how to cover that role. But if the actor feels that stage management is not sympathetic to extra personal days, even if the show is not harmed, then they will often call in sick on short notice. The idea is to control the absences—not to pretend they won't happen.

AEA RULES

Since the rules for vacations and personal days change with each new AEA contract, consult the appropriate up-to-date contract before working out your policy.

Vacations

Each actor is allowed one week of vacation for each six months of employment. All actors accumulate 4% of their salary each week in a vacation fund, which is held by management. When an actor goes on vacation, they receive no weekly salary for that week, but instead collect their accumulated vacation pay. An actor may also choose to take the accumulated vacation pay and not take a vacation.

Personal Days

Under current AEA rules, each actor is permitted to take two personal days for any reason and two additional personal days for "compelling circumstances"— family emergencies, weddings, etc. These are unpaid personal days; in other words, the actor is docked for these missed performances. Personal days may not be used to extend a vacation.

APPROVAL OF ABSENCES

Management must approve any absences by principal actors. This is especially important for stars, since advertising changes during a star's absence. It's possible another star will be brought in to cover the original's vacation. The stage manager usually approves ensemble or minor principal absences, and management is merely informed of the approved absence. Stagehands may take vacations with the approval of the technical director or house crew head, depending on what type of contract they are on.

Both application by the actor and approval by management or stage management must be in writing. Application and approval should be dated, since there are often multiple requests for time off. A copy of the approval should go to the actor and another copy put into a file for reference if needed.

Vacations and personal days are on a first-come-first-served basis. If there are multiple understudies for a role, the understudy must be informed of who is performing which performances at least two weeks prior to the vacation or personal day.

VACATION AND PERSONAL DAY CALENDAR

One of the most popular and often-viewed documents a stage manager posts is the vacation and personal day calendar. In the case of an open-ended production, this calendar should be for a full year. Once an actor or stage manager has applied for time off, the request should be included on the calendar, but marked "pending." This will hold the date so others will know it's not available. Once approved, you can remove the "pending."

This calendar should be updated each week and emailed to management, producers, and creative team so everyone will know the makeup of the cast for the foreseeable future.

SOME SUGGESTIONS REGARDING TIME OFF

Let the company know the policy regarding vacations and personal days as soon as you've worked it out with management. Is it strictly by the AEA rules or more relaxed?

Encourage actors to take their vacations rather than take the money. This keeps the show fresh, and actors are rested and relaxed. It also keeps the understudies better prepared and happier, since they make extra money when they are covering.

If an actor or stage manager calls in sick either the day before or the day after a vacation, ask them to call you back from a local landline phone number. This will let you know whether the actor has indeed returned to New York City, or wherever your show is playing.

LEAVES OF ABSENCE

This is a tricky area and requires a genuine policy decision with producers, general managers, creative team, and stage management. A leave of absence is a request to take more time off from a production than can be accommodated by a vacation. It is usually to take another short-term job or to deal with a family problem. It can be as short as three weeks or as long as a year. There is no AEA requirement or guideline for leaves of absence unless for medical reasons.

Considerations
If the person requesting the leave of absence is also an understudy, remember that you are not only replacing this one actor's track, but also their understudy track. Consider the following:

- How badly do you want to keep the actor requesting the leave?
- Can you find a replacement who fits the costumes?
- Is the potential replacement for the leave of absence a possible permanent replacement?
- If the show is a long run, the replacement actor can be added to your "bank" of available actors for the future casting.

Here is the leave of absence (LOA) policy that has worked well for me and the shows I've managed:

- Unless there is a compelling reason not to do so, I'll grant an LOA after the actor has been with the show for at least one year.
- No more than one LOA per actor per year.
- If you don't want the actor to continue in the show, turn down the LOA, even if it seems arbitrary.
- Convince management that granting LOAs keeps the show fresh.

Physical Therapy

The Idea

Everyone has their own doctor, and most actors and dancers have their own physical therapist or chiropractor. However, it is in the interests of the show for the production to provide regular, easily available physical therapy for the cast, crew, musicians, and management to address show-specific physical problems. Physical therapy is almost always needed on a musical and often on plays with multiple scenic levels.

Regular physical therapy normally is scheduled in 15-to-20-minute slots for two-hour segments twice a week. Ideally, regular physical therapy happens in the theatre—usually in a dedicated dressing room—and is paid for by the show. Any more serious physical therapy is handled in the offices of the therapist and paid for by the actor's insurance.

A Story

There is a long-running Broadway show with an excellent physical therapist who was hired even before the production went into rehearsal. The therapist asked to see the costume sketches and set design and made recommendations for modifications to both that would help to prevent injuries. The creative team felt that the physical therapist was being overly intrusive and ignored the recommendations. Soon after the opening, this production was overwhelmed by injuries, mostly sustained from the elaborate, heavy costumes. The costumes were then redesigned at great expense according to the physical therapist's recommendations. The injuries stopped.

CONSIDERATIONS IN REHEARSAL

The goal here is to prevent injuries, for the well being of the actors as well as the show.

Raked Stage
If the production has a raked stage, everyone in the company must have lessons on how to stand and walk on this incline. Pulled muscles are common on raked stages, as are back injuries.

Flying Harnesses
The design of a flying harness is often left to technicians who are properly concerned with safety and appearance. However, they give little thought to long-term bodily stress on the actor. Since each actor's body has different strengths and weaknesses, consultation with the physical therapist by both harness designer and actor is essential.

Specialty Costumes

There are a number of shows—*The Lion King, Shrek The Musical*, and *Wicked* for example—that use non-human costumes. The actors are often put into bent-over, hobbled, hot, or heavy costumes and must wear them for long periods of time. If the physical therapist is involved in the early design of these costumes, the creative team can still get the look they require without making the actor miserable.

Strenuous Choreography

Choreographers have a perfect right to create the dances they want for a production. They will have determined in auditions if the dancers are capable of executing this choreography. However, acrobatics, tumbling, and long strenuous dance numbers will tax even the youngest dancers. Having physical therapy available during rehearsal will teach the dancers how to deal with the dance requirements and keep them physically healthy during rehearsals.

DEALING WITH MANAGEMENT

Physical therapy can often seem like a frivolous, coddling expense to management, especially since this is not a one-time expense but a weekly one. You may need to lobby for the expense. Then you need to get the best therapist you can for the job.

Discuss the Need for PT Early

General managers try to stick as closely as possible to the budget they've approved with the producers. A new line item can make them very unhappy. Early discussions about the need for physical therapy and the frequency of the sessions will save later arguments.

Choosing the Physical Therapist

Management's job is to keep costs down and some PTs are more expensive than others. Here are other considerations:
- Will the regular PT sessions be at the theatre or must the actors go to a studio?
- Is the PT studio within easy reach of the theatre for any emergencies?
- Is the PT studio open on Saturdays and Sundays?
- Are both male and female PTs available to the company?
- Does the PT company deal with other Broadway shows? Do they have the time and manpower to deal with yours?
- Do the dancers trust this PT?

PT AT THE THEATRE

Dedicate a room to physical therapy so that the therapist may leave their table and other necessary equipment at the theatre set up and ready to go. Be sure the PT room is quiet and free from interruptions during sessions.

PT SCHEDULING

Physical therapy must be available to anyone working on the show—actors, dancers, singers, crew, musicians, and stage management. All these groups will need physical help at some point during a long run. The stage manager should schedule and track PT usage.

Sign-up Sheets
Post a sign-up sheet with time slots in the same place and at the same time each week. These PT slots often fill up quickly.

Injuries
Injuries must always get first priority, even if this means cancelling someone else's scheduled appointment.

Over-Use
Company members might sign up for PT every week whether they need it or not. If you see someone over-using this privilege, tell them they must make room for others unless they have a show-threatening injury.

No-Shows
If someone fails to show up for a scheduled appointment, let them know that if they do it again, their PT privileges will be revoked. Have a consistent policy for dealing with no-shows.

Working with Unions and Deputies

The Idea

The Actors' Equity deputy system was set up so that AEA members don't have to complain directly to management about union issues, which might put them at risk of being seen by management as a bad employee. The deputies are neutral reporters of problems brought to them by actors or stage managers. The deputy may call AEA directly to report problems and may also attend regular union meetings to discuss show-related issues.

Deputies can neither make policy nor set rules—they provide a conduit from the cast and stage managers to AEA. Inexperienced deputies may feel they have power and are entitled to set backstage policy. They do not.

In practice, if the stage manager has a good relationship with the deputies, problems can be solved without having to involve either the union or the show's management.

WHO ARE THE DEPUTIES?

Deputies are the members of the cast, elected by the cast and stage managers. On a play there might be only one deputy. A musical requires at least two—one principal and one chorus deputy. In practice, I prefer to have one principal, one female chorus, and one male chorus deputy. This way, all constituencies are represented.

Deputy Elections

AEA requires that deputies be elected during the first week of rehearsal through open nomination and secret ballot. I'm partial to choosing experienced, reasonable actors from each of the contract groups and asking them if they'd be willing to be deputy. If so, they then volunteer at the deputy election. The cast is happy to have an easy election and you get deputies with whom you can work.

Deputy elections must be held every six months, or whenever a serving deputy leaves the production.

DEPUTIES AND PRODUCTION STAGE MANAGERS WORKING TOGETHER

As with every other aspect of running a show, it's important that the production stage manager forge good working relationships with deputies.

Make the Deputies your Friends

As production stage manager, you want the deputies to come to you first with any hint of a problem. You do not want them calling AEA to report an issue before you've had a chance to deal with it. Remind the deputies that you are also a member of AEA and subject to union rules. You want to abide by proper procedures as laid down by both AEA and show management.

Deputies in the Dressing Rooms

Deputies are always actors and are privy to conversations that no one else is. There's almost always a certain amount of backstage griping and gossip, but dressing room conversations can turn into groundswells of complaint or rumor. Encourage the deputies to come to you at the first hint of a problem. Then, with the deputies, you can decide how to deal with the issues.

Trial Balloons

If there is to be a change in management policy, or if there is a question about how to deal with an issue, ask the deputies to come to your stage manager's office and discuss the new information with them. You can avoid a disastrous or embarrassing mistake by trying things out on the deputies.

Get the Deputies Behind You

Every show will have contentious issues, issues that cause hardships or confusion for a company. If the issues have been explained carefully to the deputies and they know that there is no union violation, they can help to explain it to the company.

DEALING WITH ACTORS' EQUITY ASSOCIATION

AEA is the union for both actors and stage managers. This presents a disadvantage in that stage managers are often called upon to discipline their fellow union members. The advantage is that stage managers can always call on their own union for advice and for rulings.

A Story

When I first joined Actors' Equity, the counselors for each area of the contract had worked as professionals in that area—the stage management counselors had been stage managers, the chorus reps had been in the chorus of Broadway shows. Now, few of the counselors have worked onstage so problems must be framed for non-theatricals, and should not assume any intimate working knowledge of a production. The counselors are all smart and dedicated union people.

Establish a Relationship with AEA Counselors

Each contract has it's own outside representatives (who work outside the AEA offices) and inside representatives (who are part of the internal bureaucracy of the union). Generally, the inside reps interpret the rules and handle issues of policy, and outside reps make determinations on extraordinary risk, payments for step-out lines, and safety and sanitary problems within the theatre building.

As stage manager, you should establish a first-name working relationship with both the inside and outside reps for your show. You must be able to call the appropriate counselor, have them take your call, and be able to talk out any issue.

The Rulebook

The rulebook for any contract is almost always vague and out-of-date. When you get a job on a new show or take over an existing show, call AEA and ask for the most recent updates to the contract. Do not assume that the rulebook given to you at the office or downloaded from the Internet is the most recent or contains all updates.

Getting Clarification or Advice

Even the most experienced stage managers need to be able to tell the cast that they have spoken with AEA and present the union ruling. Published or implied rules are always open to interpretation by both actors and management. When in doubt, call for a ruling.

DEALING WITH IATSE

This could be a book on its own. Stagehands are the skilled workers of the theatre. Having their expertise, advice, and friendship make the difference between being a stage manager who can run a show and one who cannot.

The International Alliance of Theatrical Stage Employee's union rules are truly arcane, with different sets of rules for the IATSE international employees and for local employees. The rules even vary from theatre to theatre, with house heads making up their own rules.

I'm not even going to try to break down these rules here. Your technical supervisor will explain the international and local rules that apply to your show. Discussions with the house heads will let you know the idiosyncrasies of that particular theatre. Do not fight these rules!

Show Respect

Stagehands are the only people in the theatre who will willingly risk their lives for a show. They will deal with live electricity, climb impossible heights—often in the dark—and work themselves into exhaustion to make a show work. Since computer literacy and a thorough understanding of engineering and rigging is necessary, many have advanced academic degrees.

Modern stagehands are smart, trained, and dedicated. Actors and management must treat them with respect, just as you ask stagehands to treat actors and management with respect.

A Story

I was trying out a Broadway show in New York City. We were in previews and the choreographer was giving notes to the actors in the house. Several stagehands were still onstage cleaning up from the preview performance. In discussing an issue of backstage traffic, the choreographer referred to the stagehands in a derogatory manner. Although he meant this as a harmless joke, the onstage stagehands heard the remark and it quickly spread all over Broadway. At a work call the next day I told the stagehands that this remark did not reflect the feeling of the actors or stage managers toward stagehands in general or toward our stagehands in particular. Nonetheless, the stagehands were bitter toward the creative team for the entire run of the show.

Dealing with Grievances

A disagreement may exist between the stagehands and management that cannot be worked out amicably between the parties. A grievance may be filed by either party, which leads to a formal meeting between parties, adjudicated by an official of IATSE International. Both parties present their complaint and a written ruling is handed down by the IATSE International official. There is no appeal.

Stage Managers are often in the middle of grievances, since they are part of management and direct the stagehands. Even though it seems counterintuitive that the stagehands' international union should judge a grievance involving local stagehands, this is the arrangement worked out with The Broadway League and is standard operating procedure.

IATSE International is separate from IATSE Local 1 (or whichever local is involved in the grievance) and renders amazingly fair judgments. If you're involved in a grievance, be as fair to both management and stagehands as possible in your testimony, remembering that you must first serve the interests of the production. Treat all parties with respect and honor the judgment immediately.

Extra Perks During a Run

The Idea

Extra perks are those niceties that appear in no union rulebook or management policy, but which will make everyone's backstage life easier and more fun, and better serve the theatre community.

THROWING PARTIES

The producers and management of the show will throw many parties. Opening nights, Tony Awards, the arrival or departure of a leading actor, or a closing night are all cause for parties. Management organizes these parties, and it is they who create the invitation list.

Backstage parties are usually organized by the stage managers and are thrown for no particular reason other than to relieve tension and to bring the entire production together.

Find a Conducive Spot in the Theatre

Most theatres have a large bar area in the lobby or back of house. Many have a large lower lobby or mezzanine lobby. Some have a huge basement under the stage. Find a place where approximately 50 people can gather and make a lot of noise—a place that can be cleaned up easily. Good ventilation and electrical power is necessary, too.

Get the Approval of the House Manager

You can't have a party without the house manager saying it's okay. Once the audience has left the building and the front of house is shut down, actors and stagehands are meant to leave the backstage area as soon as their professional obligations are completed. Only the house manager can waive this requirement.

Tip the Doorman

Give the doorman a tip after each party—you are asking him to stay much later than the normal hours backstage. Tipping makes them happy to see another party being scheduled.

Invite Everyone

Since the idea of backstage parties is to unite the building, everyone associated with the show should be invited. Actors, stagehands, musicians, stage managers, management, producers, ushers, concession people, house managers, publicity and press people. Everyone.

CREW DINNERS

On any show, but especially on musicals or complicated plays, the crew works impossible hours, usually 8 a.m. to midnight for weeks on end. Management will often take the entire crew out for one dinner to show their appreciation. This may seem like a small gesture, but it goes a long way to ensuring that the stagehands see the respect the management and producers feel for them.

BACKSTAGE TOURS

Unless there are well-established policies about backstage tours, it will soon become chaos —backstage and onstage—following performances. Stage management, with the approval of general and house management, must set and post clear rules for actors, crew, musicians, and management for conducting backstage tours. Here are some good rules to follow:
- There must be no more than 10 people in any tour. Groups larger than this can't be managed.
- Anyone may request a tour—actors, stagehands, musicians, management.
- Whoever has requested the tour must lead it. Otherwise, the stage managers will be the default tour leaders.
- There can be no touching of props or climbing onto scenery.
- There will be areas of the stage and backstage that are off limits.
- Tours may be cancelled if bad weather (snow or rain) means that dirt or water may be tracked onto the stage.
- There must be a stage manager on the deck whenever a tour is in progress.

Other Show-Specific Events

There's a whole range of marketing, promotional, and industry support events that a show is involved with. They all have special considerations.

TONY AWARDS

If your show is asked to perform on the Tony Awards, encourage the management to do a scene or number that includes as many cast members as possible. This is not only so that Mom and Dad can see their kid on TV, but also because it is a Screen Actors' Guild-American Federation of Television and Radio Artists (SAG-AFTRA) contract, which pays good money. If some cast members are included and some aren't, there will be resentment.

Include the swings in any large musical number. It will make the cast seem bigger and more of a spectacle, and it will make your hard-working swings feel more a part of the company.

Be sure everyone on the show is invited to the Tony party, not just the actors.

TALKBACKS

After-show talkbacks are a useful tool for long-running shows. They are a terrific selling point for group sales and great for educational groups who want to ask questions of professionals about their craft. However, they can also be a real chore for a company if not handled properly.

Like backstage tours, talkbacks work best when clear parameters such as these are set out and agreed to before performances begin:

- Tell each group that the cast will be invited to the talkback but cannot be required to be there, especially the stars.
- Invite not only the actors, but stagehands, designers, musicians, and management to participate.
- Set a minimum amount for each group to donate to charity. On my shows, we always ask for at least $100 to be donated to Broadway Cares/Equity Fights Aids. But the charity must be one that everyone backstage can agree upon.
- Plan the talkbacks at least a week in advance.
- Clear all talkbacks with the house manager.
- Actors must be out of costume, makeup, and wigs before attending the talkback.
- Limit the time of the talkback and let the groups know what that amount of time is.
- Post the talkbacks on the weekly schedule.

ALBUM

Most new musicals and revivals will record an album. Like the Tony Awards, an album is confirmation to those folks back home that their son or daughter is really working. And it is lucrative.

Because of the costs of recording an album, each actor is usually employed for only one session, even though the entire recording period may extend to multiple sessions. Encourage management to include the swings in the album. You'll get a bigger sound, but even more importantly, the swings will be made to feel a part of the company.

COMMERCIALS

Commercials are very expensive to shoot and to air, but most Broadway and touring musicals use them, as do many plays. A commercial must be as carefully organized as a technical rehearsal. And there are many more opinions to satisfy.

Shot List

Since each shot usually requires a new onstage setup, the number of shots is quite limited. Both the producers of the production and the producers of the commercial will have definite ideas of what should be included in the commercial and how many people should be involved. Before anything else can be done, an agreed-upon storyboard for the commercial must be worked out among all the various creative and financial people on the production and a shot list compiled from the storyboard.

As production stage manager, your job at these storyboard meetings is to be realistic about the number of shots possible in a day. Consider the following:

- How much time will it take to set up the scenery and lighting for each shot?
- How much time does the commercial director want to rehearse and film each shot?

- How much time is needed for costume changes?
- How much time is needed for breaks and meals?

The Schedule

The exact, hour-by-hour schedule for the commercial shoot should be worked out by the production stage manager and then adjusted and approved by the commercial director and producer.

It's important to keep the flow of scenery, props, and costumes logical for the crew, and in show order if possible. Since not all actors will be used in all shots, protect your actors by allowing some rest time between shots. Figure 13.5 is a sample schedule for a commercial shoot.

Include Swings

As with other prestige events, inclusion of the swings in the commercials will pay huge dividends during the life of the production. It's also income for the swings.

Crew Size

Since time is truly money on a commercial, be sure you've called enough crew to move quickly between scenes throughout the day. As much as management may try to cut down crew size to save money, the worst outcome on a commercial is to not get all the needed shots because setup time was too long.

Catering

Thoughtful, well-prepared meals mean that cast, crew, and management will be in a good mood throughout the shoot. Find a place to set up tables so everyone can sit and have a restful meal. Stagger the meal breaks so everyone isn't standing in line at the same time. The difference in cost between cheap meals and tasty, plentiful ones is miniscule; the productivity rewards are huge.

Contract Explanation

Since the actors will be working on a SAG-AFTRA contract for the commercial shoot, their normal AEA rules do not apply. Having the company manager or SAG-AFTRA representative meet with the cast to explain to working rules and pay will remove anxiety from the cast. The stage manager should not explain the rules of the commercial shoot to the actors.

TELEVISION APPEARANCES

In New York City and on tour, actors in both plays and musicals are asked to appear on TV shows to present scenes or songs. Near the opening of a new show there may be many of these requests. This means there can be a short turnaround from the end of an evening performance to an early morning TV call, since the TV call is not part of the AEA turnaround. These appearances are governed by SAG-AFTRA rules and not AEA. SAG-AFTRA pay rates apply for both performers and stage managers.

Since most TV appearances are early in the morning, this can mean calling the actors and crew at 5 or 6 a.m. Exhaustion is a real worry here, and recommendations need to be made to management about the overuse of actors or crew. Rotating the stage manager in charge of TV appearances means fair distribution of SAG-AFTRA money for the SMs as well as keeping all members of the team fresh.

PROMOTIONAL TRIPS AND EVENTS

These are becoming more prevalent as advertising for commercial productions becomes more sophisticated.

On-Tour Appearances

Tours routinely do promotional events in advance of arriving in a city. Interviews with the stars are common, and so travel to and from the promotional city needs to be arranged while still allowing for the actors to be fresh for the onstage performance. If an entire musical number is to be performed, the travel arrangements multiply. Crew, costumes, and props, as well as cast, must be considered.

Conferences

Broadway shows and tours like to participate in conferences of professionals who book package tours or promote tourism. These performances are usually on small, under-equipped stages. As production stage manager, you should find out the exact playing conditions well in advance in order to decide the scale of the performance that best promotes the show. Don't go in ill prepared—you want to sell the show, not to make it look foolish.

Separate Performance Units

Some long-running shows have formed units of actors not currently performing the show to travel and promote the production. These units have their own costumes, props, crew, and stage manager. They are very useful since they don't have to work within the schedule of the performing production.

DOCUMENTARIES

This whole area of shooting documentary footage is confusing and constantly changing. Most of the documentaries I've been involved in are a "maybe" project—that is, footage is being shot that may or may not be used in a documentary that may or may not happen. The new AEA media package—which extends use of actor images for commercial or promotional radio, television, or the Internet—makes this process much easier and it continues to evolve. A careful reading of the AEA contract and an explanation by an AEA representative will be necessary to make sure everyone knows about the current AEA media rules.

FUNDRAISERS

On Broadway, the most common are the Easter Bonnet Competition, Gypsy of the Year, and Broadway Bares. All of these raise money for Broadway Cares/Equity Fights Aids and are generally supported by the entire theatre community.

Money is raised in different ways by various fundraisers, but it usually involves asking for donations—either at a performance or at an event—and selling memorabilia. As production stage manager, you'll be in charge of organizing the collection of the money, the counting of the money, and the safe storage of the money.

Keeping an atmosphere of fun around these events and spreading the work over as many of the willing cast and crew as possible will raise more money and keep the fundraising from becoming a burden.

Disasters

The Idea

Theatre is a live event, and things go wrong. No matter how careful you are or how well prepared your team may be, things will go wrong. The cast, crew, and audience are all in the same room together—when things go wrong, everyone must be informed.

The production stage manager is responsible for the decision: Stop the show or keep going. There is usually no time for consultation with management. Not only safety, but also the dignity of the actors onstage should be your guide. However, remember that the audience is there to be entertained. If a show can continue safely, no matter what the disaster, keep going so the audience's enjoyment is not interrupted.

STOPPING A SHOW

While stopping a show is far from an ideal circumstance, there are some situations that warrant this action:

- *Technical malfunction.* This is the most common reason to stop a show. The audience can usually see it happening. They probably will not be surprised.
- *Illness of an actor or crew member.* If an understudy or substitute crew member can seamlessly come into the show, then continue on and make any necessary announcements at intermission. If you must stop the show, make any necessary announcements at that time.
- *Onstage or backstage accident.* Again, if you can continue, do so unless the problem is apparent to the audience.
- *Medical emergency in the audience.* Sick audience members must be dealt with ASAP. This causes quite a disruption, especially if EMS must be called. Also, the house lights usually have to be brought up to allow medical people to do their work.
- *Fire or flood.* In the case of an onstage fire, you may have to bring in the asbestos fire curtain or use the water curtain to separate the stage from the house. Be sure you know the procedure for doing this.

If you must evacuate the house, it is the law in most cities that an evacuation procedure has already been worked out with the house manager. The house manager is in charge of any evacuation—follow the house manager's lead.

Many newer theatres have deluge water curtains instead of asbestos fire curtains. In the event of fire, these deluge curtains automatically douse the stage and pit with enormous amounts of water. The play cannot continue and the house must be evacuated.

- *Power Outage.* This happens more often in New York City than in most major cities. It may also not be a complete power outage, but a brown out or voltage drop, which prevents certain computers, winches, or power racks from working properly. All theatres have emergency lighting, which will come on in the event of power failure.

  Without power, you probably won't have microphones to announce anything to the house or headsets to speak to the crew, so you'll have to immediately come onstage to speak live to the audience. Ask the audience to remain in their seats until the situation is assessed. Power is usually restored rather quickly.

Have a Plan

The house manager is required to have an evacuation plan for both the audience and for backstage. During technical rehearsals, a meeting with cast, crew, stage managers and house manager is essential to discuss these procedures.

Decide in advance who will make the announcement to the audience and how. If the stoppage is to be more than momentary, you may need to ask one of your stars to come onstage to talk to the audience to keep them entertained. Let the audience know whether or not to stay in their seats.

Coping with a disaster backstage is trickier. Since you may have lost headset communication, be sure the cast knows what the procedure will be for stopping a show. This will probably be you coming onto the stage and verbally telling everyone that the show is stopping. Get the cast to safety—they will already know the predetermined evacuation route and meeting point outside the theatre.

If the stoppage is to be more than momentary, let the cast and crew know how long the show will be stopped and how and at what point the show will be restarted. Remember that actors are in a zone of onstage reality. Stopping a show breaks that reality and they may not respond as quickly as in normal life.

It can be dangerous to stop turntables, treadmills, or any pieces of moving scenery with actors in position. Be very careful and aware of your actors' locations when ordering sudden stops. Sometimes automation can be dialed down rather than stopped abruptly. Work this out with your automation department during tech.

Don't Hesitate to Stop a Show

Keeping a show going is in the DNA of a stage manager. But if there is a serious disruption in the house or a dangerous situation backstage, don't hesitate to stop a show. Foolishly keeping a show going can result in a lawsuit, if injury is the result. If you're in doubt about whether to stop or not, stop.

Entertaining the Audience
Sometimes you gotta have a gimmick.

A Story

I staged the National Tour of *Sunset Boulevard*, which opened in Denver. At the very first preview, the sound system shut down. I jumped up onto the stage, told the audience what had happened, made a joke, and then got a signal from the soundman that all was well. We started the show again. About five minutes later, the same exact thing happened again. The sound system went down, I got up onstage and talked to the audience, got a signal from the sound department and we began again. And then it happened a third time. I thought, "I can't get up onstage again and say the same thing again. They'll kill me." The associate conductor's 11-year-old daughter was watching the show from an aisle seat. I grabbed her hand and she came up onstage with me. I said to the audience, "Hey, you can't hate someone who's holding hands with an adorable child, can you?" I got a nice laugh, the system was repaired, and the show went on without further incident.

CANCELLING A SHOW

Cancelling a performance is a big deal. Even if you know that for whatever reason the show cannot happen that night, it is management who must make this decision.

A Story

I once had to cancel a performance of *Sunset Boulevard* in New York. I came onstage to explain to the audience what had happened and to apologize. I told them returns would be available at the box office, and then went to the front of house to see if I could help. Because the audience knew what I looked like, various audience members attacked me, as if this were my fault. My advice—if you must cancel a show, do it over the god mic and not in person.

Inform Management Immediately
Be sure that the company manager, general manager, house manager, lead producer, and director know of any show-endangering problem as soon as possible. They will all need time to assess the situation and consult with each other as to action.

Box Office Returns
If a show is cancelled, the audience will want their money back. The box office needs to be prepared for this and must have cash on hand. There will also need to be crowd control at the box office. However, if a show is is cancelled during a performance, the box office may be closed. The house manager and company manager will need to be

in the lobby advising customers how to exchange tickets or get a refund.

Warn the Ushers and House Manager
They are your crowd control and will receive a lot of the wrath of the patrons. Be sure they know what's going on.

ACTOR OR CREW INCAPACITY

Of course there are a whole host of other things you might have to deal with.

Alcohol and Drug Abuse
Drinking and drug problems happen a lot less frequently these days than they used to. Neither are cool, and those who may drink or take drugs during performance time may suffer the approbation of their peers as well as the consequences of management. This is often cause for termination. Here are some helpful alcohol/drug policies:
- *Never permit it.* If you smell alcohol on a person's breath or suspect a person is using a drug, deal with it right away. A show can get away from you quickly if people suspect you are lenient on drugs and alcohol.
- *Never confront a user alone.* If you must confront an actor, be sure you have a deputy, ASM, or company manager with you. If you must confront a crew member, have a crew head with you. Witnesses will protect you from "he said/she said."

Personal Issues
These can be as devastating to performance and backstage demeanor as drugs or alcohol. Divorces, deaths, money issues, or anger management issues are very real and must be dealt with compassionately and privately. But any issue that affects performance cannot be ignored—it must be dealt with and fixed. Sometimes, just the suggestion of a few personal days or a vacation will solve the problem.

The PSM Makes the Decisions
Any backstage disciplinary action must be under the control and guidance of the production stage manager. Never ask your assistants to deal with issues of incapacity or discipline.

Sending a Person Home
If an actor or crew member is incapacitated, they must be sent home. If they cannot perform, they have no place in the building. You may have to send an ASM or company manager home with them if the incapacity is serious.

Provide Help
The best managements and producers are always willing to provide help to employees with drug, alcohol, or personal problems. As production stage manager, you should make the case to the employer for such help. If the person was valuable enough to be hired in the first place, they're valuable enough to deserve help.

TERMINATION PROCEDURE

The production stage manager does not have the right to fire anyone. You can strongly recommend that someone be removed from their job, but the actual firing must come from management.

Firing should be done quickly, privately, and with good, stated reasons. It should always be done in person—not over the phone or by email. The fewest number of people possible should know in advance about the firing. The worst situation is when the person to be fired hears about it, in advance, as gossip.

As production stage manager, be sure there is a paper trail of disciplinary events and warnings.

IF *YOU* GET FIRED

Almost everyone with a long career in show business will be fired. Most often, it's because of a personality conflict. You may also be fired because someone in power wants a favored person to have your job. Or you may inadvertently make mistakes that make it impossible for you to continue in your job. Here are some guidelines:

- Don't quit. For economic reasons, it's better for management to fire you than for you to quit. If you want to quit for personal reasons, just remember it will cost you money.
- Always tell the truth about being fired. Everyone in show business understands that unfair firings happen. The worst thing is to tell people that you quit and then for it to come out that you were fired.
- Call AEA immediately. They will advise you of your rights and will deal with management for you.
- Work out a severance. How long you will continue in your job after firing, how much severance pay is due you, and how the firing will be announced to the company are all negotiable items.
- Don't act out. Be as professional, thorough, and friendly after a firing as you were before. Your last weeks on the job are how people will remember you.

14

Production Stage Management Tips

Here, in no particular order, are some tips I've formulated over the years—use them or not—your choice:

WATCH YOUR WEEKLY GROSSES

Weekly grosses for both Broadway and touring shows are published weekly in a variety of sources. These grosses used to be published as "net"—that is, the gross take after certain expenses like credit card charges and group discounts were deducted. Grosses are now published as "gross"— the total amount taken in each week at the box office.

You can ask (or guess) what the weekly operating expenses for your show are. If you see that the weekly grosses are not as much as your weekly operating expenses, you should start looking for another job.

MEET OFTEN WITH GENERAL MANAGERS AND COMPANY MANAGERS

It's easy, and common for stage managers, to begin to see management as remote, out-of-touch business people who work in offices. Conversely, management can see stage managers as profligate spenders and complainers. A weekly face-to-face meeting between stage managers and general and company managers will go a long way toward preventing these perceptions. Email cannot convey tone. And since most communication seems to be by email, groups that don't meet regularly can misunderstand the needs of others.

Management and stage managers want the same thing—for the show to run as long, as smoothly, and as profitably as possible. Talk about it. Let them know the dangers of a show with too few swings. Let them know you appreciate the difficulty of running a show with marginal profitability. And remember—it is ultimately management's decision about how money is spent and where it is allocated.

LET THE SWINGS, UNDERSTUDIES, DEPUTIES, AND DANCE CAPTAINS KNOW YOU'RE GOING TO BAT FOR THEM

As production stage manager, you are asking these folks with offstage duties to cover you, to let you know of problems in advance, to rehearse extra hours, to perform when ill, to watch your back. Let them know you're watching their back, too. Respect them and honor their contribution to the show and they will do the same for you.

TREAT THE WHOLE CREW WITH RESPECT

If the crew does not perform with discipline and coordination, your show will look terrible. Your crew are handpicked professionals without whom you cannot do your job. Some rules to follow:
- Learn everyone's name and what job they do.
- Meet with the crew heads to ask advice on how to handle situations both onstage and offstage.
- If a technical mistake happens, never blame the crew member. If you reprimand a crew member in public, they will never trust you again. Tell whomever needs to know that you are dealing with the problem and then speak to the crew member in private to find out what went wrong.
- Remember that every theatre is different and operates under slightly different rules. Consult with your contract crew and with the house heads to get the rules straight.

DEAL WITH RUMORS

Hey, it's show business. Rumors will always fly around backstage, and some of them may actually be true. I believe in addressing rumors before they become viral. Here's some advice:
- The hair and wardrobe rooms are good places to find out what the cast is talking about.
- Posting information immediately is a great way to quell rumors. As soon as you know of a cast replacement, an award, a firing, a tour, or the closing of a show, post it on the callboard. The cast will come to trust that you will inform them of anything that concerns them as soon as you know it.
- Addressing rumors head-on by calling a company meeting or by posting the correct information on the callboard prevents rumors from spreading.
- Never spread a rumor yourself. As stage manager, you're privy to information long before the cast or crew. Don't be Rumor Central. When something can be announced, announce it. Hinting at information is nothing but gossip.

WEEKLY COMPANY MEETINGS

It is very civilizing to have a regular, once-a-week meeting to talk about the upcoming week—the cast can announce personal events, management can discuss policy issues, the creative team can stop by with general notes—and the whole cast, crew, musicians, and management personnel get together to have a relaxed talk.

DON'T MICROMANAGE YOUR TEAM

If you're the PSM, you can't do everything. And you want your first and second ASMs to be capable of taking charge. I believe in assigning each member of the stage management team individual areas of responsibility and then letting them handle those areas without interference.

PSM handles set, electrics, sound, teching, and personnel issues. First ASM handles deck and props. Second ASM handles wardrobe, hair, and opposite side props.

As PSM, you've chosen your team according to their particular skills in production—props, wardrobe, computer skills, etc. Be sure they get to use their particular skills, both in production and in running the show. Pride and uniqueness in everyone's work makes for a willing team.

A Story

I'm a believer in decorating backstage for holidays and parties. And I ask the management to help pay for the supplies. Once a general manager complained about this unnecessary expense. I explained that it costs about $5,000 or $6,000 to replace an ensemble member in a show, more for a principal. If we could keep one cast member from leaving the show because they were happy to be at the theatre, it would pay for decorations, parties, and painting for years. The GM immediately signed on to this concept and willingly contributed the money.

Another Story

As I said earlier, I often work with an ASM named Jim Woolley. Among his many talents is one for holiday decorations and cleanliness backstage. We once worked with a star whose dressing room was on the second floor backstage. The stairwell leading to this dressing room had dirty walls with peeling paint, which the theatre never got around to painting. Jim painted the stairway walls and decorated the star's door. The actor, who was notoriously difficult, was so pleased with this caring gesture that there was never a backstage problem with this actor for the entire long run of the production.

OTHER ASSORTED TASKS

In addition to running the show, the stage management team is responsible for other non-production tasks. Assign these tasks diplomatically:

- In/Out stuffers. These announcements of cast replacements require a lot of attention. They must be approved, printed, stored, and distributed to the ushers for the appropriate performances. Only one person should be responsible.
- Front of House Board. Not only the maintenance of the "ABC Board," listing the cast alphabetically but also the In/Out board of replacements should go to the same ASM responsible for the stuffers.

  Happily, this is becoming an electronic function. Rather than putting card board sliders into house board, many shows now have a lobby screen to announce Ins and Outs for a specific show. This screen can be controlled and programmed from the stage manager's office.
- Valuables. The nightly collection of valuables is a pain in the neck and should be assigned to the same ASM each night. They are also responsible for locking up and returning the valuables.
- Fundraising. Assign a willing ASM to organize any fundraising. Collecting the money, giving the nightly speech, deciding what items are to be sold, counting the money, and safely storing the money are all time-consuming items that should be organized by only one person.
- Physical Therapy. Only one ASM should be responsible for the organization and policing of physical therapy.
- Calling the Show. All Stage Managers (except subs) should be capable of calling the show. The PSM should establish a regular routine for calling the show and for running the deck. Rotating the calling and deck responsibilities keeps your team from getting bored.

ENCOURAGE VACATIONS AND PERSONAL DAYS

It's reasonable to want to save money on a show—you never know how long a show will run or when your next job will turn up. But it's a mistake to bank your vacation money rather than get away from the show on a real holiday. You want your whole team to be mentally fresh.

BACKSTAGE COMFORT

A cast will spend three to eight hours a day backstage at a theatre. The crew and SMs will spend even more time. Even when the front of house of a theatre has been renovated, the backstage often has not. Everyone wants the backstage to be as clean, comfortable and interesting as possible—just as you would your own home.

HEATING AND COOLING

Broadway and touring houses are mostly very old, with very old heating and cooling systems. And it is expensive to revamp these systems. But dancers cannot be expected to come offstage sweating after a strenuous dance number or scene and change clothes in freezing wings. And actors in *Fiddler On The Roof* cannot be expected to wear layers of wool clothing if it's 90 degrees onstage.

If the temperatures backstage are not suitable, put the complaints from actors, musicians, stagehands and stage managers in your daily and weekly reports. Create a paper trail that AEA and the theatre owners must deal with. Especially if the show is a hit, you'll be surprised how creative theatre owners can be in solving these problems.

A Story

I was doing a play in which the actors had to wear multiple layers of heavy clothing and another older actor had to wear a fat suit. We opened the show in warm weather, and the temperature onstage was often close to 90 degrees. After many complaints, the theatre owners told us that in order to replace the air conditioning units, the old units would have to be removed before the new ones could be installed—we would be without air conditioning for a long period of time. Also, we were told that the units needed required six months to order. This show won many awards and turned into a huge hit. The producer and actors threatened to move to another theatre if the AC problem were not solved. A week later, new AC was installed in one day—the day off.

GUESTS

Backstage guests are a privilege for cast and crew. I've already written about how to handle onstage guests. Ask the cast, crew, and musicians to sign a pre-printed guest list each night with the name and number of guests and the name of the company member. Then give the list to the doorman—he will let in only those on the list.

For principals, have the doorman announce the guest over the backstage PA system. The dressers will then bring the guest to the principal dressing room. For the ensemble, have the doorman announce the guest over the backstage PA, and then have the guest wait in a specific area backstage until the ensemble member is available to meet them. For stars, you may need security personnel and crowd control barriers outside the stage door.

15
My Curtain Speech

Production stage management is really a design function. In addition to all the duties and functions of stage management for a commercial production I've talked about throughout the book, you are responsible for setting the style and tone for running the show.

You will determine whether a show is to be loosely or strictly run, how information is to be distributed, what sorts of people will run the show, and how to deal with crew and management. You will set how the cues are to be called. You will determine the communication language with the crew, the organization of the cues, and how to get out of inevitable problems. You will set the rehearsal schedule, the tech schedule, the calling rotation schedule, and the vacation/personal day schedule. You will run the show. And your personality and training set the tone.

I believe that American-style stage management is the best in the world. Having one person responsible for all events onstage and backstage means that all artistic, technical, and personal issues come through one channel. The production stage manager is the only person on a production who understands everything—technical, artistic, personal, and often financial. You are the only person with the vision of the totality of a production.

My research into shows that I was about to stage manage has made me a baseball fan and reintroduced me to Charles Dickens, John Steinbeck, William Shakespeare, Anton Chekov, and Sylvester Stallone. It has made me understand the war in Vietnam, the destruction of the Warsaw Ghetto, and the effects of racism in this country. The theatre has allowed me to work with living geniuses—Mike Nichols, Tom Stoppard, Bob Crowley, Cameron Mackintosh. It has allowed me to travel the United States and the rest of the world and to understand cultural differences. The theatre is an unparalleled learning opportunity—it puts you in touch with more talented, interesting, and world-changing people, living or dead, than any other profession. And it has allowed me to raise and educate four children.

Because of the physical demands of the theatre, you must be more disciplined than in most professions. What other job asks you to work six days a week, often 16 hours a day during production? What other profession demands that your peak mental acuity is at night? And what other profession insists that if you want to keep working into middle age, you must have the stamina of a 20-year-old? Many of my friends who work in film, TV, or business make more money than I do and work fewer hours. But none of them are as interested in their work or have the stamina and discipline that I do—the theatre keeps you vital. It forces you to stay physically and mentally fit; otherwise, you simply cannot do your job.

And finally—lucky you to be a stage manager. I've been a professional stage manager for over 40 years and I'm happy to say that I'm interested in my job every day. No two days are ever alike—there are always new people, new technology, new travel, new energies to renew me. And always new stage managers questioning why I do things the way I do, and forcing me to reinvent myself every day.

Production Calendar

May

MONDAY	TUESDAY	WEDNESDAY	THURSDAY	FRIDAY	SATURDAY	SUNDAY
	1	2	3	4	5	6
7	8	9	10	11	12	13
14	25	16	17	18 Award Scenic Bids	19	20
21	22	23	24	25	26	27
28	29 Begin Scenic Build in Shop (12 Weeks)	30	31			

Scenic Build Week 1 of 12

Figure 4.1: Production Calendar/example

Production Calendar

June

MONDAY	TUESDAY	WEDNESDAY	THURSDAY	FRIDAY	SATURDAY	SUNDAY
				1	2	3
				Scenic Build Week 1		
4	5	6	7	8	9	10
		Scenic Build Week 2 of 12				
11	12	13	14	15	16	17
		Scenic Build Week 3 of 12			XXXXXXX NA	
18	19	20	21	22	23	24 XXXXX closes @ XXXXXX
				Creative Member XXXXX NA		
		Scenic Build Week 4 of 12		XXXXXXX NA		
25	26	27	28	29	30	1 **July**
		Scenic Build Week 5 of 12				
		Creative Member XXXXX NA				
		XXXXXXX NA				

Figure 4.1: Production Calendar/example-continued

Production Calendar

July

MONDAY	TUESDAY	WEDNESDAY	THURSDAY	FRIDAY	SATURDAY	SUNDAY
2	3	4	5	6	7	8
9	10	11	12	13	14	15
16	17	18	19	20	21	22
23	24	25	26	27	28	29
30	31					

Week of 2–8:
- Scenic Build Week 6 of 12
- XXXXXXX NA
- Creative Member XXXXX NA

Week of 9–15:
- Scenic Build Week 7 of 12
- PSM NA (Sunday 15)
- XXXXXXX NA
- Creative Member XXXXX NA

Week of 16–22:
- Scenic Build Week 8 of 12
- Electric Shop Work Week 1 of 5
- PSM NA
- XXXXXXX NA
- Creative Member XXXXX NA

Week of 23–29:
- Sound Shop Work Week 1 of 4
- Scenic Build Week 9 of 12
- Electric Shop Work Week 1 of 5
- PSM NA
- XXXXXXX NA

Week of 30–31:
- Sound Shop Work Week 2 of 4
- Scenic Build Week 10 of 12
- Electric Shop Work Week 3 of 5
- XXXXXXX NA

Figure 4.1: Production Calendar/example-continued

Production Calendar

August

MONDAY	TUESDAY	WEDNESDAY	THURSDAY	FRIDAY	SATURDAY	SUNDAY
		1	2	3	4	5
				XXXXXXX NA		
		Sound Shop Work Week 2 of 4				
		Scenic Build Week 10 of 12				
		Elecs Shop Work Week 3 of 5				
6	7	8	9	10	11	12
		Sound Shop Work Week 3 of 4				
		Scenic Build Week 11 of 12				
		Rehearsal Studio: #3A Available + Office #5-3				
		Elecs Shop Work Week 4 of 5				
XXXXXXX NA						
13	14	15	16	17	18	19
1st Day of Studio Rehearsal		9:30–11 NBC in 9A w/Actor & Trainer	Meet & Greet			Day Off
			Rehearsal Hall: Full Company Rehearsal Week 1 of 5			
		Sound Shop Work Week 4 of 4				
		Scenic Build Week 12 of 12				
	Rehearsal Studio: Principals Only					
		Elecs Shop Work Week 5 of 5				
20	21	22	23	24	25	26
Drummer on Contract						Actor@ Bwy Co-op in Nashville
						Day Off
		Theatre: Load-In Week 1 of 3				
		Rehearsal Hall: Full Company Rehearsal Week 2 of 5				
27	28	29	30	31		
Actor @ Bay Co-op in Nashville				9:30-11 NBC in 9A w/ Actor & Trainer		
		Theatre: Load-In Week 2 of 3				
		Rehearsal Hall: Full Company Rehearsal Week 3 of 5				

Figure 4.1: Production Calendar/example-continued

Production Calendar
September

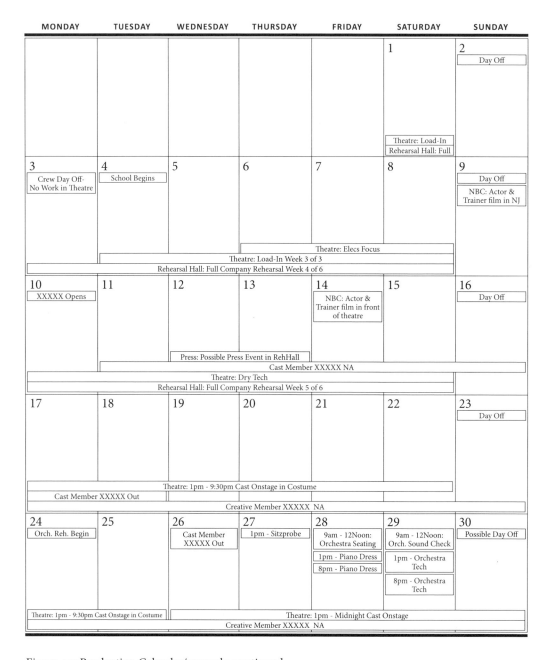

MONDAY	TUESDAY	WEDNESDAY	THURSDAY	FRIDAY	SATURDAY	SUNDAY
					1	**2** Day Off
					Theatre: Load-In / Rehearsal Hall: Full	
3 Crew Day Off- No Work in Theatre	**4** School Begins	**5**	**6**	**7**	**8**	**9** Day Off / NBC: Actor & Trainer film in NJ
				Theatre: Elecs Focus		
		Theatre: Load-In Week 3 of 3				
	Rehearsal Hall: Full Company Rehearsal Week 4 of 6					
10 XXXXX Opens	**11**	**12**	**13**	**14** NBC: Actor & Trainer film in front of theatre	**15**	**16** Day Off
		Press: Possible Press Event in RehHall				
			Cast Member XXXXX NA			
	Theatre: Dry Tech					
	Rehearsal Hall: Full Company Rehearsal Week 5 of 6					
17	**18**	**19**	**20**	**21**	**22**	**23** Day Off
		Theatre: 1pm - 9:30pm Cast Onstage in Costume				
	Cast Member XXXXX Out					
	Creative Member XXXXX NA					
24 Orch. Reh. Begin	**25**	**26** Cast Member XXXXX Out	**27** 1pm - Sitzprobe	**28** 9am - 12Noon: Orchestra Seating / 1pm - Piano Dress / 8pm - Piano Dress	**29** 9am - 12Noon: Orch. Sound Check / 1pm - Orchestra Tech / 8pm - Orchestra Tech	**30** Possible Day Off
Theatre: 1pm - 9:30pm Cast Onstage in Costume		Theatre: 1pm - Midnight Cast Onstage				
		Creative Member XXXXX NA				

Figure 4.1: Production Calendar/example-continued

Production Calendar
October

MONDAY	TUESDAY	WEDNESDAY	THURSDAY	FRIDAY	SATURDAY	SUNDAY
1 1pm - Rehearse As Needed / 8pm - Orchestra Dress	**2** 1pm - Orchestra Dress w/Photos / 8pm - Orchestra Dress w/Photos	**3** 1pm - Rehearse As Needed / 8pm - Preview #1	**4** 8pm - Preview #2	**5** 8pm - Preview #3	**6** 2pm - Preview #4 / 8pm - Preview #5	**7** Day Off

Theatre: 1pm - Midnight Cast Onstage   Theatre: 1pm - Midnight Cast Onstage
Preview Week #1
Creative Member XXXXX NA

MONDAY	TUESDAY	WEDNESDAY	THURSDAY	FRIDAY	SATURDAY	SUNDAY
8 8pm - Preview #6	**9** 8pm - Preview #7	**10** 8pm - Preview #8	**11** 8pm - Preview #9	**12** 8pm - Preview #10	**13** 2pm - Preview #11 / 8pm - Preview #12	**14** Day Off

Preview Week #2
1pm - 5pm: Onstage Rehearsal

MONDAY	TUESDAY	WEDNESDAY	THURSDAY	FRIDAY	SATURDAY	SUNDAY
15 8pm - Preview #13	**16** 8pm - Preview #14	**17** 2pm - Preview #15 / 8pm - Preview #16	**18** 8pm - Preview #17	**19** 8pm - Preview #18	**20** 2pm - Preview #19 / 8pm - Preview #20	**21** Day Off

Preview Week #3
1pm - 5pm: Onstage Rehearsal   1pm - 5pm: Onstage Rehearsal

MONDAY	TUESDAY	WEDNESDAY	THURSDAY	FRIDAY	SATURDAY	SUNDAY
22 8pm - Preview #21	**23** 8pm - Preview #22	**24** 2pm - Preview #23 / B-Roll Shoot Both Shows / 8pm - Preview #24	**25** 8pm - Preview #25	**26** 8pm - Preview #26 / Hold 2–3 Reh.Hrs. for B-Roll SetUps	**27** 2pm - Preview #27 / 8pm - Preview #28 / XXXXX TV Special Airs	**28** Day Off

Preview Week #4
1pm - 5pm: Onstage Rehearsal   1pm - 5pm: Onstage Rehearsal

MONDAY	TUESDAY	WEDNESDAY	THURSDAY	FRIDAY	SATURDAY	SUNDAY
29 Day Off	**30** 8pm - Preview #29	**31** 2pm - Preview #30 / 8pm - Preview #31				

Preview Week #5
1pm - 5pm: Onstage

Figure 4.1: Production Calendar/example-continued

Production Calendar
November

MONDAY	TUESDAY	WEDNESDAY	THURSDAY	FRIDAY	SATURDAY	SUNDAY
			1 8pm - Preview #32 / Begin Critics' Performances	**2** 8pm - Preview #33	**3** 2pm - Preview #34 / 8pm - Preview #35	**4** 3pm - Preview #36
			Preview Week #5 / 1pm - 5pm: Onstage Rehearsal			
5 8pm - Preview #37	**6** Day Off	**7** 2pm - Preview #38 / 8pm - Preview #39	**8** 6:30pm - Opening Night	**9** 8pm - Performance #2	**10** 2pm - Performance #3 / 8pm - Performance #4	**11** 11am - Record "New Deal" for Macy's / 3pm - Performance #4
1pm - 5pm: Onstage						
12 Day Off	**13** 7pm - Performance #6	**14** 2pm - Performance #7 / 8pm - Performance #8	**15** 7pm - Performance #9	**16** 8pm - Performance #10 / XXXXX PD / XXXXX Out / XXXXX ON	**17** 2pm - Performance #11 / Actor XXXXX PD (M & E) / 8pm - Performance #12	**18** 3pm - Performance #13 / XXXXX Opens
19 7pm - Performance #14	**20** 10:15 - 11:30pm XXXXX Rehearsal / 7pm - Performance #15	**21** 2pm - Performance #16 / XXXXX Out/ XXXXX ON / 8pm - Performance #17	**22** Day Off / XXXXX Parade	**23** 2pm - Performance #18 / 8pm - Performance #19	**24** 2pm - Performance #20 / 8pm - Performance #21	**25** Day Off
26 Day Off	**27** 7pm - Performance #22 / Stagehand XXXXX Out / XXXXX IN	**28** 2pm - Performance #23 / 8pm - Performance #24	**29** 7pm - Performance #25	**30** 8pm - Performance #26 / XXXXX Out / XXXXX ON		

Figure 4.1: Production Calendar/example-continued

Production Calendar

December

MONDAY	TUESDAY	WEDNESDAY	THURSDAY	FRIDAY	SATURDAY	SUNDAY
					1	**2**
3 Day Off	**4** 7pm - Performance #30	**5** 2pm - Performance #31 8pm - Performance #32 XXXXX interviews w/XXXXX between shows	**6** 7pm - Performance #33	**7** 8pm - Performance #34	**8** 2pm - Performance #35 XXXXX Out / XXXXX ON 8pm - Performance #36	**9** 3pm - Performance #37 XXXXX Event w/ Actor XXXXX
10 Day Off	**11** 7pm - Performance #38	**12** 2pm - Performance #39 8pm - Performance #40	**13** 7pm - Performance #41 Swing Out: Ensemble XXXXX	**14** 8pm - Performance #42	**15** 11:30 - 12:30 Amex at Pearl 2pm - Performance #43 8pm - Performance #44	**16** 3pm - Performance #45 SM XXXXX PD Stagehand XXXXX Final Perf
					Stagehand XXXXX OUT / XXXXX IN	
17 Day Off	**18** 7pm - Performance #46 PSM PD Stagehand XXXXX becomes AutoFly Operator	**19** 2pm - Performance #47 8pm - Performance #48	**20** 7pm - Performance #49	**21** 1pm - XXXXX Event at JFK 8pm - Performance #50	**22** 2pm - Performance #51 8pm - Performance #52	**23** 3pm - Performance #53 Sarah Sodie PD
24 Day Off **31** Day Off	**25** Day Off	**26** 2pm - Performance #54 8pm - Performance #55	**27** 2pm - Added Performance 7pm - Performance	**28** 8pm - Performance	**29** 2pm - Performance 8pm - Performance	**30** 1pm - Performance 6:30pm - Performance

Figure 4.1: Production Calendar/example-continued

PSM's Casting Notes

Name	Date	Acting Notes	Vocal Notes
	2/7/08	5'11"/Love Him/TE-vocally covered	Song Like This
	1/15/07	5'11"/Young,Smart/Looks studious/Well-Spoken/R-4	3/"To Be a Dike"
	10/27/06	5'6"? - says he's 5'8"/Asian/Adorable/Stock actor/R-2-3	
	LA 8/2/06	5'10"?/Asian/Well-built/Smart/R-3+	3+/Moment
	2/8/08	5'10"/Simple, real reading/Self-satisfied/Normal/NF but reveals script	"Jew Song"
	LA 6-2-06	6'/Black/Handsome/Appealing/Not cooked yet/ R-2+	3/"Out There"
	10/27/2006+1/15/07	5'10"/Can't whistle/Wants to be cute/Funny in Song/Didn't Read	3/"Out There"
	3/21/08	5'11"/Young blonde/Working class face/R-3+as Lance/Gal-No	???
	LV 9/29/07	6'/Small, breathy voice but connects/Lyrics+/Robin-real&clear/Took dir	4/"Sensitive Song"/
	8/28/07	6'/Solid performer without a lot of personality	3-/???
	8/28/07	6'1"/Black/Sweet/R-2	3+/????
	1/15/07	6'?/Leading Man/Contemporary/TG-muscled out top notes/explore legit	3+/"Ur Nothing w/o Me"
	8/28/07	5'10"/Balding now/Professional & solid/I trust him/R-3+	3+/"Big D"
	8/28/07	6'/Can't act at all	3+ Tenor/????
	10/27/06	5'9"/A bit soft & modern/Took dir/Matthew Bourne guy/R-3	3/???
	10/27/06	5'9"/Big ears/Better Herb than Hist/R-3+ (slightly Chorus)	
	8/28/07	6'/Greg Reuter/Handsome/Spontaneous/R-4	3+/???
	LA 1-25-08	5'8"?/"S"/Hist-Good/Herb-OK but not whacked/Patsy-Sweet & Connects	Enjoy Being a Girl
	1/15/07	6'1"/Leading Man w/ char/Smooth, wolfin look/Very useful guy/R-4+	4-/"They Can't Take That Away"
	5/23/06	5'8"/Dark, cute, Tenor/Good interior life as actor/R-3+	3+/"Astoria Gloria"/ ↑Bb
	1/15/07	5'10"/Dark & Young/Can't Act/R-2	3+/"I Am Happiness"
	5/23/06	5'10"/Black/Masculine/Rhythm?	3-/"Pirate King"
	5/23/2006+7/5/06	5'11"/Char.face w/nose/Huge Bari/Funny/Also came to principal call	4/"Proud Lady"
	1/15/07	5'11"/Has age & char./Great face/Can't sing low enuf for King//R-2+	3/"I Honestly Love You?
	4/8/05+LV6-1-06	5'7"/Black, small/I loved him	3/"Puberty"
	3/21/08	6'?/Slim & Fair/R-4 Lance-Funny & Orig ST - Bad Russian	3+/???
	1/15/07	6'/Tall w/ char/Funny/Spam underwear/R-3-	3-/"Street Where U Live"

Bank			
	8/28/07	5'9"/Dark/Energetic/Way too busy & unfocussed/Cute but relies on it/R-3-	3/"I Believe in You"
	5/28/04	6'1"/Looks like Beaker	3+/"Camelot+Noble Cock"
	6/1/04	5'9"/Bald, slim/Unexpectedly funny in song/Missed style in scene	?/"Hair"/Bari w/Falsetto
	9/1/05	5'10"/No center as an actor/PL didn't like/ CN did	3/"Where Was I"
	5/28/04	5'10"?/Black/Great energy	3+/"Ain't Misbehavin"
	5/23/06	5'8.5"/Good News/Cute/Wants to mug but stopped w/dir./R-3+	3/"Gummy Bears"
	10/27/06	5'9"/Funny Historian/OTT but worth it/R-3+ (needs work session)	3/
	10/27/06	6'/Not cooked yet/Strange & Funny/R-2 (follow this guy)	3/
	6/1/04	5'9"/Young, eager, funny/	4/"Come w/Me" Strong Bari
	9/1/05	5'11"?/ Not an actor but dizzy & funny	3/"That's Where I'm Going"
	9/1/05	5'11"/Not an actor but an adorable, strong dancer	2+/"Dream Lover"
	5/23/06	5'9"/A guy/Very appealing/Brownies/"S"/R-2	3/"Use What U Got"
	9/1/05	5'11"?/Girly readings/Humor not in words	3+/"Big Black Man"
	8/28/2007+2-7-08	6'1"/Funny Face but doesn't use it/Not gd this time/Needs experience/R-4-	3+/"Proud Lady"

Figure 4.3: PSM's casting notes/example

Dance	Role
D-3+/P-4	Bed/Lance u/s
D-3/P-3	Brian w/ Robin or Herbert
D-4/P-3	Brad Bradley w/No cover
D-4/P-3	Scott Taylor/Robin u/s
We Know Him	Robin u/s
D-3/P-4	Ens. w/No u/s
D-4/P-3	Swing Only
D-3/P-3	Lance u/s (Robin?Herb?)
D-3/P-2/Taps	Rob Moffat (P-3 from Peter)
D-3/P-3	Swing
D-3+/P=4	No Covers
D-3/P-3	Greg w/ Galahad u/s
D-3+/P-3+	Robin u/s
D-3/P-2+	Swing
D-4/P-3	Robin u/s (not 1st choice)
	Shepard w/ Herb u/s
D-3+/P-3+	Galahad u/s
D-4/P-4	Ens. W/Patsy u/s/
D-3/P-2	Stand-by/Gal,King,Bed u/s
D-3/P-3	Darryl w/Herbert
D-4/P-3	Swing
D-4/P-3	Scott or Swing
D-3/T-3	Greg/Kevin w/Herb u/s
D-3/P-2	Kevin or Scott w/Bed u/s
D-4/P-4	Swing/Brad w/Patsy u/s??
D-3/P-3	Lance or Gal u/s
D-4/P-3	Swing Any Co.

D-3/P-3	Lance u/s
D-3/P-4	PrinceH/Dennis
D-4/P-3+	Robin
D-4/P-4	NYC — Brian
D-4/P-4	Dancer/No Cover
D-3/P-3	Herb u/s
D-3/P-3	Herb u/s
D-3/P-3	Herb u/s
D-3/P-2+	Lance
D-4/P-4	NYC Brian
D-4/P-4	NYC No u/s
D-3/T-3	No u/s
D-4/P-3+	NYC Scott No u/s
D-3/P-3	Galahad u/s Tour or Vegas

Daily Rehearsal Report
Name of Show

Day: _____

Date: _____

Daily Stage Managers' Report

Name of Studio: _____   Rehearsed: _____

Actor	Called	Released	
PRINCIPALS (11)			**ROOM A – BIG ROOM**
Actor	10	6	**10 – 12** Staging - "XXXXXXXX" scene & number
Actor	10	6	
Actor	10	3	**12 – 2** Music - "XXXXXXXX"
Actor	10	6	
Actor	9	6	
Actor	10	6	**2 – 3** Lunch
Actor	10	3	
Actor	No Call		**3 – 3:30** "XXXXXXXX"
Actor	10	6	
Actor	10	6	
Actor	No Call		**4 – 4:45** Choreo - "XXXXXX"
ENSEMBLE WOMEN (10)			
Actor	10	6	**4:45 – 5** Music - "XXXXXXX"
Actor	10	6	
Actor	10	6	**5 – 6** Music - Give "XXXXXX" & "XXXXXXX"
Actor	10	6	to Orchestrators
Actor	10	6	
Actor	11	3:30	**ROOM B – CHOREO ROOM**
Actor	10	6	
Actor	10	6	
Actor	10	6	
ENSEMBLE MEN (10)			
Actor	10	6	**3:30 – 4** Choreo - "Hot"
Actor	10	6	
Actor	10	6	
Actor	10	6	
Actor	10	6	
Actor	10	6	
Actor	10	6	**ROOM C – VOCAL ROOM**
Actor	10	6	
Actor	10	6	**1 – 2** Music - "Fare Thee Well" w/Ens. Women 1, 2 & 3
Actor	9:45	6	Principal 1 & 2
CONFLICTS:			
			3:30 – 4:30 Music - "Let Her In"

PRESS:
Actor NA 12:15–2

NOTES:

Mgmt: Actor went to Empire Theatre & chose Dressing Rm 7
the large dressing room on 2nd Floor @ end of hallway
Actor has taken Dressing Rm 1 — 1st floor @ end of hallway.
6:30–8   Production Meeting
Actor 1st day back in reh. After LOA

FITTINGS:

9–10 Actor @Tricorne	12:45–1:30 Actor @Parsons
9:45–10:30 Actor @Parsons	3:30–4:30 Actor @Parsons
10–11 Actor @Parsons	5–6 Actor @Parsons
10:30–11:15 Actor @Parsons	
11:15–12 Actor @Parsons	
11:30–12:30 Actor @Parsons	
12–12:45 Actor @Parsons	
12:30–1:45 Actor @Parsons	

Wardrobe: 5–5:30 Chin fittings in 4C
Change — All Ensemble into Dogs for King entrance (II-40 to 42) not possible
w/current script. We need 3 min. We have about 30 sec currently.

Props: Horse meeting cancelled today.

Figure 5.1: Daily rehearsal report/example

Wardrobe Breakdown

	ACT I-1	I-2	I-3	I-4	I-5	I-6	I-7	I-8
	Vaudeville Theatre Seattle	Kitchen Frame House	Road Seattle to Los Angeles	Backstage Vaudeville Dallas	Onstage Vaudeville L.A.	Hotel Room Akron	Chinese Restaurant N.Y.	Granztiger's P N.Y.
MAMA ROSE	COAT/HAT	REPEAT	REPEAT	COAT/DRESS		ROBE/PJS	BLANKET COAT	COAT/DRES
HERBIE				COAT/SUIT		COAT/SUIT	REPEAT	REPEAT
LOUISE					UNCLE SAM	PAJAMAS	BLANKET COAT	COW
DAINTY JUNE					STATUE OF LIB	NIGHTGOWN	BLANKET COAT	DAINTY/CO
MALE #1	STAGEHAND				ARMY	PAJAMAS		ETON BOY
FEMALE #1	JOCKO MOM							
FEMALE #2	JOCKO MOM							
FEMALE #3	JOCKO MOM							CRATCHITT
MALE #2	UNCLE JOCKO		RICH MAN			GUEST IN ROBE		
MALE #3	PIANIST		CHAUFFEUR			GOLDSTONE		LIGHT OP.
MALE #4	POKER PLAYER	POP				KRINGELEIN		
BABY JUNE	DUTCH GIRL	ADD COAT	NEW TROUSERS		STATUE OF LIB			
BABY LOUISE	DUTCH BOY	ADD COAT	NEW DRESS		UNCLE SAM			
FEMALE #4	WARDROBE							
FEMALE #5							WAITRESS	COW HEAD
FEMALE #6								
FEMALE #7								STAGEHANI
FEMALE #8	WARDROBE							COW REAR
FEMALE #9								STAGEHANI
FEMALE #10	JOCKO SISTER					GUEST IN ROBE		
MALE #5	FLY FLOOR	SCENE CHANGE	DIORAMA		AVIATOR			FARM/ETON
MALE #6	POKER PLAYER	SCENE CHANGE	TROOP LEADER		NAVY			FARM/ETON
MALE #7	GEORGIE	SCENE CHANGE	SIGN HOLDER?					FARM/ETON
MALE #8	SCENE CHANGE	SCENE CHANGE						FARM/ETON
MALE #9	FLY FLOOR	SCENE CHANGE	TROOP LEADER					FARM/ETON
MALE #10	POKER PLAYER	SCENE CHANGE		WEBER		GUEST IN ROBE		STAGEHANI
FEMALE CHILD #1	BALLOON GIRL							
MALE CHILD #1	COWBOY		BOY SCOUT		NEWS/NAVY			
MALE CHILD #2	KEYSTONE COP		RICH BOY		NEWS/ARMY			
MALE CHILD #3	CLARENCE		TAP URCHIN		NEWS/AVIATOR			
MALE UNDERSTUDY #1								
FEMALE SWING #1								
CHILD SWING								
MALE UNDERSTUDY #2								
ROSE STANDBY								
FEMALE SWING #2								

Figure 6.1: Wardrobe breakdown/example

I-9	I-10	I-11	ACT II-1	II-2	II-3	II-4	II-5	II-6
tiger's Office N.Y.	Theatre Alley Buffalo	R.R. Platform Omaha	Desert County, Texas	Burlesque, Wichita	Backstage Corridor	Wichita, Detroit, Phila, Minsky's	Louise's Dressing Room	Bare Stage After Show
AT		COAT/DRESS	DRESS	COAT/DRESS		COAT/DRESS	COAT/DRESS	REPEAT/FUR
T	REPEAT	REPEAT		VEST/PANTS	COAT/SUIT	REPEAT	COAT/SUIT	
LEGS	COAT/PANTS	MATADOR		COAT/PANTS		COAT/GOWNS	G-STRING/ROBE	DRESS/STOLE
AT	REMOVE JKT							
			MAZEPPA					
			TESSIE TURA	WRAPPER				
AT			ELECTRA					
			CIGAR	REPEAT	REPEAT			
			PASTEY	REPEAT	REPEAT			
			TORREADORA	COAT/DRESS	REPEAT	MINSKY'S		
			TORREADORA	COAT/DRESS		MINSKY'S		
			TORREADORA	COAT/DRESS				
			TORREADORA	COAT/DRESS		MINSKY'S		
			TORREADORA	COAT/DRESS		MINSKY'S		
			TORREADORA	COAT/DRESS		MINSKY'S		
				STRIPPER			MAID	
		COAT						
		COAT						
							B-COCHON	
				WILLY			PHIL	
						MINSKY'S		

Prop List
2012 *Annie* Revival

PROP	WHO USES	PRESET	NOTES
ACT 1		pg 1	"Overture" (#1)
SCENE 1: Orphanage - Girls Annex		pgs 1–5	"Maybe" (#2), "Annie's Escape" (#3)
Bed Orphans	USL		
Big Bed Sheets & Blankets			Bottom sheet, 2 top sheets, 1 blanket
Drawer Bed Sheet			Top sheet
3 Crumpled Notes	Annie	USL	2 in sweater, 1 on bed
Silver Locket—Broken	Annie	USL	Costumes
Sack of Clothing	Annie	Under Stairs	
SCENE 1: Orphanage - Girls Annex		pgs 7–14	"Hard Knock Life" (#4)
Stuffed Bear	Molly	SL 3	Wrist strap
4 Pillows in Pillow Cases	Orphans	Bed / Stairs	Cases easy to remove & opening marked
Blankie	Tessie	Bed	
Broom	Pep/Duf/Annie	SL 1	
Galvanized Tub	Duffy / Annie	Under Stairs	
4 Mop Backpacks	Mol, Kate, Tes	in Tub	3 worn, 1 not worn
Plunger	Tessie	Under Stairs	
Toilet Brush	Tessie	Under Stairs	
2 Dresses	Kate / July	Stairs (4/5)	Not worn, items orphans are cleaning up
Wicker Laundry Basket	Kate / July	SL 1	Girl cartwheels into / over
4 Hand Scrub Brushes	Molly / Kate	Bed Shelf	
Cleaning Rag	Annie	Top Stairs	
Workbench w/	Orphans	SL 1	
Rick Rack Spool w/ 2 Lengths			
Red Box Fabric			
Green Flower Fabric			
Green Shirt			
Purple Dress			
Pink Polka Dot Fabric			
Sewing Machine			Lever up
Basket w/Reindeer Fabric			
Iron			
Ironing Board		SL 1	
Kitty & Balls Fabric		SL 1	
Green Lantern Fabric	Pepper	SL 1	
Plaid Fabric			
Stripes Fabric			
Forest Fabric			
B&W Fabric			
Flask	Hannigan	USL	
Whistle on String	Hannigan	USL	Around neck
Laundry Hamper	Bundles	USL	Annie gets in and is wheeled out
Pile of Sheets & Towels - Folded	Bundles	USL	
SCENE 2: LES Street		pgs 15–19	"Tomorrow" (#6)
Apple Seller Tray w/ 5 Apples	Jane	SL 3	Rotten apples - 2 removable
Lunch Pail	Ryan	SL 3	
Heavy Bundle—Rags	Gavin	SL 1	Carried on actor's shouler
Milk Bottles in Wire Rack	Joel	SR 3	
Bundled Baby	Sarah	SL 3	Baby not seen
Bag of Groceries	Sarah	SL 3	
Wheeled Dog Cart	Ryan	SR 1	Pulled

Figure 7.1: Prop list/2012 *Annie* revival

Prop List
2012 *Annie* Revival

PROP	WHO USES	PRESET	NOTES
Dog Catcher's Net	Gavin	SR 3	
Hooverville Crate	Crew	SL 3	
2 Trash Cans (Sm w/ Dog Treat)	Crew	SL 3	Crew strikes
2 Night Sticks	Den / Kev	SL 3	
SCENE 3: Hooverville		pgs 19–25	"Hooverville" (#7) / "Hooverville Raid" (#8)
Box w/	Merwin	SR 1	
Hammer	Ryan	SR 1	
Scrap Wood		SR 1	
Small Rug	Liz	SR 1	
Whisk Broom	Liz	SR 1	
Gold Lantern	Liz	SR 1	
Camp Stool	Amanda	SL 3	
Red Lantern	Amanda	SL 3	
Oil Drum w/	Ashley	SL 1	
Pot of Soup	Ashley	SL 1	
Ladle for Stew	Ashley	SL 1	
Basin w/	Sarah	SR 3	
11 Bowls for Soup	Sarah	SR 3	
Apple Tray	Jane	SL 3	Repeat
Cane & Newspaper	Joel	SR 1	
Hoover Poster	All	SR 2	Inside Hooverville unit
Deck of Cards	Gavin	SR 1	
Short Newspaper Stack	Crew	SR 3	
Crate	Jeremy	SL 3	Repeat from LES scene
Crate	Ryan	SR 1	
2 Nightsticks	Den / Kev		Repeat
SCENE 4: Orphanage - Office		pgs 25–35	"Little Girls" (#9) / "Little Girls Reprise" (#10)
Desk & Chair w/		SR 1	
Drawer 1 w/ Gin Bottle, Glass, Mirror			Acrylic glass
Drawer 3 w/ Gin Bottle, Glass			Acrylic glass
Phone			
File Box w/ Tweezers, Hair Brush			
Wine Bottle & Tea Towel			
Jewelry Box w/ Nail File			
3 Pens			
Bound Book			
Clipboard w/ Roster			
Messy Papers			
Hankie on top			
Whistle	Hannigan	SR 3	Repeat
Tracked Mouse	Georgi	SL 1	
Yo-Yo	Pepper	SR 3	
Night Stick	Dennis	SL 3	Repeat
Briefcase w/	Grace	SL 3	
Document & Pencil	Grace	Briefcase	
SCENE 4 INTO 5: Shopping Transition		pg 35	
Window Frame & Dress Form		SR 2	
Reciept	Jeremy	SR 2	
Walking Stick	Gavin	SR 1	
Shirt Box	Keven	SL 1	
Hat Box	Ashley	SL 1	

Figure 7.1: Prop list/2012 *Annie* revival-continued

Prop List
2012 *Annie* Revival

PROP	WHO USES	PRESET	NOTES
Gift Box	Jane	SR 1	
SCENE 5: Warbucks Mansion		pgs 36–49	"I Think I'm Gonna Like It Here" (#11)
3 Folded Shirts	Ashley	SL 1	
Small Ledger & Pen	Amanda	SL 3	
Stack of Sheets (#1)	Jane	SR 3	
2 Stack of Sheets (#2, #3)	Keven	SR Balcony	
Flower Group #1	Sarah	SL 1	
Flower Group #2	Amanda	SR 3	
Flower Group #3	Ashley	SR 1	
Vase Jane	SL 3		
Painting	Mer, Den	SR 1	
2 Forks	Gavin	SL 1	2 Different options
Vacuum Cleaner w/ Long Cord	Jane, Ashley	SR 3	Official jump rope
3 Feather Dusters	Sarah, Ash, Am	SL 3	Rigged on pedestal
Pedestal on Casters w/ Bust	Sarah	SL 3	
Bottle of Wine	Merwin	SL 3	
Wine Glass	Merwin	SL 3	
Sauce Pan w/ Ladle Spoon	Liz	SR 2	
Hankie	Mrs. Pugh	SL 1	
Menu	Mrs. Pugh	SL 1	2 menus?
Plate w/	Gavin	SL 3	
Dessert			Not practical
Spoon			Repeat
Large Napkin	Gavin / Annie	SL 3	3' x 3' - for Annie's neck
Pile of Dirty Sheets	Keven / Ryan	SR 1	
Bathtub w/ Towel & Bubbles	Keven / Ryan	SL 1	
Large Ledger & Pen	Sarah	SR 2	
Cleaning Rag #1	Keven	SR 1	
Cleaning Rag #2	Ryan	SR 1	Mop floor with this rag
Cleaning Rag #3	Amanda	SR 1	
Cleaning Rag #4	Sarah	SL 1	
Cleaning Rag #5	Ashley	SL 3	
Cleaning Rag #6	Keven	SR Balcony	
2 Suitcases	WB / Gavin	SL 3	
Speed Graphic Camera	Ryan	SR 1	Flash
Shelf w/ Phone w/		SR 2	
Message Pad, Pen		SR 2	
SCENE 6: NYC		pgs 49–53	"NYC" (#12)
Walking Stick	Merwin	SL 1	Costumes
Beggar Cup & Coins	Gavin	SR 1	
Shoe Shine Box & Rag		SR 2	Slides across floor
27 Helium Balloons		SR & SL	9 groups of 3—2 tall, 7 regular
Organ Grinder w/		SR 3	
2 Removable Helium Balloons			
Monte Table w/	Den / Kev	SL 3	Magnetic top and cups
3 Cups, Candy, Paper Money	Keven	SL 3	
Paper Money	Gra, Kev, WB	SL 3	
Salvation Army Bucket & Bell	Gav / Sarah	SR 1	
Suitcase & Cosmetic Bag	Star to be	SL 3	
Crystal Ball on Pillow	Liz	SR 3	
Camera	Jane	SR 2	

Figure 7.1: Prop list/2012 *Annie* revival-continued

Prop List
2012 *Annie* Revival

PROP	WHO USES	PRESET	NOTES
Grey Hat Box	Jane	SL 1	
3 Tickets	Warbucks	SL 3	In coat pocket, torn each show
Roxy Seats - 3		SL 1	
Dog Catcher's Net	Ryan	SL 1	Repeat
Grace Calling Card	Grace	SR 3	Gives to dog catcher
SCENE 7: Orphange - Office		pgs 53–62	"Easy Street" (#13)
Desk & Chair w/		SR 1	Repeat
Drawer 1 & 3 w/ Gin Bottle, Glass, Mirror			Repeat
Phone			
File Box w/ Tweezers, Hair Brush, Hankie			
Jewelry Box w/ Nail File			
3 Pens			
Bound Book & Clipboard			
Messy Papers			
2 Magazines			
Whistle	Hannigan	SR 1	Repeat
Radio		SR Wall	Repeat
Briefcase w/	Grace	SR 3	Repeat
Adoption Document	Grace	SR 3	
Lily Purse w/ Hankie	Lily	SR 3	
Compact & Lipstick	Lily	SR 3	
Expanding Car		SR 1	
SCENE 8: Warbucks Office		pgs 62–69	"You Won't Be an Orphan for Long" (#15)
Phone	Grace	SR 1	
Large Ledger & Pen	Joel	SL 1	Repeat from Like It Here
Desk & Chair w/	Warbucks	SR 2	
Blotter, Stamper, Mag Glass	Warbucks		
Check Book & Pen	Warbucks		
Pen Set	Warbucks		
Writing Paper	Warbucks		
Steno Pad & Pen	Grace		
Tiffany's Box, Ribbon w/	Warbucks	Desk	Hooked onto desk?
Silver Locket		Desk	
Brandy Glass w/ Tea	Warbucks	SR 3	
Stack Of Sheets	Ryan	SL Balcony	Repeat
ACT 2		pg 70	"Entr'acte" (#16)
SCENE 1: NBC Radio Studio		pgs 70–76	"Fully Dressed" (#17)
Foley Table w/	Keven	SL 1	
Door Open and Close Effect			
Squeaky Shoes & Board			
Applause Sign			
Head Set			
NBC Chimes & Mallet			
Triangle on String & Mallet			
Other Foley Noise Props			
NBC Script Packet (Red)			
Oxydent Sign			
Ventroliquist Dummy "Wacky"	Joel	Bench	
3 Microphones			All lowered
Bench	WB, Annie, Grace		

Figure 7.1: Prop list/2012 *Annie* revival-continued

Prop List
2012 *Annie* Revival

PROP	WHO USES	PRESET	NOTES
Apple Box	Annie		Stands on
4 Script Packets	Ry x 2, Den, Bert		
Head Set	Ryan		
SCENE 2: Orphanage - Office		pgs 76–83	"Fully Dressed" (#18) / "Easy Street" (#19)
Basket or Drawer w/	Stairs		
3 Fans & 3 Hankies	Basket		Corners
Girdle	Basket		Straps down — side
Lipstick	Basket		Side
2 Nighties - Lightweight	Basket		Over edge
3 Pairs Panties	Basket		Bottom — to stuff
2 Camis	Basket		Bottom — to stuff
Hankie (Set w/ Lipstick)	Basket		Bottom — to stuff
Boa	Basket		Costumes?
Yo-Yo	Georgi		Repeat
Broom	Duffy	Under Stairs	Repeat
Desk & Chair w/		SR 1	Repeat
Drawer 1 w/ Gin Bottle, Glass, Mirror			Cracked open
Bra			Velcroed
Phone			
File Box w/ Tweezers, Hair Brush, Hankie			
Jewelry Box w/ Nail File			
3 Pens			
Bound Book			
Clipboard w/ Roster			
Messy Papers			
Whistle	Hannigan	USL	Repeat
Radio		SR Wall	Repeat
SCENE 3: White House		pgs 83–93	"Cabinet Tomorrow" (#21) / "Cab End" (#22)
WB Desk		SR 2	
6 Chairs		SL 3 & SR 2	Joined 3 & 3
Flag Stand		SR 3	
Wheelchair	FDR	SL 3	
Newpaper	Morganthau	Table	Washington Post
6 Legal Folders w/ Papers	All	Table	Figures
Pen Ickes	Table		
Cigarette in Holder	FDR	SL 3	
Telegram	Howe	SL 3	
SCENE 4: Warbucks		pgs 93–98	"Something Was Missing" (#24)
Warbucks Desk			On from previous scene
Warbucks Chair	Joel	SL 3	Repeat
Stack of Applications #1	Joel	SL 3	
Stack of Applications #2	Amanda	SR 1	
Stack of Applications #3	Sarah	SR 1	
Stack of Applications #4	Ashley	SR 1	
FBI Envelope on Tray w/	Ryan / Drake	SL 3	5" x 8" sized envelope
Letter			
Annie Silver Locket			
SCENE 5: Warbucks		pgs 98–111	"I Don't Need Anything But You" (#25)
Presents Stack #1	Dennis	SR 1	Sled w/ box, bear, Grace present
Presents Stack #2	Sarah	SR 1	1 medium

Figure 7.1: Prop list/2012 *Annie* revival-continued

Prop List
2012 *Annie* Revival

PROP	WHO USES	PRESET	NOTES
Presents Stack #3	Keven	SR 1	Piano w/ dolls
Presents Stack #4	Jeremy	SR 1	1 medium
Presents Stack #5	Ryan	SR 1	1 large, 1 medium
Presents Stack #6	Jeremy	SR 1	1 medium
Giraffe	Joel	SR 1	
Toy Box w/ Lollipops	Dennis	SR 2	
Bear Pallet w/ Blue Ball	Ryan	SR 2	
Doll House	Dennis	SL 1	
Rocking Horse	Joel	SL 1	
Present Tier	Joel	SL 1	
Red Wagon w/			
Presents			
Yellow Ball			
Lollipops			
6 Shoe Box Presents w/ Taps	Dennis	SL 2	7 shoe boxes — 1 for each orphan exc Molly
Molly Box w/ Jingle Bells	Molly	SL 2	Shakes — does not open
6 Sweater Boxes w/ Sweater	Am, Sarah	SL 2	Orphans exc Annie
Garland - Double	Liz, Sarah, Jane	SL 2	Blue end is the lead end
Garland - Single	Crew	SR 2	On WB stairs @ Intermission
2 Wreaths	Dennis / Liz	SR Balcony	
3 Wreaths	Kev / Ry / Jer	SR 3	
Bible	Rooster	SR 1	
2 Driver's Licenses	Rooster & Lily	SR 1	
Birth Certificate	Rooster	SR 1	
Silver Locket (2nd Half)	Rooster	SR 1	
Tray w/ 5 Champagne Glasses	Jane	SR 1	
Tray w/ 5 Champagne Glasses	Amanda	SR 2	
Wheelchair	FDR	SR 1	Repeat
2 Long Stem Roses	Gavin	SR 1	
Long Stem Rose	Joel	SR 1	Velcroed in wing
Long Stem Rose	Liz	WB Stair 3	
Long Stem Rose	Jane	WB Stair 7	
2 Long Stem Roses	Ash, Am	SL 3 / SL 1	1 w/ shoe boxes, 1 w/ doll house
SCENE 6: Warbucks		pgs 112–125	"New Deal for Christmas" (#28)
Annie Suitcase	Annie	SL Balcony	Big sitable
Whistle	Hannigan	SR 1	Repeat
Envelope w/ "Mudge Report"	Drake	SR 1	
"The jig is up" Check x 2	Warbucks	SL 1	Torn up every show
Wheelchair	FDR	SL 1	Repeat
2 Handcuffs	Han, Roos, Lil	SL 1	
Canape Tray	Jeremy	SR 3	Dropped on floor
Canape Tray	Jane	SR 3	Dropped on floor
Canape Tray w/ 2 Champ Glasses	Ashley	SL 2	
Yo-Yo	Pepper	SR 1	Repeat
Tray w/	Jane	SR 3	
2 Champagne Bottles			
2 Spoons			

Figure 7.1: Prop list/2012 *Annie* revival-continued

Tech Table Map

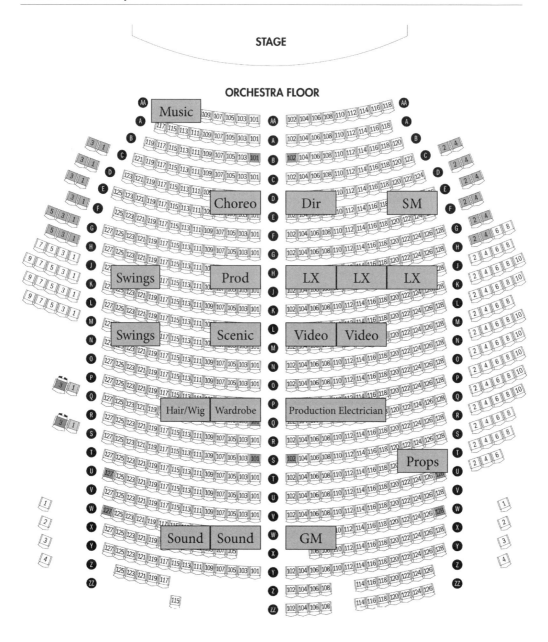

Figure 9.1: Tech table layout 2012 *Annie* revival

AUTO FLY CUE TO BEGIN DRY TECH
SPAMALOT

CUE	PIECE	SPEED
ACT 1 PRESET		
	Portcullis ↓	
	DS Blackout Drop ↓ Low	
	Cloud Headers 1–4 ↑ to High	
	FOY Line ↓ and SL	
HISTORIAN → FINLAND (ACT I SCENE 1 → ACT I SCENE 2)		
AUTO FLY 500 - RED	Blackout ↑	FAST
AUTO FLY 501 - WHITE	Portcullis ↑	FAST
FINLAND → MUD CASTLE (ACT I SCENE 2 → ACT I SCENE 3)		
AUTO FLY 505 - RED	Clouds 2–4 ↓ Int.	Medium
POST PLAGUE VILLAGE		
AUTO FLY 507 - RED	Clouds 2–4 ↑ to Act 1 Preset	
AUTO FLY 508 - RED	Clouds 2–4 ↓	
WITCH VILLAGE → CAMELOT (ACT I SCENE 7 → ACT I SCENE 10)		
FOY 52	Tension	
FOY 53	↑ to Preset	
FOY 54	Fly L to R	
AUTO FLY 509 – RED	Portcullis ↓	
	Blackout ↓	
CAMELOT (ACT I SCENE 10)		
AUTO FLY 513 – BLUE	Camelot Hanger ↓	
	Clouds 2 – 4 ↑	
AUTO FLY 514 – RED	Blackout ↑	
AUTO FLY 515 – WHITE	Portcullis ↑	

Figure 9.3: Auto fly cue to begin dry tech/*Spamalot*

CUE	PIECE	SPEED

GOD'S FEET → FIND THE GRAIL
(ACT I SCENE 11 → ACT I SCENE 12)

CUE	PIECE	SPEED
AUTO FLY 520 – RED	Clouds 1–4 ↓	
	God's Feet ↓	
	Camelot Hanger ↑	
AUTO FLY 523 – RED	Spread God's Feet	
AUTO FLY 524 – WHITE	Close God's Feet	
AUTO FLY 525 – BLUE	God's Feet ↑	
AUTO FLY 526 – RED	Clouds 1–4 ↑	

FRENCH CASTLE → END OF ACT
(ACT I SCENE 13 → END OF ACT I)

CUE	PIECE	SPEED
AUTO FLY 528 – RED	Clouds 1–4 ↑	
AUTO FLY 529 – RED	Clouds 1–4 ↑	

INTERMISSION

ACT 2 PRESET

CUE	PIECE	SPEED
	Clouds 1–4 ↓ (1 Foot)	
	Blackout ↑	
	FOY ↑ and off L	

HISTORIAN → FOREST
(ACT 2 SCENE 1 → ACT 2 SCENE 2)

CUE	PIECE	SPEED
AUTO FLY 601 – RED	Portcullis ↑	

JEW SONG
(ACT 2 SCENE 4)

CUE	PIECE	SPEED
AUTO FLY 602 – RED	Cloud 1 ↑	

JEW SONG → FOREST
(ACT 2 SCENE 4 → ACT 2 SCENE 5)

CUE	PIECE	SPEED
AUTO FLY 603 – WHITE	Cloud 1 ↓	

FOREST → WHATEVER HAPPENED TO MY PART
(ACT 2 SCENE 5)

CUE	PIECE	SPEED
AUTO FLY 605 – RED	Blackout ↓	
AUTO FLY 606 – WHITE	Clouds 2–4 ↑	

Figure 9.3: Auto fly cue to begin dry tech/*Spamalot*-continued

CUE	PIECE	SPEED
PRINCE HERBERT (ACT 2 SCENE 6)		
AUTO FLY 607 – RED	Blackout ↑	
	Cloud 1 ↑	
AUTO FLY 609 – RED	Clouds 1–2 ↑	
FOY 10	Hook Up	
FOY 10.1	Tension	
FOY 10.2	Lift to Preset	
AFTER "ALL ALONE"		
AUTO FLY 611 – RED	Clouds 1–4 ↓	
COCONUT SHENANIGANS (ACT 2 SCENE 7A)		
FOY 11 AUTO FLY 612 – RED	Fly Tim the Enchanter to Center Clouds 1–4 ↓ (to deck)	
AUTO FLY 613 – BLUE	Clouds 1–4 ↑	
KILLER RABBIT → FINALE (ACT 2 SCENE 8 → ACT 2 SCENE 9)		
FOY 12	Fly Foy offstage L	
FOY 13	Foy to Deck	
FOY 14	Foy Rig out to store	
AUTO FLY 620 – RED	Hand of God ↓	
AUTO FLY 621 – WHITE	Hand of God ↑	
	Portcullis ↓	
	Blackout ↓	
FINALE		
AUTO FLY 625 – BLUE	Camelot Hanger ↓	
	Clouds 1–3 ↑	
	Cloud 4 ↓	
AUTO FLY 626 – RED	Blackout ↑	
AUTO FLY 627 – WHITE	Portcullis ↑	
BOWS		
AUTO FLY 635 – RED	Camelot Hanger ↑	
	Cloud 1 ↑	
AUTO FLY 640 – RED	Clouds 1–3 ↓ (Projections)	
AUTO FLY 645 – WHITE	Portcullis ↓	
	Blackout ↓	

Figure 9.3: Auto fly cue to begin dry tech/*Spamalot*-continued

MANUAL FLY CUES TO BEGIN DRY TECH
SPAMALOT

CUE	PIECE	SPEED
PRESET		
	Tab open to Broadway Portal Finland Drop ↓	
		Next move:
FINLAND → MUD CASTLE (ACT I, SCENE 2 → ACT I, SCENE 3)		
FLY A - RED	Finland Drop ↑	
LAKER GIRLS → THE SONG THAT GOES LIKE THIS (ACT I, SCENE 6)		
FLY D - RED	Chandelier ↓ Low	Medium Speed
		Next move:
THE SONG THAT GOES LIKE THIS → WITCH VILLAGE (ACT I, SCENE 6 → ACT I, SCENE 7)		
FLY E - RED	Chandelier ↑	Medium Speed
		Next move:
ALL FOR ONE → KNIGHTS OF THE ROUND TABLE (ACT I, SCENE 9 → ACT I, SCENE 10)		
FLY G - RED	Camelot Wheel ↓	
		Next move:
KNIGHTS OF THE ROUND TABLE → AT THE FEET OF GOD (ACT I, SCENE 10 → ACT I, SCENE 11)		
FLY H - RED	Camelot Wheel ↑	
		Next move:
INTERMISSION		
FLY AA - RED	U/S Blackout Drop ↓ Forest Drop U/S Blackout Drop ↑	
		Next move:
YOU WON'T SUCCEED ON BROADWAY (ACT II, SCENE 4)		
FLY CC - RED	Broadway Portal ↓	
		Next move:

Figure 9.4: Manual fly cues to begin dry tech/*Spamalot*

MANUAL FLY CUES TO BEGIN DRY TECH
SPAMALOT

CUE	PIECE	SPEED

YOU WON'T SUCCEED ON BROADWAY
(ACT II, SCENE 4)

FLY DD - WHITE	Star ↓	
		Next move:

YOU WON'T SUCCEED ON BROADWAY → FOREST
(ACT II, SCENE 4 → ACT II, SCENE 5)

FLY EE - BLUE	Star ↑	
FLY FF - AMBER	Broadway Portal ↑	
FLY HH- RED	Forest Drop ↑	
		Next move:

HERBERT'S BEDROOM → GREAT HALL
(ACT II, SCENE 6 → ACT II, SCENE 7)

FLY KK - RED	Prince Herbert Drop ↑	
	#5 Elec. ↑	
		Next move:

RIO
(ACT II, SCENE 6)

FLY LL - RED	#5 Electric ↓	
FLY LL - RED	#5 Electric ↑	
		Next move:

FINALE
(ACT II, SCENE 9)

FLY NN - RED	Wedding Hanger ↓	
		Next move:

FINALE
(ACT II, SCENE 9)

FLY PP - RED	Finale Hearts ↓	
FLY QQ - WHITE	Broadway Portal ↓	
	Wedding Hanger ↑	
	AutoFollow: Finale Hearts ↑	
FLY SS - RED	Broadway Portal ↓	

Figure 9.4: Manual fly cues to begin dry tech/*Spamalot*-continued

AUTO DECK CUES
TO BEGIN DRY TECH

AT HALF HOUR		
Preset	Winch 1	Dog Off SL
	Winch 2	Dog Off SR
	Winch 3	Dog Off SR Preset & Knifed w/Mud Castle
	Winch 4	
	Winch 5	
	Winch 6	Dog at Center (preset for Castle A)
	Winch 7	Dog DS Pre-Set & Knifed w/Castle A

Next move: **Approx. 2 min from Top of Show**

CUE	EFFECT	DIRECTION	WINCH	TARGET	SPEED

FINLAND → MUD CASTLE (ACT I SCENE 2 → ACT I SCENE 3)					
Winch 100	Finland Legs	IN		Deck	Fast drop to deck
Winch 101	Mud Castle	ON	3	Center	

Next move: **Approx. 4 min**

MUD CASTLE → PLAGUE VILLAGE (ACT I SCENE 3 → ACT I SCENE 4					
Winch 103	Mud Castle	Off SR	3	Off To Pre-Set	

Next move: **Approx. 4 min**

PLAGUE VILLAGE → MUD VILLAGE (ACT I SCENE 4 → ACT I SCENE 5)					
Winch 111	Castle A	DS	7	Track 6 Pos.	
	Reeds	ON (SR)	1	Full	
	Reeds	ON (SL)	2	Full	

Next move: **Approx. 1 min**

MUD VILLAGE (ACT I SCENE 5)					
Winch 115	Spin Turtle 90°	Under Unit			Called by Carp.
	Winch 7 Dog	US	7	Boat Position	

Next move: **Approx. 3 min**

MUD VILLAGE → LADY OF THE LAKE (ACT I SCENE 5 → ACT I SCENE 6)					
Winch 120	Hyd.Pump On				
Winch 121	Sunroof	OPEN			
	Castle A	OFF (SL)	6	Off Extreme L3	
Winch 122	Elevator	UP		Stage	

Next move: **Approx. 3 min**

Figure 9.5: PSM's auto deck cues to begin dry tech/*Spamalot*

CUE	EFFECT	DIRECTION	WINCH	TARGET	SPEED
LADY OF THE LAKE (ACT I SCENE 6)					
Winch 124	Boat	DS	7	Elevator	
Winch 124.5	Reeds	OFF (SL)	1	Off Int.	
	Reeds	OFF (SR)	2	Off Int.	
Winch 125	Winch 7 Dog	US	7	Extreme US	
Winch 126	Elevator	DOWN			
Winch 126.5	Sunroof	CLOSE			
Winch 127	Castle A	ON (SL)	6	Center	
	Reeds	OFF (SL)	1	Off Extreme	
	Reeds	OFF (SR)	2	Off Extreme	

Next move: **Approx. :30 sec**

CUE	EFFECT	DIRECTION	WINCH	TARGET	SPEED
LADY OF THE LAKE → WITCH VILLAGE (ACT I SCENE 6 → ACT I SCENE 7)					
Winch 128	Winch 7 Dog	DS	7	Winch 6 Pos.	Carp Called
Winch 128.5	Spin Turtle 90°	Under Unit			Carp Called

Next move: **Approx. 3 min**

CUE	EFFECT	DIRECTION	WINCH	TARGET	SPEED
WITCH VILLAGE (ACT I SCENE 7)					
Winch 129	Scales	ON (SR)	2		
Winch 129.5	Scales	OFF (SL)	2		
	Castle A	US	7		

Next move: **Approx. 13 min**

CUE	EFFECT	DIRECTION	WINCH	TARGET	SPEED
WITCH VILLAGE → KNIGHTS (ACT I SCENE 8 → ACT I SCENE 9)					
Winch 131	Castle A	US	7	Dock	Slow!
	Winch 1 Dog	Preset to L	1		
	Winch 2 Dog	Preset to R	2		

Next move: **Approx. 10 min**

CUE	EFFECT	DIRECTION	WINCH	TARGET	SPEED
GOD'S FEET (ACT I SCENE 11)					
Winch 131.5	SR Mountain	ON (preset)	1	Preset	Slow
	Winch 2 Dog	ON (preset)	2	Preset	Slow
Winch 132	Pump	ON			

Next move: **Approx. 1 min**

Figure 9.5: PSM's auto deck cues to begin dry tech/*Spamalot*-continued

CUE	EFFECT	DIRECTION	WINCH	TARGET	SPEED

GOD'S FEET → GRAIL
(ACT I SCENE 11 → ACT I SCENE 12)

CUE	EFFECT	DIRECTION	WINCH	TARGET	SPEED
Winch 133	Elevator (SR)	UP		Deck	
SM Call to Preset	SL Mountain	ON	2	Preset	
Winch 134	Elevator (SR)	DOWN			

Next move: **Approx. 1 min**

GRAIL
(ACT I SCENE 12)

CUE	EFFECT	DIRECTION	WINCH	TARGET	SPEED
Winch 135	SR Mountain	ON (SR)	1	SR of Center	
	SL Mountain	ON (SR)	2	SR of Center	
Winch 136	SR Mountain	BACK SL	1	Center	
Auto Follow	SL Mountain	BACK SL	2	Center	
Winch 137	Sunroof	OPEN			
Winch 138	Elevator	UP DECK		Deck	
Winch 139	Scissor Lift	UP			

Next move: **Approx. 1 min**

GRAIL → FRENCH CASTLE
(ACT I SCENE 12 → ACT I SCENE 13)

CUE	EFFECT	DIRECTION	WINCH	TARGET	SPEED
Winch 140	Scissor Lift	DOWN			
	Elevator	DOWN			
Winch 141	Sunroof	CLOSE			
Winch 142	SR Mountain	OFF (SR)	1	Off Extreme	
	SL Mountain	OFF (SL)	2	Off Extreme	
	Castle A	DS	7		
Winch 143	Winch 2 Dog	SR	2		

Next move: **Approx. 6 min**

FRENCH CASTLE
(ACT I SCENE 13)

CUE	EFFECT	DIRECTION	WINCH	TARGET	SPEED
Winch 150	Castle A turtle	Rotate CCW	7	180°	
Winch 151	Lamp post	ON (SL)	2		
Winch 152	Lamp post	OFF (SR)	2	Off Extreme	
Winch 153	Castle A	Rotate CW	7	180°	
Winch 154	Castle A	US	7	DS Intermediate	

Next move: **Approx. 2 min**

Figure 9.5: PSM's auto deck cues to begin dry tech/*Spamalot*-continued

INTERMISSION					
Preset	Winch 1 ON SL 15' with tree knifed				
	Winch 2 ON SR 15' with tree knifed				
	Winch 3 ON SR 12' with tree knifed				
	Winch 4 ON SL 12' with tree knifed				
	Winch 5 Dog Preset off SR				
	Winch 6 Dog Preset off SL				
	Winch 7 Castle A US, not docked				

Next move: **Approx. 9 min for Top of Act II**

CUE	EFFECT	DIRECTION	WINCH	TARGET	SPEED

Into: BRAVE SIR ROBIN
(ACT II SCENE 3)

CUE	EFFECT	DIRECTION	WINCH	TARGET	SPEED
Winch 200	Castle A	DS	7		

Next move: **Approx. 3 min**

End of: BLACK KNIGHT
(ACT II SCENE 3)

CUE	EFFECT	DIRECTION	WINCH	TARGET	SPEED
Winch 201	Castle A	US	7		

Next move: **Approx. 3 min**

Into: YOU WON'T SUCCEED ON BROADWAY
(ACT II SCENE 4)

CUE	EFFECT	DIRECTION	WINCH	TARGET	SPEED
Winch 222	Tree	OFF (SL)	1	Off Extreme	
	Tree	OFF (SR)	2	Off Extreme	
	Tree	OFF (SR)	3	Off Extreme	
	Tree	OFF (SL)	4	Off Extreme	

Next move: **Approx. 6 min**

THE FOREST (During Whatever Happened to My Part?)
(ACT II SCENE 5)

CUE	EFFECT	DIRECTION	WINCH	TARGET	SPEED
Winch 235	Castle A	DS	7		
	Castle A	Rotate CW	7	180°	
Winch 237	Castle A	DS	7		

Next move: **Approx. 1 min**

FOREST → PRINCE HERBERT'S CASTLE
(ACT II SCENE 5 → ACT II SCENE 6)

CUE	EFFECT	DIRECTION	WINCH	TARGET	SPEED
Winch 241	Footlights	UP			

Next move: **Approx. :30 sec**

Figure 9.5: PSM's auto deck cues to begin dry tech/*Spamalot*-continued

CUE	EFFECT	DIRECTION	WINCH	TARGET	SPEED
PRINCE HERBERT'S CASTLE (ACT II SCENE 6)					
Winch 242	Footlights	DOWN			
Winch 243	Footlights	UP			
Winch 244	Footlights	DOWN			
Winch 245	Footlights	UP			
Winch 246	Footlights	DOWN			
Winch 247	Footlights	UP			
Winch 248	Footlights	DOWN			
Winch 253	Castle A	Rotate CCW	7	180°	
Winch 253.5	Footlights	UP			
Winch 254	Castle A	US	7		
	Winch 2 Dog	To Preset	2		
	Winch 4 Dog	To Preset	4		

Next move: **Approx. 4 min**

Into: I'M ALL ALONE (ACT II SCENE 7)					
Winch 258	Castle A	DS	7		
	Castle A	Rotate CW	7	90°	
	Footlights	DOWN			
Winch 259	Castle A	US	7		
	Castle A	Rotate CCW	7	90°	

Next move: **Approx. 1 min**

Into: KILLER RABBIT (ACT II SCENE 8)					
Winch 260	Rabbit Mound	ON (SR)	4	Center	

Next move: **Approx. 4 min**

Into: HOLY GRAIL'S BEEN FOUND (ACT II SCENE 7)					
Winch 262	Rabbit Mound	OFF (SL)	4	Off Extreme	
	Castle A	US	7	Dock	

Next move: **Approx. 4 min**

Into: FINALE					
Winch 270	Castle A	DS	7		

Figure 9.5: PSM's auto deck cues to begin dry tech/*Spamalot*-continued

Annie

Dry Tech Goals

MONDAY, SEPT. 10	Top of Show thru I-4 Newsreel w/Laundry Moves Orphanage Bedroom Lower East Side ("Tomorrow")
TUESDAY, SEPT. 11	I-4 thru I-7 Hannigan's Office Bergdorf's Warbucks' Mansion "NYC"
WEDNESDAY, SEPT. 12	I-7 thru II-2 Hannigan's Office ("Easy Street") Car & Car Exit Warbucks Office Intermission Change
THURSDAY, SEPT. 13	II-1 thru II-4 NBC & Hannigan's Office ("Fully Dressed") Newsreel to White House White House Warbucks' Office
FRIDAY, SEPT. 14	II-4 thru II-6 Warbucks' Office Warbucks' Mansion Christmas
SATURDAY, SEPT. 15	Hold to Complete Dry Tech if Needed

Dry Tech hours at the theatre will be 2:30 p.m. to 5:00 p.m. and 6:00 p.m. to 10:00 p.m. with a dinner break from 5:00 p.m. to 6:00 p.m.

Figure 9.6: Dry tech goals/2012 *Annie* revival

Tech Notes to Actors

1. Computer & Printer in Production Office
2. Valuables at half-hour.
3. If anyone needs a new script or new pages, please ask me.
4. As in rehearsal, Pam is stage right. Amanda is stage left.
5. Pam & Amanda will work out off-stage traffic.
6. Off-stage masking is still to come. Legs in #3 are all we currently have.
7. Use hallway cross-over—no onstage cross-over.
8. We're trying to have all QCs in hallways.
9. Please don't give notes to the crew—give to SM.
10. No food or liquid onstage, except water.
11. Nothing will ever move unless you see it move first.
12. Once we've set a move, please keep your timing the same. We'll assume all is well unless you point out a problem.
13. When we get to a move:
    a. We'll stop the rehearsal
    b. Move cast downstage or into the house.
    c. Move set in worklight with no actors onstage.
    d. If you're satisfied, we'll put you onstage & move set in worklight again.
    e. If satisfied, we'll move the set in stage light.
    f. We'll move in any condition as often as you need to feel safe.
14. Rovers & Shinbusters won't change positions unless we rehearse them.
    a. If you need an SM flashlight for any entrance or exit, just ask for it.
15. Wardrobe
    a. As you know, we are teching in wardrobe
    b. Please no eating or drinking in wardrobe
    c. Try not to sit around in theatre seats in wardrobe.
    d. Work out QCs as we go.
    e. No open-toed shoes onstage—if you don't have wardrobe shoes.

Mic Demo

Figure 9.7: Notes to actors/tech day one/small show

Tech Rehearsal Goals
2012 *Annie* Revival

Cast Call: 1:00 p.m. to 9:30 p.m.

MONDAY, SEPT. 17	Newsreel	
	1st Orphanage	Maybe / HKL / Bundles
		HKL Reprise
	Lower East Side	Tomorrow / Lt. Ward
TUESDAY, SEPT. 18	Lower East Side	Tomorrow / Lt. Ward
	Hooverville	
	Into 2nd Orphange	Little Girls / Lt. Ward
		Grace's 1st Visit
WEDNESDAY, SEPT. 19	2nd Orphanage	Little Girls / Lt. Ward
		Grace's 1st Visit
	Bergdorf	
THURSDAY, SEPT. 20	1st Warbucks	Gonna Like It Here
		Warbucks is Home
	NYC	NYC
FRIDAY, SEPT. 21	NYC	NYC
	2nd Orphanage	Grace's 2nd Visit
		Easy Street
SATURDAY, SEPT. 22	1 – 5:30	Work-Thru 1st Act
	7 – 9:30	NYC into 3rd Orphanage
SUNDAY, SEPT. 23	Day Off	
MONDAY, SEPT. 24	1:00 – 5:30	3rd Orphange – Easy Street
		2nd Mansion – Won't Be Orphan
	7:00 – 9:30	NBC Maybe Reprise
		Fully Dressed
TUESDAY, SEPT. 25	Newsreel	
	White House	Tomorrow Reprise w/Annie
		Tomorrow Reprise w/Cabinet
	3rd Warbucks	Something Was Missing
		Wants to Adopt Annie
		Anything But You

Figure 9.8: Tech rehearsal goals/2012 *Annie* revival

Tech Rehearsal Goals
2012 *Annie* Revival

Cast Call: Begin 10 out of 12 Days – 12:30 p.m. to midnight

WEDNESDAY, SEPT. 26	3rd Warbucks	Mudge's Visit to End of Show
THURSDAY, SEPT. 27	1:00 p.m.	Sitzprobe
	7:00 p.m.	Half-Hour Call
	7:30 p.m.	Work-Thru Show
FRIDAY, SEPT. 28	1:00 p.m.	Half-Hour Call
	1:30 p.m.	Piano Dress
	7:00 p.m.	Piano Dress
SATURDAY, SEPT. 29	1:00 p.m.	Half-Hour Call
	1:30 p.m.	Orchestra Tech
	7:00 p.m.	Half-Hour Call
	7:30 p.m.	Orchestra Tech
SUNDAY, SEPT. 30	POSSIBLE DAY OFF – Please Hold This Day	
MONDAY, OCT. 1	1:00 p.m.	Rehearse as Needed
	7:00 p.m.	Half-Hour Call
	7:30 p.m.	Orchestra Dress
TUESDAY, OCT. 2	1:00 p.m.	Half-Hour Call
	1:30 p.m.	Orchestra Dress with Photos
	7:00 p.m.	Half-Hour Call
	7:30 p.m.	Orchestra Dress with Photos (Invited Dress?)
WEDNESDAY, OCT. 3	1:00 p.m.	Rehearse as Needed
	7:30 p.m.	Half-Hour Call
	8:00 p.m.	Preview #1

Figure 9.8: Tech rehearsal goals/2012 *Annie* revival-continued

Calling Script for *Annie*

MAN 2

(Reading from newspaper)
> Hey, listen to this...

(General crowd noise)

#7 – Hooverville (2:53)

MAN 2 (Cont'd)

> "Former President Herbert Hoover said today in an interview 'Though I was in no way personally responsible for the 1929 stock-market crash...

(CROWD groans)

> I have the deepest sympathy for the millions of Americans who are now ragged, hungry and homeless.'"

MAN 1

(Raising HIS hand)
> Ragged!

WOMAN 3 & WOMAN 4

(Raising hands)
> Hungry!

MAN 3 & All

(Raising hands)
Homeless!   Cond. Punch-In   Elec. #171

Figure 10.1: Calling script/2012 *Annie* revival/example

ALL
TODAY WE'RE LIVING IN A XX SHANTY   Elec. #171.5
TODAY WE'RE SCROUNGING FOR A MEAL   Elec. #172

SOPHIE
TODAY I'M STEALING COAL FOR FIRES.
WHO KNEW I COULD STEAL - 2 – 3 – 4 – 1   Elec. #173

MEN
I USED TO WINTER IN THE TROPICS   Elec. #174

WOMEN
I SPENT MY SUMMERS AT THE SHORE.

MAN (W/ PAPERS)
I USED TO THROW AWAY THE PAPERS -

ALL
HE DON'T AN Y MORE- 2 – 3 – 4 – 1   Elec. #175

(MAN 2 stuffs newspapers under his coat. ALL sing sarcastically)

WE'D LIKE TO THANK YOU, HERBERT HOOVER
FOR REALLY SHOWING US THE WAY
WE'D LIKE TO THANK YOU, HERBERT HOOVER
YOU MADE US WHAT WE ARE TODAY.
PROSPERITY WAS 'ROUND THE COR NER   Elec. #176
A COZY COTTAGE BUILT FOR TWO
IN THIS BLUE HEAVEN THAT YOU GAVE US
YES! WE'RE TURNING BLUE – 2 – 3 – 4 – 1

THEY OFFERED US AL SMITH AND HOOVER
WE PAID ATTENTION AND WE CHOSE   Elec. #177
NOT ONLY DID WE PAY ATTENTION
WE PAID THROUGH THE NOSE – 2 – 3 – 4 – 1   Elec. #178

SOPHIE
IN EV'RY POT HE SAID "A CHICKEN"

ALL
BUT HERBERT HOOVER HE FORGOT   Elec. #179
NOT ONLY DON'T WE HAVE THE CHICKEN

ANNIE
YOU AIN'T GOT THE POT!

ALL
HEY HER BIE ,   Elec. #180

Figure 10.1: Calling script/2012 *Annie* revival/example-continued

24.

WOMEN (1) YOU LEFT BEHIND A GRATEFUL NATION	MEN GROUP (2) GRATEFUL NATION

WOMEN GROUP (4)
HERB, OUT HATS ARE OFF.

MEN GROUP (3)
SO HERB, OUR HATS
ARE OFF TO YOU.

Warn:	ADeck	#224 - Red
		225 - Blue
		226 - Green
		226.5 - Yel
	AFly	#520 - Red
		521 - Blue
	Fly K - Red	

ALL (CONT'D)
WE'RE UP TO HERE WITH ADMIRATION

ANNIE
YOU THINK HE'D LIKE A LITTLE STEW?

WOMEN
COME DOWN AND SHARE SOME CHRISTMAS DINNER,

MEN
HO, HO, HO.

WOMEN
BE SURE TO BRING THIS MISSUS TOO,

MEN
BRING THE MISSUS TOO.

ALL
WE GOT NO TURKEY FOR OUR STUFFIN'.
WHY DON'T WE STUFF YOU?   Elec. #181
_____

WE'D LIKE TO THANK YOU, HERBERT HOOVER   Elec. #182
FOR REALLY SHOWING US THE WAY.
YOU DIRTY RAT,
YOU BUREAUCRAT,
YOU MADE US WHAT WE ARE TODAY   Elec. #183
– 2 – 3 – 4 – 5 – 6 – 7 – 8
1 – 2 – 3 – 4
COME AND GET IT, HERB !   Elec. #184

Cond. Downbeat   Elec. #185
_____
                                          ADeck #224 – Red   R&L Lads ↑

MAN 3 (GAVIN)
Sshhh.

WOMAN 3 (JANE)
(Scared)
   'Evening.

LT. WARD
Yeah, evening. All right. Move along, all you bums outta here.

Figure 10.1: Calling script/2012 *Annie* revival/example-continued

ANNIE

They're not bums!

LT. WARD

We're tearing down this junk pile, now.

	w/ Conductor	Elec. #186
1 - 2 - 3 - 4	Now!	
2 - 2 - 3 - 4		
3 - 2 - 3 - 4 - 5 - 6 - 7 - XX	Sandy Off	Elec. #186.5
1 - 2 - 3 - 4 - 5 - 6 - 7 - 8		
XX - 2 - 3 - 4 - 5 - 6 - 7 - 8	Annie Moves	Elec. #187
		ADeck #225 – Blue H-Ville OFF
		AFly #520 - Red Q-Boro ↑
1 – 2 – 3 – 4 – 5 – 6 – 7		
1 – 2 – 3 – 4 – 5 – 6 – 7		
1 – 2 – 3 – 4 – XX – 6 – 7		Elec. #188
2 – 2 – 3 – 4 – 5 – 6 – 7		
XX – 2 – 3 – 4 – 5 – 6 – 7 – 8		ADeck #226 – Gn. Orph ON/Open
		AFly#521 – Blue Lndry 1&2 ↓
1 – 2 – 3 – 4 – 5 – 6 – 7 – 8		
2 – 2 – 3 – 4 – 5 – 6 – 7 – 8		Elec. #189
	"Clear"	ADeck #226.5 - Yel LES1 ↓
		R Lad ↓

LIGHTS ONLY

1 – 2 – 3 – 4 – 5 – 6 – 7 – 8		Warn: ADeck #227 - Red
1 – 2 – 3 – 4 – 5 – 6 – 7 – 8	*It's the Hard Knock Life*	228 - Blue
1 – 2 – 3 – 4 – 5 – 6 – 7 – 8	*It's the HKL/Stab Her with a Safety Pin*	229 - Gn.
1 – 2 – 3 – 4 – 5 – 6 – 7 – 8	*No One Cares for You A* Smidge	ADeck #227 – Red LES 1,2,3 ON
		Desk ON
1 – 2 – 3 – 4 – 5 – 6 – 7 – 8	*When You're in an* (Whistle)	Elec. #190
	Wall Clear of Light	Fly K – Blue Office Lt ↓
	Door Opens	Elec. #191
	Hannigan Speaks	ADeck #228 – Blue MouseOn
	Girls Clear of Mouse	ADeck #229 – Gn MouseOff

Scene 4 (10:25)
#9 - Little Girls

MISS HANNIGAN

All right. That's all the fresh air you're gettin' for the month.

Figure 10.1: Calling script/2012 *Annie* revival/example-continued

Dance Calling Script

SCENE THREE:	The Best Damn Town
Music No 11:	"SAN DIEGO" (6:38)

	1st Native Entrance - Ahhhhhs		

HORN 1 – 2 &a3

Count			
1 – 2 – 3 – 4 – 5 – 6 – 7 – 8		Principals Exit/Table & Chairs Off Rt	
2 – 2 – 3 – 4 – 5 – 6 – 7 – 8		" "	
3 – 2 – 3 – 4 – 5 – 6 – 7 – 8		IntroSingers Enter R & L	
4 – 2 – 3 – 4 – 5 – 6 – 7 – 8		IntroSingers Enter R & L	
5 – 2 – 3 – 4 – 5 – 6 – 7 – 8			
1 – 2 – 3 – 4 – 5 – 6 – 7 – 8	Aah	Boys Slide Ent. DS/Reach Kick	
2 – 2 – 3 – 4 – 5 – 6 – 7 – 8	Aah	Attitude/Attitude	
3 – 2 – 3 – 4 – 5 – 6 – 7 – 8		Boys & Girls in 1 line	
4 – 2 – 3 – 4 – 5 – 6 – 7 – 8		Girls roll over Boys' back	
5 – 2 – 3 – 4 – 5 – 6 – 7 – 8	Aah	1st Group Lift	
6 – 2 – 3 – 4 – 5 – 6 – 7 – 8	Aah	All travel to Center	
7 – 2 – 3 – 4 – 5 – 6 – 7 – 8	Aah	Boy leader lift	
8 – 2 – 3 – 4 – 5 – 6 – 7 – 8	Aah	Girls circle Lift	
9 – 2 – 3 – 4 – 5 – 6 – 7 – X	Aah	Boy lowers/Reveal Dance #1	Elec. #122

SAN DIEGO!
HELLUVA TOWN
WHERE THE NAVY'S AT ANCHOR
AND THE LOCALS HAVE NO RANCOR
'CAUSE THE BREEZES MAKE YOU HANKER

X – 3 – 4 – 5 – 6 – 7 – 8	Dancer #2 taps #3	Elec. #123
2 – 2 – 3 – 4 – 5 – 6 – 7	Point SR	

SAN DIEGO – SAN DIEGO
HELLUVA TOWN
WHERE YOU BASK IN THE SUNSHINE
AND DRINK ALL THAT GREAT WINE
MAKES THE LIVING JUST SO FINE

2 – 3 – 4 – 5 – 6 – 7 – 8	
1 – 2 – 3 – 4 – 5 – 6 – 7 – 8	Dancer #2 taps #4/Points SL

AT NIGHT THE MOON ON THE OCEAN
LIGHTS THE LOVERS IN MOTION
AND THE WAVES BLEND WITH THEIR SIGHS.

2 – 3 – 4 – 5 – 6 – 7 – 8	
1 – 2 – 3 – 4 – 5 – 6 – 7	Dancer #2 falls

SAN DIEGO
HELLUVA TOWN
WHERE THE FOOD IS DELICIOUS
AND THE GIRLS ARE CAPRICIOUS
BUT NEVER PERNICIOUS

2 – 3 – 4 – 5 – 6 – 7 – 8	
1 – 2 – 3 – 4 – 5 – 6 – 7	Dancer #2/#5 to Pineapple

AS THEY SWING AND THEY SWAY
BY THE TWINKLING LIGHTS OF THE BAY

Figure 10.2: Dance calling script/example

AND THEY WHISPER I MAY
AND SO DO I.

2 – 3 – 4 – 5 – 6 – 7 – 8		
1 – 2 – 3 – 4 – 5 – 6 – 7 – 8		
2 – 2 – 3 – 4 – 5 – 6 – X		Elec. #124

Ballet – 1st Raid

X – 2 – 3 – 4 – 5 – 6 – 7 – 8	Dancers Enter R & L	Elec. #125
2 – 2 – 3 – 4 – 5 – 6 – 7 – 8	Kick/Jump/HA!	
3 – 2 – 3 – 4 – 5 – 6 – X – 8	Singers exit R & L/Villagers thrown R & L	Elec. #126
4 – 2 – 3 – 4 – 5 – 6 – 7 – 8	" " "/Triplet/Chicken Dance	
5 – 2 – 3 – 4 – 5 – 6 – 7 – 8	Tug of War/Bag tossed	
6 – 2 – 3 – 4 – 5 – 6 – 7 – 8	Handbag/Steal/Steal/Steal	
7 – 2 – 3 – 4 – 5 – 6 – 7 – 8	1st Parade w/Purse to SL	
8 – 2 – 3 – 4 – 5 – 6 – 7 – 8	Bag Toss/Toss/Toss/Toss – Exit R1	
9 – 2 – 3 – 4 – 5 – 6 – 7 – 8		
10 – 2 – 3 – 4 – 5 – 6 – 7 – X		Elec. #127

Pas De Quatre – 1st Tango

HOLD		
7 – X		Elec. #128
1 – 2 – 3 – 4 – 5 – 6 – 7 – 8	Dancer #6/#7 Flip from Rt/Leap	
2 – 2 – 3 – 4 – 5 – 6 – 7 – 8		**Warn: End of Act 1**
3 – 2 – 3 – 4 – 5 – 6 – 7 – 8	Lift Girl/Pendulum Lift	
4 – 2 – 3 – 4 – 5 – 6 – 7 – 8	Dancer #8 under girl lift/Christ Lift	
5 – 2 – 3 – 4 – 5 – 6 – 7 – 8	Girl on Dancer #6 shoulder/Back flip out	
6 – 2 – 3 – 4 – 5 – 6 – 7 – 8	Death Drop forward/Backward	
7 – 2 – 3 – 4 – 5 – 6 – 7 – 8	Girl dives onto Dancer #6 shoulder	
8 – 2 – 3 – 4 – 5 – 6 – 7 – 8	Girl side flick/Repeat	
9 – 2 – 3 – 4 – 5 – 6 – 7 – X	Flip Girl to Arabesque/Drag Rt	Elec. #129

2nd Raid

1 – 2 – 3 – 4 – 5 – 6 – 7 – 8	Singers enter from SR to SL – Crazy Cross	
2 – 2 – 3 – 4 – 5 – 6 – 7 – X	Villagers Freeze to Center	Elec. #130
3 – 2 – 3 – 4 – 5 – 6 – 7 – 8	Tug L & R of Villagers/Singers Exit R & L	
4 – 2 – 3 – 4 – 5 – 6 – 7 – 8	Butt Dance	
5 – 2 – 3 – 4 – 5 – 6 – 7 – 8	Scarf around neck/Conga Line	
6 – 2 – 3 – 4 – 5 – 6 – 7 – X	Conga Line off Rt w/DL chasing	Elec. #131

Pas De Deux

1 – 2 – 3 – 4 /– 5 – 6 – 7 – 8	Intro – #6 enter SR/#1 lifts head	
2 – 2 – 3 – 4 /– 5 – 6 – 7 – 8	Intro – #6 lifts Girl	
3 – 2 – 3 – 4 – 5 – 6 – 7 – 8	Girl runs/#6 stops	
4 – 2 – 3 – 4 – 5 – 6 – 7 – 8	Tango Pulse/#6 approaches girl	
5 – 2 – 3 – 4 – 5 – 6 – X – 8	#6 touches Girl	Elec. #132
1 – 2 – 3 – 4 – 5 – 6 – 7 – 8	Embrace	
2 – 2 – 3 – 4 – 5 – 6 – 7 – 8	Drop	
3 – 2 – 3 – 4 – 5 – 6 – 7 – 8	Attitude Turn/Promenade	
4 – 2 – 3 – 4 – 5 – 6 – 7 – 8	Hold	
5 – 2 – 3 – 4 – 5 – 6 – 7 – 8	Swoop	

Figure 10.2: Dance calling script/example-continued

6 – 2 – 3 – 4 – 5 – 6 – 7 – [X]	Lift	Elec. #133
[7] – 2 – [3 – 4] – 5 – 6 – 7 – 8	Kick/Drop	
8 – 2 – 3 – 4 – 5 – 6 – 7 – 8	Roll across back	
9 – 2 – 3 – 4 – [5] – 6 – 7 – [X]	Both move SR/Tourjette	Elec. #134
[10] – 2 – 3 – 4 – [5] – 6 – 7 – 8	Lift/Girl Spin	
[11] – 2 – 3 – 4 – [5] – 6 – 7 – 8	Lift/Girl Spin	
12 – 2 – 3 – 4 – [5 – 6 – 7 – 8]	Drag SR on Man's back	
13 – 2 – [3 – 4 – 5 – 6 – 7 – 8]	Girl falls back	
[14] – 2 – 3 – 4 – 5 – 6 – 7 – 8	Girl jump wrap	
[15] – 2 – 3 – 4 – [X] – 6	Bird Lift	Elec. #135

Fight		
2 – 2 – 3 – 4 – 5 – 6	Intro/#8/#7/#6 flip from Left	
5 – 6 – 7 – 8		**Warn: House Curtain**
[3] – 2 – 3 – 4 – 5 – 6 – 7 – 8	Running Legs	
[4] – 2 – [3] – 4 – [5 – 6 – 7 – 8]	Pull/Pull/#8&#6 Flip	
5 – 2 – 3 – 4 – [5 – 6 – 7 – 8]	#4 over #6, Forward roll	
6 – 2 – [3 – 4] – [5] – 6 – [7 – 8 – 9 – 10]	#8,#6 Bump/#6 Flip/#9 Aerial	
[7] – 2 – 3 – 4 – 5 – 6 – [7 – 8]	Girl Tug/Fireman's Lift	
8 – 2 – 3 – 4 – 5 – 6	#1 to DSL	
9 – 2 – 3 – [4 – 5] – 6 – 7 – 8	Punch & Flip	
10 – 2 – 3 – 4 – 5 – 6 – 7 – 8	Man runs SL	
1 – 2/3		
Held Horn Note	#6 above head into 1R	

Wedding Procession – Jordan/Ashley @C		
[X] – 2 – 3 – 4 – 5 – 6 – 7 – 8	Embrace	Elec. #138
2 – 2 – 3 – 4 – 5 – 6 – 7 – 8	Ensemble enter R & L	
3 – 2 – 3 – 4 – 5 – 6 – 7 – 8	Form Tableau	
4 – 2 – 3 – 4 – 5 – 6 – 7 – 8	#1 receives engagement	
5 – 2 – 3 – 4 – [5] – 6 – [7 – 8]	#1 lift/Embrace	
Where the nuts come from.		
1 and a [X]	Pose	Elec. #139
		Hse Curt ↓
Curtain Hits Deck		Elec. #140
		House ↑
		Works ↑

Figure 10.2: Dance calling script/example-continued

DAILY PERFORMANCE REPORT

Name of Show

Name of Theatre: Date:

City: Perf. #

	Up	Down	Time
Act 1	8:08	9:14	1:06:33
Intermission			:15
Act 2	9:29	10:30	1:00:55
Playing Time			2:07:28
Running Time			2:22:28

Calling SM	XXXX
SM Track 1	XXXX
SM Track 2	XXXX
Mix	XXXX
Observing	XXXX
Conductor	XXXX

NAME	ON	ROLE	REASON
XXXX	XXXX	XXXX	Swing out - Do Not Dock

INJURY

Actor	Repetitive Stress on back

OVERTIME

2Hrs	Actor - MakeUp
1Hr	Actor - MakeUp

TODAY'S REHEARSAL CALL

Onstage:
1:00–3:00   Choreo rehearsal w/ xxxxxxx & SM
Lower Lobby:
3:30–5:30   Music Brush Up rehearsal w/ Actor, Ensemble and Swings w/ MD

LATE

Actor	20min to rehearsal - had to be called. Misread the call

NOTES

Repeated CO_2 leakage during xxxxx number, and a long CO_2 leakage from the onstage tanks just after the curtain fell. Also, the Hair room is complaining of the room filling w/ fog.

The tilt in the winched flower is broken and will be fixed before tomorrow's performance.

An inspired show – especially from xxxxx & xxxxx. Cheering, screaming standing ovation at curtain call.

Swing had a very solid show in xxxxx's track.

Figure 13.1: Daily performance report/example

STAGE MANAGER'S WEEKLY REPORT

Name of Show

Theatre — City   Dates (Month, Day thru Month, Day)

Performances #

ATTENDANCE			
DAY/DATE	**OUT**	**REASON**	**ON**
Tues, Jan. 27	XXXX	Personal Day	XXXX
	XXXX	Vacation	XXXX
	XXXX	Vacation	XXXX
Wed Mat, Jan. 28	XXXX	Vacation	XXXX
	XXXX	Swung Out - Do Not Dock	XXXX
	XXXX	Vacation	XXXX
Wed Eve, Jan. 28	XXXX	Vacation	XXXX
	XXXX	Vacation	XXXX - PSM XXXX - 1st XXXX
Thurs, Jan. 29	XXXX	Vacation	XXXX
	XXXX	Vacation	XXXX - PSM XXXX - 1st XXXX
	XXXX	Vacation	XXXX
Fri, Jan. 30	XXXX	Vacation	XXXX
	XXXX	Ill	XXXX
	XXXX	Ill	XXXX
			XXXX
	XXXX	Vacation	XXXX
	XXXX	Vacation	XXXX - PSM XXXX - 1st XXXX
	XXXX	Vacation	XXXX
Sat Mat, Jan. 31	XXXX	Vacation	XXXX
	XXXX	Ill	XXXX
	XXXX	Ill	XXXX
	XXXX	Ill	XXXX
Sat Mat, Jan. 31	XXXX	Vacation	XXXX - PSM XXXX - 1st XXXX

Figure 13.2: Stage manager's weekly report/example

STAGE MANAGER'S WEEKLY REPORT

Name of Show

Theatre — City

DAY/DATE	OUT	REASON	ON
	XXXX	Vacation	XXXX
Sat Eve, Jan. 31	XXXX	Vacation	XXXX
	XXXX	Ill	XXXX XXXX
	XXXX	Ill	XXXX
	XXXX	Ill	XXXX
	XXXX	Vacation	XXXX
	XXXX	Vacation	XXXX - PSM XXXX - 1st XXXX
Sun, Feb. 1	XXXX	Vacation	XXXX
	XXXX	Ill	XXXX
	XXXX	Ill	XXXX
	XXXX	Vacation	XXXX - PSM XXXX - 1st XXXX
	XXXX	Vacation	XXXX

LATE			
DAY/DATE	NAME	COMMENT	
Wed, Jan 28	XXXX	5 min late to ½ Hr.	Called
Sat, Jan 31	XXXX	5 min late to ½ Hr.	No Call

ACCIDENTS			
DAY/DATE	NAME	DESCRIPTION	C-2 FILED?
Sat, Jan 31	XXXX	Tweaked right knee during Morning Person	Yes

CONDUCTOR	
DAY/DATE	WHO?
Tues, Jan. 27 (1 perf)	XXXX
Wed, Jan. 28 (1 perf)	XXXX
Wed, Jan. 28–Sun, Feb 1 (6 perfs)	XXXX

Figure 13.2: Stage manager's weekly report/example-continued

STAGE MANAGER'S WEEKLY REPORT

Name of Show

Theatre — City

REHEARSAL CALL

DAY/DATE	TIME	SCENE/SONG	WHO?
Wed, Jan 28	1:00 to 1:30	Bunny Ears	XXXX
Wed, Jan 28	7:00 to 7:30	Bunny Ears	XXXX
Thurs, Jan. 29	1:00 to 5:00	Photo Documentation	XXXX
Thurs, Jan 29	7:00 to 7:30	Bunny Ears	XXXX
Fri, Jan. 30	1:00 to 5:00	Photo Documentation	XXXX
Fri. Jan. 30	4:00 to 6:00	Dance Rehearsal	XXXX
Sat. Jan. 31	7:00 to 7:30	Bunny Ears	XXXX

CREW CALLS

Tues, Jan 27	1:00–5:00	DC Podcast Interview	House Elec.
Wed, Jan. 28	8–12 Noon	Regular Work Call	Full Show Crew
Thurs, Jan. 29	10:30–12 Noon	Photo Doc Call	(2)Pink / (2)Local Prop House Elec. + 1
Thurs, Jan. 29	1:00–5:00	Photo Doc	(2)Pink / (2)Local Prop House Elec. + 1
Fri, Jan. 30	1:00–5:00	Photo Doc	(2)Pink / (2)Local Prop House Elec. + 1

OVERTIME

DAY/DATE	NAME	# HOURS
Tues	XXXX – Makeup	2
	XXXXXXX	1
Wed Mat	XXXX – Makeup	2
	XXXX & XXXX	1
Wed Eve	XXXX & XXXX	1
Thurs	XXXX – Makeup	2
	XXXX & XXXX	1
Fri	XXXX – Makeup	2
	XXXX & XXXX	1
Sat Mat	XXXX – Makeup	2
	XXXX & XXXX	1
Sat Eve	XXXX & XXXX	1
Sun	XXXX – Makeup	2
	XXXX & XXXX	1

Figure 13.2: Stage manager's weekly report/example-continued

STAGE MANAGER'S WEEKLY REPORT

Name of Show

Theatre — City

PRESS		
DAY/DATE	**NAME**	**DESCRIPTION**
Tues, Jan 27	DC Theatre Scene Podcast interview	XXXX in Dressing Room
Wed, Jan 28	TheatreMania.com Interview	XXXX in Dressing Room
Thurs, Jan 29	Food Network Contestants watched show	Filmed arrival and departure
Fri, Jan 30	Food Network Interviews	XXXX in Mezzanine level

TECHNICAL NOTES
Tues, Jan 27 – Switched XXXX movements over to XXXX. Going very well.
Wed, Jan 28 – Began switching XXXXX movements over to XXXX. We have switched the XXXXX Arrival and the Arrival to XXXX ear movements over as of Saturday. We will continue to rehearse the remaining moves next week.
Fri, Jan 30 – XXXXXX prop broke on the button of 'XXXXX. A screw came loose and wardrobe repaired by the next show.
Sat, Jan 31 – XXXXXX went out a cue early during Act I. Operator advanced a cue instead of hitting go. Then hit go when trying to go back.
XXXX trained on XXXX Auto Fly track from Tuesday to Saturday night. On Sunday, he decided that he needs to learn the track at a slower pace. He has spoken with XXXX.
Sun, Feb 1 – At 5 minute call, one of the sound computers crashed. Sound identified the problem and will fix at a work call on Tuesday.

MANAGEMENT NOTES	
Wed Eve, Jan 28	Lots of company concern about switching over the XXXXX. XXXX came by to talk to everyone and by the end of the week, the company seems in better spirits about it.
Sat Mat, Jan. 31	Company complaints of coldness. The garage door wasn't overhauled. Quickly corrected and SMs will now check pre-show.

GENERAL NOTES
Cold and sickness going around the company! Lots of outs this week and lots of people pushing through and fighting on coming colds. All 4 swings on for 2 performances this week and fantastic jobs by all!
Prop replacements are going in at a slow pace. Seems to make the cast more comfortable with it. We are really taking the time to rehearse the moves with all prop crew.
XXXX in all week and did a fantastic job! Fully trained on both SM deck tracks. The company was thrilled to see him.
A great week all in all.

Figure 13.2: Stage manager's weekly report/example-continued

Name of Show
Weekly Schedule

Month, Day thru Month, Day

MONDAY, FEBRUARY 16			DARK	

TUESDAY, FEBRUARY 17

Press: "The View"   *8:00 a.m. Cast Call/11:53 a.m. On Air*

7:00 p.m. Performance #74	Out:	XXXX	On:	XXXX
		XXXX		XXXX

WEDNESDAY, FEBRUARY 18

Crew Call
8:00 a.m.-12 Noon   Work Call   Full Show Crew

2:00 p.m. Performance #75	Out:	XXXX	On:	XXXX
		XXXX		XXXX
8:00 p.m. Performance #76	Out:	XXXX	On:	XXXX
		XXXX		XXXX

THURSDAY, FEBRUARY 19

Rehearsal Call   *Crew Call*
1:00–5:00 Understudy Rehearsal   1:00–5:00 Props (2)
Identify each Actor

8:00 p.m. Performance #77	Out:	XXXX	On:	XXXX
		XXXX		XXXX

FRIDAY, FEBRUARY 20
8:00 p.m. Performance #78   *Talk-Back:*   *Group from Indianapolis*

SATURDAY, FEBRUARY 21
2:00 p.m. Performance #79   LOA: XXXX (until 8/30/09)   Sub: XXXX

8:00 p.m. Performance #80

SUNDAY, FEBRUARY 22

3:00 p.m. Performance #81	Out:	XXXX	On:	XXXX
		XXXX		XXXX

Vacations:	Out:	On:
	XXXX	XXXX

Personal Days:	Out:	On:
Tues & Wed	XXXX	XXXX
	XXXX	XXXX
Thursday	XXXX	XXXX
		XXXX
	XXXX	XXXX
Sunday	XXXX	XXXX
	XXXX	XXXX

Figure 13.3: Weekly schedule/example

Cast History

Full Name	Social Security #
	xxx-xx-xxxx
Telephone	Date of Birth
xxx.xxx.xxxx	
Email	Address

Emergency Contact

Medical Information

First Rehearsal:
First Performance:

Costume Fittings

Pre-rehearsal	10 minutes	Measurements @ xxx
Pre-rehearsal	20 minutes	Wig Measurements @Marquis Theatre
9/15/09	2 hours	Fitting @ xxx (5:00pm–7:00pm)
9/18/09	1 hour	Fitting @ xxx (5:30pm–6:30pm)
10/8/09	30 minutes	Fitting @ xxx (6:00pm–6:30pm)

Injury

12/17/09	Hurt L. Knee & Rt. Wrist in collision w/ xxx in basement. He was late for an entrance.

Lateness

9/27/09	35 minutes late (called—train problems)
12/27/09 Eve	8 min. late to ½ Hr. (called—traffic)

Illness

Vacation

Personal Days

10/10/09	Out—bereavement

Violations

On For

Other

12-09-09	Swung Out

Figure 13.4: Cast history/example

Commercial Shoot Schedule

Day 1 - Monday, March 16

CAST MAKEUP CALLS for Monday, March 29

12 Noon	Princ 5, Princ 4, Ens 1, Ens 2, Ens 3, Ens 4
1:00 p.m.	Princ 1, Full Ensemble
3:30 p.m.	Princ 3
5:00 p.m.	All 3 Princ 2s

Time	Shot	Scene/Song	What	Who	Time
Set to Scene A (ADeck 320/AFly 17/Fly D/Elec.86)	Re-light		Ensemble into Ens 4, Ens 1		15 min
1:00 p.m.	1 Mic-PRINC 5, Ens 3,Ens 2 Princ 4 1a 1b	Scene A	Top of Scene thru "Check This Out" which includes: Ens 1, Ens 3 Ens 3 on Guerney – "Who are you?" "This is your wife"	PRINC 5, Ens 4, Mirror	45 min
1:45 p.m.	Set to Scene B (ADeck 420/AFly 26/Fly J1/ Elec.86)		Re-light	Ens 4, Ens 1, Ens 3 PRINC 5 into Duloc	15 min
2:00 p.m.	2 3 4	Scene B	Entire Number X3 Pick-ups within number SteadiCam PRINC 5 shots	PRINC 5 & Full Ensemble PRINC 5 & Full Ensemble PRINC 5 & Full Ensemble	90 min
3:30 p.m.	Change Set to Scene C (ADeck #170/AFly#13/Fly A/Elec.14)			Into Dragonettes, Skeletons	15 min
3:45 p.m.	5 6 7 8	Scene C Mic - Princ 1 Princ 1 w/ Rabbit End of Number	Woods "Look Out" Sign	Princ 1 Princ 1 Princ 1 Princ 1	30 min
4:15 p.m.	Change Set to Scene D (ADeck 525/AFly 32/ Fly Q/Elec.191)				15 min
4:30 p.m.	9 10	Princ 3 Hawaii Mic - Princ 3	"Hula with Me…" Button of # (Hawaii @C.stage) w/simplified staging	All Hawaiian Ens Princ 3, Princ 4, Maidens,NO TRIO	30 min
5:00 p.m.		DINNER BREAK FOR CAST & CREW			
6:00 p.m.		Change set to Scene E (ADeck 370/AFly 22/Fly G/Elec.105)			15 min
6:15 p.m.	11	Princ 2's Hut "I Know It's For Me" Mic – All 3 Princ 2s	"I Know It's For Me"	3 Princ 2s	45 min
7:00 p.m.		RELEASE KIDS Change Set to Scene F (ADeck1010/AFly 53/Fly DD/Elec.311.5)Ensemble into Lemming			15 min
7:15 p.m.	12 13	Over the Cliff Mic - Princ 2	Lemming (after Curtain ↑) Lemming w/SteadiCam	Princ 2 & Ensemble Princ 2 & Ensembl	60 min
8:15 p.m.		RELEASE CAST exc. Trio, Princ 1, Princ 3 & Princ 2 Change Set to Scene G (ADeck1100/AFly 55/Fly HH/Elec.351)		xxx, xxx & xxx into Trio 	 15 min

Figure 13.5: Commercial shoot schedule/example

Commercial Shoot Schedule
Day 1 - Monday, March 16

8:30 p.m.	14	Maui Mic – All Princ 1, Princ 2, Princ 3, Mice	Air Guitar Entrance	Princ 1, Princ 2, Princ 3	45 min
	15	"My Home"	Trio Reveal	Princ 3, 3 Blind Trio	
	16		Princ 1, "You an't see me rt now"	Princ 3, Princ 1 & Princ 2	
	(17)	(If Time Allows)	Princ 1 & Princ 2 on Log	Princ 1 & Princ 2	
	(18)	(If Time Allows)	Princ 3 pushes Princ 1 @Button	Princ 3, Princ 1 & Princ 2	
	(19)	(If Time Allows)	Princ 2 – "I spent my whole life on this island …"	Princ 2	
	(20)	(If Time Allows)	"Maybe you shouldn't judge …"	Princ 2, Princ 1, Princ 3	

9:15 p.m.		RELEASE Trio Change Set to Scene H (ADeck 250/AFly 14/Fly A/Elec.72)	15 min

9:30 p.m.	21	Swamp "Hold My Hand" Mic – Princ 1 & Princ 3	Entire scene from Princ 3 ent.	Princ 1 & Princ 3 which includes:	45 min
	21a		"I'm like a canoe"	Princ 1 & Princ 3	
	21b		""Off on a walk…"	Princ 1 & Princ 3	
	22		"Help the maiden"	Princ 1 & Princ 3	
	23		"To the edge" - Vaudeville (No change in set)	Princ 1 & Princ 3	
	(24)	(If Time Allows)	"Fun" (from "Sliding")	Princ 1 & Princ 3 Princ 1 & Princ 3	

10:15 p.m.		RELEASE PRINC 3 Change set to Scene I (ADeck 630/AFly 35/Fly Q/Elec.210)	15 min

10:30 p.m.	25	Princ 2's Hut Mic – Princ 1 & Princ 2	Princ 2 arm pumps	Princ 2	30 min
	26		"…it's raining"	Princ 1 & Princ 2	
	27		"Where have you been?"	Princ 2 & Princ 1	

11:00 p.m.	Break For The Day

Figure 13.5: Commercial shoot schedule/example-continued

Commercial Shoot Schedule

Day 2 - Tuesday, March 17

CAST MAKEUP CALLS for Tuesday, March 30

9:00 a.m.	Full Ensemble, Princ 4, Princ 1
12 Noon	Princ 2, Princ 3

Time	Shot	Scene/Song	What	Who	Time
Set to Scene J (ADeck 1240/AFly 59.5/Fly OO/ Elec.379)					
10:00 a.m.	28	Under Volcano "Hot"	Hot X3	FTCs	120 min
		Mic – Princ 4, Ensemble 1 3, 4, 5, 7, 8, 9, 10			
	29		Chorus Line	FTCs	
	30		"What are you doing with that sandwich?"	FTCs, Princ 1	
	31		Princ 4 Hair Flip	Princ 4, Princ 1, Ens as Above	
12:00 Noon		LUNCH BREAK FOR CAST & CREW			
1:00 p.m.		Change Set to Finale (ADeck 1310/AFly 63/Fly XX/Elec.460)			15 min
1:15 p.m.	32	Finale	"It's Magic"	Full Company (exc.PRINC 5, Kids)	60 Min
			Rain		
		Mic - ??			
	33		"Moon" – "Sun" – from Wedge		
2:15 p.m.		RELEASE COMPANY exc. PRINC 1, PRINC 3 & PRINC 2			
		Change set to Scene K (ADeck 790/AFly 38/Fly W/ Elec.237)			15 min
2:30 p.m.	34	Cliffs	"Bring it To Me X3	Princ 1, Princ 2 & Princ 3	45 min
		Mic – Princ 1, Princ 3, Princ 2			
	35		Crane shots for Trio	Princ 1, Princ 2 & Princ 3	
3:15 p.m.		RELEASE PRINC 1, PRINC 3 & PRINC 2			
		Wrap			

Figure 13.5: Commercial shoot schedule/example-continued

Commercial Shoot Schedule

Monday, March 16

6:30 a.m.	Full show crew + additional props for seats
	Off-load camera equipment
	Pull orchestra seats in center section of Rows I, J & K
12 Noon	CREW LUNCH
	Actors' makeup call
1:00 p.m.	1st shot
5 p.m.	CREW & CAST DINNER
6 p.m.	Continue shooting
11 p.m.	Break for Day 1 9 shooting hours

Tues, March 17

9 a.m.	Full show crew
	Actors' makeup call
10 a.m.	1st shot
12 Noon –1:00 p.m.	CREW & CAST LUNCH
1:00 p.m.	Continue shooting
3:15 p.m.	End of shooting 4¼ shooting hours
3:15 p.m. – 5:30 p.m.	Restore house/stage
5:30 p.m.	Crew sets up show
6:30 p.m.	½ hr call
7:00 p.m.	Curtain

Figure 13.5: Commercial shoot schedule/example-continued

Appendix:
Unions and Associations

Here are some of the unions and associations you may need to work with, or at least know about, as a production stage manager for the professional theatre. For each I've provided a brief description along with a URL address for further information.

ACTORS' EQUITY ASSOCIATION (AEA OR EQUITY)

Founded in 1913, Equity is the labor union that represents more than 49,000 actors and stage managers in the United States. Equity seeks to advance, promote, and foster the art of live theatre as an essential component of our society. Equity negotiates wages and working conditions and provides a wide range of benefits, including health and pension plans, for its members. Actors' Equity is a member of the AFL-CIO, and is affiliated with the International Federation of Actors (FIA), an international organization of performing arts unions.

actorsequity.org

AMERICAN FEDERATION OF MUSICIANS (AFM)

The American Federation of Musicians of the United States and Canada is the largest organization in the world representing the interests of professional musicians. Whether negotiating fair agreements, protecting ownership of recorded music, securing benefits such as health care and pension, or lobbying legislators, the AFM is committed to raising industry standards and placing the professional musician in the foreground of the cultural landscape.

afm.org

ASSOCIATION OF THEATRICAL PRESS AGENTS AND MANAGERS (ATPAM)

ATPAM members are press agents, publicity and marketing specialists, company managers, and house and facilities managers who are devoted to the health, vitality and success of staged entertainment of all types. ATPAM is part of the International Alliance of Theatrical and Stage Employees, Moving Picture Technicians, Artists and Allied Crafts of the United States, Its Territories and Canada, AFL-CIO, and CLC. As Local 18032 of the IATSE, ATPAM enjoys membership in the largest union governing the entertainment business and, with that, finds itself as part of vital, growing industry that encompasses stage, screen, and television.
atpam.com

CASTING SOCIETY OF AMERICA

The Casting Society of America (CSA) was created in February of 1982 and was at that time called the American Society of Casting Directors. It was founded to establish a recognized standard of professionalism in the casting field and providing its members with a support organization to further their goals and protect their common interests. At this time, CSA boasts more than 600 members. CSA Casting Directors and Associates work around the world, with members based in the United States, Canada, Europe, Australia and Africa. Today CSA acts as a global resource for producers, directors and creative teams seeking casting professionals, promotes the image of casting directors and associates worldwide, engages in a number of charitable activities, and supports its members by sharing important and helpful professional information of common interest.

DRAMATISTS GUILD OF AMERICA

The Dramatists Guild of America was established in the early 20th century, and is the only professional association that advances the interests of playwrights, composers, lyricists, and librettists writing for the live stage. The Guild has over 6,000 members nationwide, from beginning writers to the most prominent authors represented on Broadway, Off-Broadway, and in regional theaters.
dramatistsguild.com

INTERNATIONAL ALLIANCE OF THEATRICAL STAGE EMPLOYEES (IATSE)

The International Alliance of Theatrical Stage Employees, Moving Picture Technicians, Artists and Allied Crafts of the United States, its Territories and Canada was founded in 1893 to establish fair wages and working conditions for stage hands. The union has evolved to embrace new entertainment mediums, craft expansion, technological innovation and geographic growth. Today, members work in all forms of live theatre, motion picture and television production, trade shows and exhibitions, television broadcasting, and concerts as well as the equipment and construction shops that support all these areas of the entertainment industry. IATSE represents virtually all the behind-the-scenes workers in crafts ranging from motion picture animator to theatre usher.
iatse.net

HERE ARE A FEW OF THE IATSE LOCALS YOU'LL LIKELY HAVE CONTACT WITH:

Local 1 represents stagehands in New York City and Westchester and Putnam counties.

Local 4 represents stagehands in Brooklyn and Queens.

Local 706 represents makeup artists and hair stylists in the Los Angeles area.

Local 764 is the Theatrical Wardrobe Union for the New York City Area.
See also Theatrical Wardrobe Union, Local 764 IATSE.

Local 768 is the Theatrical Wardrobe Union for the Los Angeles area.

Local 784 is the Theatrical Wardrobe Union for the San Francisco Bay area.Local 798 represents makeup artists and hair stylists in the New York City area.

Local USA 829 represents designers, artists, and craftspeople.
See also United Scenic Artists Local USA 829.

Local 18032 represents theatrical press agents and managers.

INTERNATIONAL FEDERATION OF ACTORS (FIA)

From the vision of two pioneers in the early 1950s—Jean Darcante of the Syndicat National des Acteurs Français and Gerald Croasdell of British Actors' Equity—FIA has emerged as an international organization speaking on behalf of performers' unions, guilds, and professional associations on all continents. FIA strives to promote and protect the artistic, economic, social, and legal interests of the performers they represent, wherever they live and work.
fia-actors.com

LEAGUE OF RESIDENT THEATRES (LORT)

LORT is the largest professional theatre association of its kind in the United States, with 74 member theatres located in every major market in the United States, including 29 states and the District of Columbia. LORT Theatres collectively issue more Equity contracts to actors than Broadway and commercial tours combined.

LORT administers the primary national not-for-profit collective bargaining agreements with Actors' Equity Association (AEA), the Stage Directors and Choreographers Society (SDC), and United Scenic Artists (USA). They also deal directly with personnel and management issues involving theatre staff, artists, and craftspeople. LORT members communicate collectively via LORT Counsel's office in New York.
lort.org

OCCUPATIONAL SAFETY AND HEALTH ADMINISTRATION (OSHA)

With the Occupational Safety and Health Act of 1970, Congress created the Occupational Safety and Health Administration (OSHA) to assure safe and healthful working conditions for working men and women by setting and enforcing standards and by providing training, outreach, education, and assistance. OSHA covers most private sector employers and their workers, in addition to some public sector employers and workers in the 50 states and certain territories and jurisdictions under federal authority.
osha.gov

PLAYBILL

Playbill's free Website offers breaking news about the theatre industry, focusing on New York shows but including regional, touring and international stage happenings. It also has a casting and job listing section.

playbill.com

SCREEN ACTORS' GUILD AND THE AMERICAN FEDERATION OF TELEVISION AND RADIO ACTORS (SAG-AFTRA)

SAG and AFTRA joined forces in 2012 and represents more than 165,000 actors, announcers, broadcasters journalists, dancers, DJs, news writers, news editors, program hosts, puppeteers, recording artists, singers, stunt performers, voiceover artists, and other media professionals. With national offices in Los Angeles and New York, and local offices nationwide, SAG-AFTRA members work together to secure the strongest protections for media artists into the 21st century and beyond.

sagaftra.org

STAGE DIRECTORS AND CHOREOGRAPHERS SOCIETY (SDC)

The SDC is the theatrical union that unites, empowers, and protects professional stage directors and choreographers throughout the United States. The stated mission is to foster a national community of professional stage directors and choreographers by protecting the rights, health, and livelihoods of all members. SDC facilitates the exchange of ideas, information and opportunities, while educating the current and future generations about the role of directors and choreographers and providing effective administration, negotiations, and contractual support.

sdcweb.org

STAGE MANAGERS' ASSOCIATION (SMA)

SMA is a New York-based association for stage mangers whose stated purpose is to protect and promote the interests of professional stage managers; to serve as a resource and networking hub for the dissemination and advancement of ideas and developments in the craft of stage management; and to educate and advise those interested in the art and techniques of stage management.

stagemanagers.org

THEATRICAL WARDROBE UNION, LOCAL 764 IATSE

The Theatrical Wardrobe Attendants in New York City first organized in 1919 as a federal union affiliated with the American Federation of Labor (AFL). In 1942, this union was granted a charter to become part of the International Alliance of Theatrical Stage Employees, Moving Picture Technicians, Artists and Allied Crafts of the United States, its Territories and Canada. In 1982 the Local was issued a new charter as "Theatrical Wardrobe Union, Local 764 of the I.A.T.S.E." The local currently has members working

in all aspects of costume and wardrobe work in the New York City area in virtually every major live entertainment venue in the city, as well as on television shows and motion pictures shooting within a 50-mile radius of Columbus Circle.
ia764.com

UNITED SCENIC ARTISTS LOCAL USA 829

Local USA 829 is a labor union and professional association of designers, artists, and craftspeople organized to protect craft standards, working conditions, and wages for the entertainment and decorative arts industries. The members of Local USA 829 are artists and designers working in film, theatre, opera, ballet, television, industrial shows, commercials and exhibitions. USA 829 is a local of IATSE.
usa829.org

Index

rotation 105, 116–117
substituting 16, 116
Stage Managers' Association
17, 204
standbys 86, 87, 118, 119
stars, casting decisions and 22
stopping a show 136–138
Sunset Boulevard 138
swings 6, 35, 50, 60, 66, 85, 86,
87, 118–120, 121, 132, 133, 134,
141, 142–143

T

talkbacks 132–133
taping the rehearsal floor 68–70
tech tables 84–85
layout 2012 *Annie* revival 168
locating 84–85
technical director 11, 51, 79, 123
technical rehearsals *see rehearsal,
technical*
technical supervisor 40–42, 130
television appearances 134–135
termination procedure 140
Theatrical Wardrobe Union 9, 12,
204–205
Tony Awards 120, 132, 133
Twitter 17

U

understudies 35, 36, 60, 87, 112,
115, 118–120, 121, 124, 136
union notification for rehearsal
start 73
unions and deputies, working
with 127–131
United Scenic Artists IATSE
Local USA 829 7, 8, 9, 10, 205
US-style production stage
manager 1

V

vacation days 122–124, 144
video and projection
design 38–40
emerging technology 38–39
designer 9–10
interaction with director 39
interaction with general
manager 40
interaction with lighting
designer 40
interaction with scenic
designer 39
video monitors 91–92
video, backstage 32

W

Wandelprobe 33
wardrobe 11, 28, 36, 37, 49, 51, 52,
53, 55, 59, 62, 93, 94, 95, 97,
98, 104, 143
breakdown 60
breakdown example 160–161
chart 60
crew 12
facilities 35, 86–87, 142
fittings 60
production calendar 35
records 60
rehearsal 51, 65
supervisor 35, 86, 112, 120
weekly grosses 141
weekly reports 114
example 191–194
weekly schedules 114
Wiz, The 9
Wolff, Rachel 16–17
Woman in White 39
Woolley, Jim 16, 55, 71, 143
wrangler, animal 11
wrangler, child 11

Acknowledgments

I owe a debt of gratitude to all the stage managers with whom I've worked and from whom I've learned. Jim Woolley has been my friend and associate for over 30 years. Rachel Wolff and Mahlon Kruse have teched many shows with me and bailed me out of many jams. Pamela Remler, Mary Katharine Flynt, Lisa Chernoff, Sarah Whitham, Kristen Harris, Neveen Mahmoud, Jovon Shuck, Barrie Moss, Bryan Rountree and Derric Nolte each have many skills which I lack and have helped me tremendously. Richard Hester, John Brigleb, Karen Moore and Tom Bartlett have assisted me on multiple shows and gone on to PSM and Supervise huge hits of their own. Chad Lewis, Greta Minsky, Linda Fox, Bob Bruyr, Ed Isser, Judy Binus, Robert Altshuler, Henry Velez, Kate Croasdale, B.J. Allen, Carrie Meconis, David Blackwell, Terry Witter and Mindy Farbrother have all been invaluable colleagues on shows stretching back over 40 years.

There are many stage managers who have never assisted me, but with whom I have a strong collegial bond. Anne Keefe, Frank Lombardi, Charlie Blackwell, Els Collins, Mary Hunter belong in this distinguished group and to whom I am indebted. And most importantly in this group is Harvey Medlinsky, who took a chance on me when I knew nothing and taught me everything.

I have many mentors, many of whom are mentioned in this book. But they shaped my life and career in so many important ways that I wanted to acknowledge them again. I am grateful to the directors Mike Nichols, Sam Mendes, Gene Saks, Alex Timbers, Zoe Caldwell, Marcia Milgrom Dodge, James Lapine, Graciela Daniele, Trevor Nunn, Joe Layton, Martin Charnin and Charles Nelson Reilly. I am equally grateful to the choreographers Jerry Mitchell, Bob Avian, Casey Nicholaw, Josh Prince, Peter Gennaro, Andy Blankenbuehler and Sonya Tayeh. And to the designers Tony Walton, Derek McLane, Tim Hatley, Rob Howell, John Napier, Santo Loquasto, Anthony Ward, Tony Straiges, John Lee Beatty, Jules Fisher, Peggy Eisenhower, Tharon Musser, Marilyn Renegal, Don

Holder, Hugh Vanstone, Ken Billington, Paul Gallo, Andrew Bridge, Jennifer Tipton, Susan Hilferty, William Ivey Long, Ann Hould-Ward, Anthony Powell, Joseph G. Aulisi, Ann Roth, Peter Hylenski, Mark Menard, Tom Clark, Nevin Steinberg, Brian Ronan, Otts Munderloh, Richard and Peter Fitzgerald, Scott Lehrer and Dan Moses Schreier. The casting director Vinnie Liff, Geoff Johnson, Tara Rubin, Merry Sugarman, Julie Hughes, Barry Moss, Carrie Gardner, Jim Carnahan, Bernie Telsey, Fran Kumin and Meg Simon have been invaluable in my continuing stage managerial education.

This book could never have been completed or printed without the patient, professional and loving prodding of Ralph Pine, the publisher of this book, and of Pat MacKay, who edited every line. They love books and the theatre in equal measure.

I never would have been exposed to the theatre at all if it had not been for my Mom and Dad. They took me to my first Broadway show when I was 11 years old and made me understand that the theatre is not just entertainment, but literature.

And finally, I owe my love of the theatre to Ms. Miriam Sayre, who was my high school drama teacher in Galion, Ohio, and who took seriously my adolescent yearnings toward the stage. She was both inspirational and practical. Miss Sayre made me understand that the theatre was vital to our lives.

About the Author

Peter Lawrence is a stage manager with over 40 years of experience in the commercial theatre. Working as production stage manager, he originated over 25 Broadway productions, among them *Spamalot, Hurlyburly, Sunset Boulevard, Shrek The Musical,* and five new plays by Neil Simon. Production stage manager assignments have seen him working in dinner theatre, stock, regional theatres, Broadway, off-Broadway, and national tours.

Lawrence has and continues to work with many of the great directors of our time including Mike Nichols, Gene Saks, James Lapine, Sam Mendes, Trevor Nunn, Joe Layton, John Doyle, Marcia Milgrom Dodge, Michael Kidd, Jonathan Kent, and many more. Scenic designers Tony Walton, Santo Loquasto, John Napier, Tim Hatley, David Korins, Rob Howell, and Derek McLane, and lighting designers Tharon Musser, Ken Billington, Jennifer Tipton, Jules Fisher, Peggy Eisenhauer, Don Holder, Hugh Vanstone, and Andrew Bridge have all been part of the design teams of Lawrence's shows. He has also worked with costume designers Theoni V. Aldredge, Susan Hilferty, Tim Hatley, Anthony Powell, William Ivey Long, and Ann Roth, and with sound designers Otts Munderloh, Peter Hylenski, Acme Sound Partners, Abe Jacob, Scott Lehrer, Dan Moses Schreier, and Ken Travis.

Lawrence has managed shows for producers Cameron Mackintosh, Emanuel Azenberg, Fran and Barry Weissler, Kevin McCollum, Ariel Tepper Madover, Bill Haber, Bob Boyett, Robert Whitehead, Robert Fox, and many others. He is the first stage manager ever to have been honored by the Tony Awards and is a recipient of the Del Hughes Lifetime Achievement Award from the Stage Managers' Association.

And when there's time, Peter Lawrence enjoys teaching and giving seminars in production stage management at drama departments around the country including Columbia University, University of North Carolina School of the Arts, and the University of Hawaii. He lives in New York City and has four children—only one of whom has gone into the theatre.